Space Exploration
Biographies

Space Exploration Biographies

Peggy Saari

Deborah J. Baker,
Lawrence W. Baker,
and Sarah Hermsen,
Project Editors

U.X.L
A part of Gale, Cengage Learning

GALE
CENGAGE Learning

Detroit • New York • San Francisco • New Haven, Conn • Waterville, Maine • London

Space Exploration: Biographies
Peggy Saari

Project Editors
Deborah J. Baker and Sarah Hermsen

Rights Acquisitions and Management
Ann Taylor

Imaging and Multimedia
Dean Dauphinais, Lezlie Light, Dan Newell

Product Design
Pamela Galbreath

Composition
Evi Seoud

Manufacturing
Rita Wimberley

Library of Congress Cataloging-in-Publication Data
Saari, Peggy.
Space exploration. Biographies / Peggy Saari ; Lawrence W. Baker, Sarah Hermsen, and Deborah J. Baker, project editors.
     p. cm. — (Space exploration reference library)
    Includes bibliographical references and index.
    ISBN 0-7876-9212-3 (hardcover : alk. paper)
    1. Astronauts—Biography—Juvenile literature. I. Title. II. Series.
    TL789.85.A1S23 2004
    629.45′0092′2—dc22
                                        2004015822

Printed in the United States of America
4 5 6 7 8 9 14 13 12 11 10 09 08

Contents

Reader's Guide

Fascinating and forbidding, space has drawn the attention of humans since before recorded history. People have looked outward, driven by curiosity about the vast universe that surrounds Earth. Unaware of the meaning of the bright lights in the night sky above them, ancient humans thought they saw patterns, images in the sky of things in the landscape around them.

Slowly, humans came to realize that the lights in the sky had an effect on the workings of the planet around them. They sought to understand the movements of the Sun, the Moon, and the other, brighter objects. They wanted to know how those movements related to the changing seasons and the growth of crops.

Still, for centuries, humans did not understand what lay beyond the boundaries of Earth. In fact, with their limited vision, they saw a limited universe. Ancient astronomers relied on naked-eye observations to chart the positions of stars, planets, and the Sun. In the third century B.C.E., philosophers concluded that Earth was the center of the universe. A few dared to question this prevailing belief. In the face of overwhelming opposition and ridicule, they persisted in trying to understand the truth. This belief ruled human affairs until the scientific revolution of the seventeenth century, when scientists used the newly invented telescope to prove that the Sun is the center of Earth's galaxy.

Over time, with advances in science and technology, ancient beliefs were exposed as false. The universe ever widened with humans' growing understanding of it. The dream to explore its vast reaches passed from nineteenth-century fiction writers to twentieth-century visionaries to present-day engineers and scientists, pilots, and astronauts.

The quest to explore space intensified around the turn of the twentieth century. By that time, astronomers had built better observatories and perfected more powerful telescopes. Increasingly sophisticated technologies led to the discovery that the universe extends far beyond the Milky Way and holds even deeper mysteries, such as limitless galaxies and unexplained phenomena like black holes. Scientists, yearning to solve those mysteries, determined that one way to accomplish this goal was to penetrate space itself.

Even before the twentieth century, people had discussed ways to travel into space. Among them were science fiction writers, whose fantasies inspired the visions of scientists. Science fiction became especially popular in the late nineteenth century, having a direct impact on early twentieth-century rocket engineers who invented the fuel-propellant rocket. Initially developed as a weapon of war, this new projectile could be launched a greater distance than any human-made object in history, and it eventually unlocked the door to space.

From the mid-twentieth century until the turn of the twenty-first century, the fuel-propellant rocket made possible dramatic advances in space exploration. It was used to propel unmanned satellites and manned space capsules, space shuttles, and space stations. It launched an orbiting telescope that sent spectacular images of the universe back to Earth. During this era of intense optimism and innovation, often called the space age, people confidently went forth to conquer the distant regions of space that have intrigued humans since early times. They traveled to the Moon, probed previously uncharted realms, and contemplated trips to Mars.

Overcoming longstanding rivalries, nations embarked on international space ventures. Despite the seemingly unlimited technology at their command, research scientists, engineers, and astronauts encountered political maneuvering, lack of funds, aging spacecraft, and tragic accidents. As the world settled into the twenty-first century, space exploration faced an uncertain future. Yet, the ongoing exploration of space continued to represent the "final frontier" in the last great age of exploration.

Space Exploration: Biographies captures the height of the space age in twenty-five entries that profile astronauts, scientists, theorists, writers, and spacecraft. Included are astronauts Neil Armstrong, John Glenn, Mae Jemison, and Sally Ride; cosmonaut Yuri Gagarin; engineer Wernher von Braun; writer H. G. Wells; and the crew of the space shuttle *Challenger*. The volume also contains profiles of the Hubble Space Telescope and the International Space Station. Focusing on international contributions to the quest for knowledge about space, this volume takes readers on an adventure into the achievements and failures experienced by explorers of space.

Features

The entries in *Space Exploration: Biographies* contain sidebar boxes that highlight topics of special interest related to the profiled individual. Each entry also offers a list of additional sources that students can go to for more information. More than sixty black-and-white photographs illustrate the material. The volume begins with a timeline of important events in the history of space exploration and a "Words to Know" section that introduces students to difficult or unfamiliar terms. The volume concludes with a general bibliography and a subject index so students can easily find the people, places, and events discussed throughout *Space Exploration: Biographies*.

Space Exploration Reference Library

Space Exploration: Biographies is only one component of the three-part Space Exploration Reference Library. The other two titles in this set are:

- *Space Exploration: Almanac* (two volumes) presents, in fourteen chapters, key developments and milestones in the continuing history of space exploration. The focus ranges from ancient views of a Sun-centered universe to the scientific understanding of the laws of planetary motion and gravity, from the launching of the first artificial satellite to be placed in orbit around Earth to current robotic explorations of near and distant planets in the solar system. Also covered is the development of the first telescopes by men such as Hans Lippershey, who called his device a "looker" and thought it would be useful in war, and Galileo Galilei, who built his own device to look at the stars. The work also details the construction of great modern observatories, both on ground and in orbit around Earth, that can peer billions of light-years into space and, in doing so, peer billions of years back in time. Also examined is the development of rocketry; the work of theorists and engineers Konstantin Tsiolkovsky, Robert H. Goddard, and others; a discussion of the Cold War and its impact on space exploration; space missions such as the first lunar landing; and great tragedies, including the explosions of U.S. space shuttles *Challenger* and *Columbia*.

- *Space Exploration: Primary Sources* (one volume) captures the highlights of the space age with full-text reprints and lengthy excerpts of seventeen documents that include science fiction, nonfiction, autobiography, official reports, articles, interviews, and speeches. Readers are taken on an adventure spanning a period of more than one hundred twenty-five years, from nineteenth-century speculations about space travel through twenty-first century plans for human flights to Mars. Included are excerpts from science fiction writer Jules Verne's *From the Earth to the Moon;* Tom Wolfe's *The Right Stuff,* which chronicles the story of America's first astronauts; astronaut John Glenn's memoirs; and president George W. Bush's new vision of space exploration.

- A cumulative index of all three titles in the Space Exploration Reference Library is also available.

Comments and Suggestions

We welcome your comments on *Space Exploration: Biographies* and suggestions for other topics to consider. Please write: Editors, *Space Exploration: Biographies,* U•X•L, 27500 Drake Rd. Farmington Hills, Michigan 48331-3535; call toll-free: 1-800-877-4253; fax to (248) 699-8097; or send e-mail via http://www.gale.com.

Timeline of Events

c. 3000 B.C.E. Sumerians produce the oldest known drawings of constellations as recurring designs on seals, vases, and gaming boards.

c. 3000 B.C.E. Construction begins on Stonehenge.

c. 700 B.C.E. Babylonians have already assembled extensive, relatively accurate records of celestial events, including charting the paths of planets and compiling observations of fixed stars.

c. 550 B.C.E. Greek philosopher and mathematician Pythagoras argues that Earth is round and develops an early system of cosmology to explain the nature and structure of the universe.

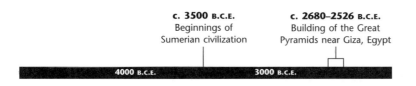

c. 3500 B.C.E.
Beginnings of
Sumerian civilization

c. 2680–2526 B.C.E.
Building of the Great
Pyramids near Giza, Egypt

4000 B.C.E.   3000 B.C.E.

c. 370 B.C.E. Eudoxus of Cnidus develops a system to explain the motions of the planets based on spheres.

c. 280 B.C.E. Greek mathematician and astronomer Aristarchus proposes that the planets, including Earth, revolve around the Sun.

c. 240 B.C.E. Greek astronomer and geographer Eratosthenes calculates the circumference of Earth with remarkable accuracy from the angle of the Sun's rays at separate points on the planet's surface.

c. 130 B.C.E. Greek astronomer Hipparchus develops the first accurate star map and star catalog covering about 850 stars, including a scale of magnitude to indicate the apparent brightness of the stars; it is the first time such a scale has been used.

140 C.E. Alexandrian astronomer Ptolemy publishes his Earth-centered or geocentric theory of the solar system.

c. 1000 The Maya build El Caracol, an observatory, in the city of Chichén Itzá.

1045 A Chinese government official publishes the *Wu-ching Tsung-yao* (*Complete Compendium of Military Classics*), which details the use of "fire arrows" launched by charges of gunpowder, the first true rockets.

1268 English philosopher and scientist Roger Bacon publishes a book on chemistry called *Opus Majus* (*Great Work*) in which he describes in detail the process of making gunpowder, becoming the first European to do so.

1543 Polish astronomer Nicolaus Copernicus publishes his Sun-centered, or heliocentric, theory of the solar system.

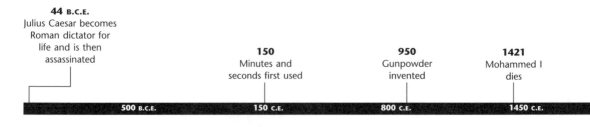

44 B.C.E.
Julius Caesar becomes Roman dictator for life and is then assassinated

150
Minutes and seconds first used

950
Gunpowder invented

1421
Mohammed I dies

500 B.C.E.   150 C.E.   800 C.E.   1450 C.E.

November 1572 Danish astronomer Tycho Brahe discovers what later proves to be a supernova in the constellation of Cassiopeia.

1577 German armorer Leonhart Fronsperger writes a book on firearms in which he describes a device called a *roget* that uses a base of gunpowder wrapped tightly in paper. Historians believe this resulted in the modern word "rocket."

c. late 1500s German fireworks maker Johann Schmidlap invents the step rocket, a primitive version of a multistage rocket.

1608 Dutch lens-grinder Hans Lippershey creates the first optical telescope.

1609 German astronomer Johannes Kepler publishes his first two laws of planetary motion.

1609 Italian mathematician and astronomer Galileo Galilei develops his own telescope and uses it to discover four moons around Jupiter, craters on the Moon, and the Milky Way.

1633 Galileo is placed under house arrest for the rest of his life by the Catholic Church for advocating the heliocentric theory of the solar system.

1656 French poet and soldier Savinien de Cyrano de Bergerac publishes a fantasy novel about a man who travels to the Moon in a device powered by exploding firecrackers.

1687 English physicist and mathematician Isaac Newton publishes his three laws of motion and his law of universal gravitation in the much-acclaimed *Philosophiae Naturalis Principia Mathematica* (*Mathematical Principles of Natural Philosophy*).

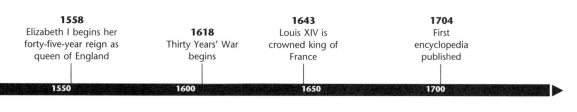

1558
Elizabeth I begins her forty-five-year reign as queen of England

1618
Thirty Years' War begins

1643
Louis XIV is crowned king of France

1704
First encyclopedia published

1550   1600   1650   1700

1781 English astronomer William Herschel discovers the planet Uranus using a reflector telescope he had made.

1804 English artillery expert William Congreve develops the first ship-fired rockets.

1844 English inventor William Hale invents the stickless, spin-stabilized rocket.

1865 French writer Jules Verne publishes *From the Earth to the Moon,* the first of two novels he would write about traveling to the Moon.

1895 English writer **H. G. Wells** publishes *The Time Machine.* Establishing Wells as a best-selling science fiction novelist, the book tells the tale of an inventor who creates a machine that can be navigated into the past or the future.

1895 Russian rocket scientist **Konstantin Tsiolkovsky** describes travel to the Moon, other planets, and beyond in his paper titled "Dreams of the Earth and Sky and the Effects of Universal Gravitation." He also introduces the concept of an artificial Earth.

1897 The Yerkes Observatory in Williams Bay, Wisconsin, which houses the largest refractor telescope in the world, is completed.

1898 H. G. Wells writes his best-known novel, *The War of the Worlds,* which describes a Martian invasion of Earth.

1903 Russian scientist and rocket expert Konstantin Tsiolkovsky publishes an article titled "Exploration of the Universe with Reaction Machines," in which he presents the basic formula that determines how rockets perform.

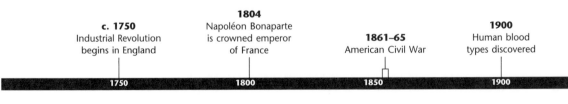

c. 1750 Industrial Revolution begins in England	**1804** Napoléon Bonaparte is crowned emperor of France	**1861–65** American Civil War	**1900** Human blood types discovered
1750	1800	1850	1900

1919 **Robert Goddard** publishes "A Method of Reaching Extreme Altitudes," an article about propelling rockets into space. In the conclusion he suggests the possibility of sending a multi-stage rocket to the Moon.

1923 German physicist **Hermann Oberth** publishes a ninety-two-page pamphlet titled *Die Rakete zu den Planetenräumen* (*The Rocket into Interplanetary Space*) in which he explains the mathematical theory of rocketry, speculates on the effects of spaceflight on the human body, and theorizes on the possibility of placing satellites in space.

1924 Using the 100-inch telescope at Mount Wilson near Los Angeles, California, American astronomer Edwin Hubble observes billions of galaxies beyond the Milky Way.

1926 American scientist Robert Goddard launches the world's first liquid-propellant rocket.

March 16, 1926 American physicist and space pioneer Robert H. Goddard launches the world's first liquid-propellant rocket.

1927 Romanian-born German scientist Hermann Oberth founds the German Rocket Society. He is a mentor to university student **Wernher von Braun.**

1928 Hermann Oberth publishes *The Rocket into Planetary Space.* He discusses liquid-propellant rockets, speculates on the effects of space flight upon humans, and proposes the idea of a space station.

1929 Konstantin Tsiolkovsky writes about placing rockets into space by arranging them in packets, or "cosmic rocket trains." This becomes known as "rocket staging."

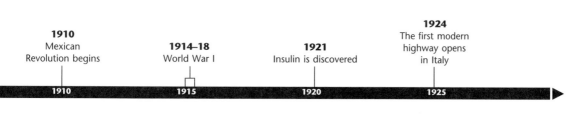

1910
Mexican
Revolution begins

1914–18
World War I

1921
Insulin is discovered

1924
The first modern
highway opens
in Italy

1910   1915   1920   1925

1929   Using the Hooker Telescope at the Mount Wilson Observatory in southern California, U.S. astronomer Edwin Hubble develops what comes to be known as Hubble's law, which describes the rate of expansion of the universe.

1930   The International Astronomical Union (IAU) sets the definitive boundaries of the eighty-eight recognized constellations.

1938   American actor Orson Welles and his Mercury Theater players broadcast a live radio dramatization of *The War of the Worlds*. The performance is so realistic that listeners in New Jersey flee their homes in panic, believing Earth is actually being invaded by Martians.

1942   German rocket scientist **Wernher von Braun** leads the Peenemünde team in the first successful launch of the V-2 rocket. By the end of World War II, Germany has fired approximately six thousand V-2s on Allied targets.

September 8, 1944 Germany launches V-2 rockets, the first true ballistic missiles, to strike targets in Paris, France, and London, England.

1945   After World War II the United States and the Soviet Union begin the Cold War, one result of which is the space race.

1947   The 200-inch-diameter Hale Telescope becomes operational at the Palomar Observatory in southern California.

1950   Now living in the United States, Wernher von Braun and his team of exiled German scientists start work on the Redstone missile. The Redstone eventually plays a significant role in America's early space program.

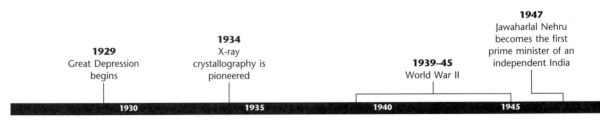

1929
Great Depression begins

1934
X-ray crystallography is pioneered

1939–45
World War II

1947
Jawaharlal Nehru becomes the first prime minister of an independent India

1930   1935   1940   1945

1952 Wernher von Braun begins his famous series of articles on space travel in *Collier's* magazine.

March 9, 1955 German-born American engineer Wernher von Braun appears on "Man in Space," the first of three space-related television shows he and American movie producer Walt Disney create for American audiences.

1957 Soviet rocket scientist **Sergei Korolev** directs the successful launch of the R-7 rocket. It becomes the most widely used rocket in the world.

1957 The Soviet Union surprises the world by launching *Sputnik 1,* the first artificial satellite. The space race intensifies between the Soviets and the United States.

July 1, 1957, to December 31, 1958 During this eighteen-month period, known as the International Geophysical Year, more than ten thousand scientists and technicians representing sixty-seven countries engage in a comprehensive series of global geophysical activities.

1958 The United States establishes the National Aeronautics and Space Administration (NASA), which integrates U.S. space research agencies and starts an astronaut training program.

1958 American engineer **Christopher Kraft** joins NASA as a member of the Space Task Group, which is developing Project Mercury.

January 31, 1958 *Explorer 1,* the United States's first successful artificial satellite, is launched into space.

March 17, 1958 The U.S. Navy launches the small, artificial satellite *Vanguard 1.* The oldest human-made object in space, it remains in orbit around Earth.

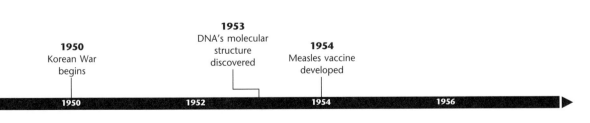

1950
Korean War
begins

1953
DNA's molecular
structure
discovered

1954
Measles vaccine
developed

1950   1952   1954   1956

1959 Sergei Korolev directs the launch of *Luna 3,* a probe satellite that provides the first views of the far side of the Moon. The *Luna 3* flight bolsters the prestige of the Soviet Union throughout the world.

January 2, 1959 The Soviet Union launches the space probe *Luna 1,* which becomes the first human-made object to escape Earth's gravity.

April 9, 1959 NASA announces the selection of the Mercury 7 astronauts: Malcolm Scott Carpenter, Leroy G. "Gordo" Cooper Jr., **John Glenn**, Virgil I. "Gus" Grissom, Walter M. "Wally" Schirra Jr., Alan B. Shepard Jr., and Donald K. "Deke" Slayton.

September 13, 1959 The Soviet space probe *Luna 2* becomes the first human-made object to land on the Moon when it makes a hard landing east of the Sea of Serenity.

1960 The first of the **Mercury 13** women aviators secretly begins testing for the Mercury astronaut training program.

August 18, 1960 The United States launches *Discoverer 14,* its first spy satellite.

October 23, 1960 More than one hundred Soviet technicians are incinerated when a rocket explodes on a launch pad. Known as the Nedelin catastrophe, it is the worst accident in the history of the Soviet space program.

1961 NASA cancels the women's astronaut testing program.

April 12, 1961 Soviet cosmonaut **Yuri Gagarin** orbits Earth aboard *Vostok 1,* becoming the first human in space.

May 5, 1961 U.S. astronaut **Alan Shepard** makes a suborbital flight in the capsule *Freedom 7,* becoming the first American to fly into space.

1957
U.S. Congress
passes the Civil
Rights Act

1959
Hawaii
proclaimed 50th
state

1957   1958   1959   1960

May 25, 1961 U.S. president John F. Kennedy announces the goal to land an American on the Moon by the end of the 1960s.

1962 A Congressional hearing is held on discrimination against women in the U.S. space program. NASA announces that the Mercury 13 did not qualify as astronauts because they had not received jet-pilot training. No American woman travels in space until 1983.

February 20, 1962 U.S. astronaut John Glenn becomes the first American to circle Earth when he makes three orbits in the *Friendship 7* Mercury spacecraft.

August 27, 1962 *Mariner 2* is launched into orbit, becoming the first interplanetary space probe.

June 16, 1963 Soviet cosmonaut **Valentina Tereshkova** rides aboard *Vostok 6,* becoming the first woman in space.

November 1, 1963 The world's largest single radio telescope, at Arecibo Observatory in Puerto Rico, officially begins operation.

March 18, 1965 During the Soviet Union's *Voskhod 2* orbital mission, cosmonaut Alexei Leonov performs the first spacewalk, or extravehicular activity (EVA).

February 3, 1966 The Soviet Union's *Luna 9* soft-lands on the Moon and sends back to Earth the first images of the lunar surface.

January 27, 1967 Three U.S. astronauts—Gus Grissom, Roger Chaffee, and Edward White—die of asphyxiation when a fire breaks out in the capsule of *Apollo 1* during a practice session as it sits on the launch pad at Kennedy Space Center, Florida.

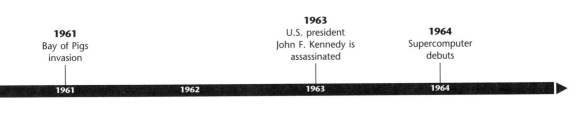

1961
Bay of Pigs
invasion

1963
U.S. president
John F. Kennedy is
assassinated

1964
Supercomputer
debuts

1961   1962   1963   1964

April 24, 1967 Soviet cosmonaut Vladimir Komarov becomes the first fatality during an actual spaceflight when the parachute from *Soyuz 1* fails to open and the capsule slams into the ground after reentry.

1968 Yuri Gagarin dies in a jet-plane crash during low-level maneuvers.

December 24, 1968 *Apollo 8,* with three U.S. astronauts aboard, becomes the first manned spacecraft to enter orbit around the Moon.

July 20, 1969 U.S. astronauts **Neil Armstrong** and **Buzz Aldrin** become the first humans to walk on the Moon.

April 14, 1970 An oxygen tank in the *Apollo 13* service module explodes while the craft is in space, putting the lives of the three U.S. astronauts onboard into serious jeopardy.

December 14, 1970 U.S. astronauts Eugene Cernan and Harrison Schmitt lift off from the Moon after having spent seventy-five hours on the surface. They are the last humans to have set foot on the Moon as of the early twenty-first century.

December 15, 1970 The Soviet space probe *Venera 7* arrives at Venus, making the first-ever successful landing on another planet.

April 19, 1971 The Soviet Union launches *Salyut 1,* the first human-made space station.

November 13, 1971 The U.S. probe *Mariner 9* becomes the first spacecraft to orbit another planet when it enters orbit around Mars.

1972 Former U.S. astronaut Buzz Aldrin founds Starcraft Booster, Inc., a company promoting space tourism and travel to Mars.

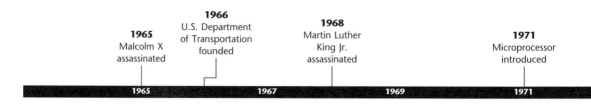

1965 Malcolm X assassinated

1966 U.S. Department of Transportation founded

1968 Martin Luther King Jr. assassinated

1971 Microprocessor introduced

1965　　1967　　1969　　1971

January 5, 1972 U.S. president Richard M. Nixon announces the decision to develop a space shuttle.

May 14, 1973 NASA sends the *Skylab* space station into orbit. It is visited by three crews of astronauts, but only remains in space for one year.

December 4, 1973 The U.S. space probe *Pioneer 10* makes the first flyby of Jupiter.

March 29, 1974 The U.S. space probe *Mariner 10* makes the first of three flybys of Mercury.

July 15 to 24, 1975 The Apollo-Soyuz Test Project is undertaken as an international docking mission between the United States and the Soviet Union.

July 20, 1976 The lander of the U.S. space probe *Viking 1* makes the first successful soft landing on Mars.

September 17, 1976 The first space shuttle orbiter, known as OV-101, rolls out of an assembly facility in Palmdale, California.

January 26, 1978 NASA launches the International Ultraviolet Explorer, considered the most successful UV satellite and perhaps the most productive astronomical telescope ever.

July 11, 1979 *Skylab* falls into Earth's atmosphere and burns up over the Indian Ocean.

October 1979 The United Kingdom Infrared Telescope, the world's largest telescope dedicated solely to infrared astronomy, begins operation in Hawaii near the summit of Mauna Kea.

November 12, 1980 The U.S. probe *Voyager 1* makes a flyby of Saturn and sends back the first detailed photographs of the ringed planet.

1973
U.S. troops pull
out of Vietnam

1977
Star Wars is
released

1978
Test-tube
baby born

1972   1974   1976   1978

April 12, 1981 U.S. astronauts John W. Young and Robert L. Crippen fly the space shuttle *Columbia* on the first orbital flight of NASA's new reusable spacecraft.

1982 Johnson Space Center director Christopher Kraft retires from NASA. During his twenty-four-year career, he headed mission control of nearly all NASA manned space flights.

June 18, 1983 U.S. astronaut **Sally Ride** becomes America's first woman in space when she rides aboard the space shuttle *Challenger*.

August 30, 1983 U.S. astronaut **Guy Bluford** flies aboard the space shuttle *Challenger*, becoming the first African American in space.

January 25, 1984 U.S. president Ronald Reagan directs NASA to develop a permanently manned space station within a decade.

1986 Former U.S. astronaut Neil Armstrong is appointed deputy chair of the Rogers Commission to investigate the explosion of the space shuttle ***Challenger***, which exploded seventy-three seconds after launch killing all seven astronauts aboard.

1986 On June 6 the Rogers Commission releases a report stating that the *Challenger* explosion was caused by defective O-rings. It recommends major changes at NASA, and an American shuttle is not launched again until 1988.

February 20, 1986 The Soviet Union launches the core module of its new space station, *Mir,* into orbit.

May 4, 1989 The space shuttle *Atlantis* lifts off carrying the *Magellan* probe, the first planetary explorer to be launched by a space shuttle.

1979–80
Fifty-two
Americans are held
hostage in Iran

1981
AIDS is first
recognized

1983
U.S. invades
Grenada

1985
DNA fingerprinting
developed

1980   1982   1984   1986

April 25, 1990 Astronauts aboard the space shuttle *Discovery* deploy the **Hubble Space Telescope.**

April 7, 1991 The Compton Gamma Ray Observatory is placed into orbit by astronauts aboard the space shuttle *Atlantis.*

September 12, 1992 U.S astronaut **Mae Jemison** becomes the first female of African descent to go into space.

1993 **Franklin Chang-Díaz** is named director of the Advanced Space Propulsion Laboratory at the Johnson Space Center. He heads research on plasma rocket engines.

1993 U.S. astronaut **Ellen Ochoa** becomes the first Latina in space.

December 1993 Astronauts aboard the space shuttle *Endeavour* complete repairs to the primary mirror of the Hubble Space Telescope.

February 3, 1995 The space shuttle *Discovery* lifts off under the control of U.S. astronaut Eileen M. Collins, the first female pilot on a shuttle mission.

December 2, 1995 The Solar and Heliospheric Observatory is launched to study the Sun.

December 7, 1995 The U.S. space probe *Galileo* goes into orbit around Jupiter, dropping a mini-probe to the planet's surface.

March 24, 1996 U.S. astronaut **Shannon Lucid** begins her 188-day stay aboard *Mir,* a U.S. record for spaceflight endurance at that time.

October 1996 The second of the twin 33-foot Keck telescopes on Mauna Kea, Hawaii, the world's largest optical and infrared telescopes, begins science observations. The first began observations three years earlier.

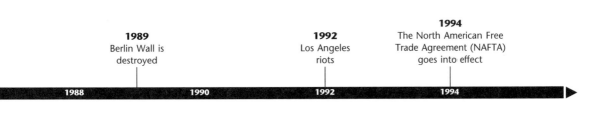

1989
Berlin Wall is destroyed

1992
Los Angeles riots

1994
The North American Free Trade Agreement (NAFTA) goes into effect

1988   1990   1992   1994

July 2, 1997 The U.S. space probe *Mars Pathfinder* lands on Mars and releases *Sojourner,* the first Martian rover.

October 15, 1997 The *Cassini-Huygens* spacecraft, bound for Saturn, is launched.

January 6, 1998 NASA launches the *Lunar Prospector* probe to improve understanding of the origin, evolution, current state, and resources of the Moon.

October 29, 1998 At age seventy-seven, U.S. senator John Glenn, one of the original Mercury astronauts, becomes the oldest astronaut to fly into space when he lifts off aboard the space shuttle *Discovery*.

November 11, 1998 Russia launches Zarya, the control module and first piece of the **International Space Station**, into orbit.

1999 Ellen Ochoa is a member of the *Discovery* crew when the shuttle makes its first visit to the International Space Station.

1999 Former U.S. astronaut **Mae Jemison** founds BioSentient Corporation to explore the commercial applications of Autogenic Feedback Training Exercise (AFTE).

July 23, 1999 The Chandra X-ray Observatory is deployed from the space shuttle *Columbia*.

2001 French astronaut **Claudie Haigneré** becomes the first European woman to visit the International Space Station and the first non-Russian woman to be a Soyuz flight engineer.

February 21, 2001 The U.S. space probe *NEAR Shoemaker* becomes the first spacecraft to land on an asteroid.

March 23, 2001 After more than 86,000 orbits around Earth, *Mir* enters the atmosphere and breaks up into several large pieces and thousands of smaller ones.

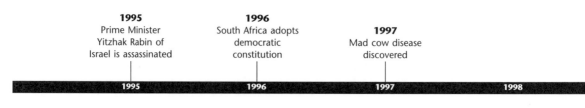

1995
Prime Minister
Yitzhak Rabin of
Israel is assassinated

1996
South Africa adopts
democratic
constitution

1997
Mad cow disease
discovered

1995   1996   1997   1998

April 28, 2001 U.S. investment banker Dennis Tito, the world's first space tourist, lifts off aboard a Soyuz spacecraft for a week-long stay on the International Space Station.

2002 Claudie Haigneré is appointed minister for research and new technologies in the French government.

2002 U.S. astronaut Franklin Chang-Díaz takes his seventh trip into space, tying a world record for the number of space flights set by fellow U.S. astronaut Jerry Ross.

2003 The space shuttle *Columbia* breaks apart in flames above Texas, sixteen minutes before it is supposed to touch down in Florida, because of damage to the shuttle's thermal-protection tiles. All seven astronauts aboard are killed.

2003 Former U.S. astronaut Sally Ride is appointed to the Columbia Accident Investigation Board to investigate the crash of the space shuttle *Columbia*. The board recommends limiting space shuttle flights.

Mid-2003 Further construction on the International Space Station is delayed following the crash of the space shuttle *Columbia*. The future of the space station is uncertain.

June 2003 The Canadian Space Agency launches MOST, its first space telescope successfully launched into space and also the smallest space telescope in the world.

August 25, 2003 NASA launches the Space Infrared Telescope Facility, subsequently renamed the Spitzer Space Telescope, the most sensitive instrument ever to look at the infrared spectrum in the universe.

October 15, 2003 Astronaut **Yang Liwei** lifts off aboard the spacecraft *Shenzhou 5*, becoming the first Chinese to fly into space.

1999
The first nonstop around-the-world balloon trip is made

2000
George W. Bush narrowly defeats Al Gore in controversial U.S. presidential election

2001
Terrorists attack the World Trade Center and the Pentagon

2002
U.S. Justice Department launches investigation into the bankruptcy scandal involving energy giant Enron

1999   2000   2001   2002

2004 NASA cancels the final service mission to the Hubble Space Telescope, citing the dangers of shuttle flights after the *Columbia* crash. Supporters of the orbiting telescope vow to keep it in space.

2004 The Chinese space agency announces plans to recruit women astronauts.

2004 Twin robots, part of NASA's Mars Exploration Rover program, transmit photos to scientists back on Earth as the agency studies the geology of the red planet.

January 14, 2004 U.S. president George W. Bush outlines a new course for U.S. space exploration, including plans to send future manned missions to the Moon and Mars.

June 21, 2004 Civilian pilot Mike Melvill flies the rocket plane *SpaceShipOne* to an altitude of more than 62.5 miles, becoming the first person to pilot a privately built craft beyond the internationally recognized boundary of space.

June 30, 2004 The *Cassini-Huygens* spacecraft becomes the first exploring vehicle to orbit Saturn.

2003
The United States
declares war on Iraq

2003   2004

Words to Know

A

Allies: Alliances of countries in military opposition to another group of nations. In World War II, the Allied powers included Great Britain, the Soviet Union, and the United States.

antimatter: Matter that is exactly the same as normal matter, but with the opposite spin and electrical charge.

apogee: The point in the orbit of an artificial satellite or Moon that is farthest from Earth.

artificial satellite: A human-made device that orbits Earth and other celestial bodies and that follows the same gravitational laws that govern the orbit of a natural satellite.

asterism: A collection of stars within a constellation that forms an apparent pattern.

astrology: The study of the supposed effects of celestial objects on the course of human affairs.

astronautics: The science and technology of spaceflight.

astronomy: The scientific study of the physical universe beyond Earth's atmosphere.

atomic bomb: An explosive device whose violent power is due to the sudden release of energy resulting from the splitting of nuclei of a heavy chemical element (plutonium or uranium), a process called fission.

aurora: A brilliant display of streamers, arcs, or bands of light visible in the night sky, chiefly in the polar regions. It is caused by electrically charged particles from the Sun that are drawn into the atmosphere by Earth's magnetic field.

B

ballistic missile: A missile that travels at a velocity less than what is needed to place it in orbit and that follows a curved path (trajectory) back to Earth's surface once it has reached a given altitude.

bends: A painful and sometimes fatal disorder caused by the formation of gas bubbles in the blood stream and tissues when a decrease in air pressure occurs too rapidly.

big bang theory: The theory that explains the beginning of the universe as a tremendous explosion from a single point that occurred about thirteen billion years ago.

Big Three: The trio of U.S. president Franklin D. Roosevelt, Soviet leader Joseph Stalin, and British prime minister Winston Churchill; also refers to the countries of the United States, the Soviet Union, and Great Britain.

binary star: A pair of stars orbiting around one another, linked by gravity.

black hole: The remains of a massive star that has burned out its nuclear fuel and collapsed under tremendous gravitational force into a single point of infinite mass and gravity from which nothing escapes, not even light.

Bolshevik: A member of the revolutionary political party of Russian workers and peasants that became the Communist Party after the Russian Revolution of 1917.

brown dwarf: A small, cool, dark ball of matter that never completes the process of becoming a star.

C

capitalism: An economic system in which property and businesses are privately owned. Prices, production, and distribution of goods are determined by competition in a market relatively free of government intervention.

celestial mechanics: The scientific study of the influence of gravity on the motions of celestial bodies.

celestial sphere: An imaginary sphere of gigantic radius with Earth located at its center.

Cepheid variable: A pulsating star that can be used to measure distance in space.

chromatic aberration: Blurred coloring of the edge of an image when visible light passes through a lens, caused by the bending of the different wavelengths of the light at different angles.

Cold War: A prolonged conflict for world dominance from 1945 to 1991 between the two superpowers: the democratic, capitalist United States and the Communist Soviet Union. The weapons of conflict were commonly words of propaganda and threats.

Communism: A system of government in which the nation's leaders are selected by a single political party that controls almost all aspects of society. Private ownership of property is eliminated and government directs all economic production. The goods produced and wealth accumulated are, in theory, shared relatively equally by all. All religious practices are banned.

concave lens: A lens with a hollow bowl shape; it is thin in the middle and thick along the edges.

constellation: One of eighty-eight recognized groups of stars that seems to make up a pattern or picture on the celestial sphere.

convex lens: A lens with a bulging surface like the outer surface of a ball; it is thicker in the middle and thinner along the edges.

corona: The outermost and hottest layer of the Sun's atmosphere that extends out into space for millions of miles.

cosmic radiation: High-energy radiation coming from all directions in space.

D

dark matter: Virtually undetectable matter that does not emit or reflect light and that is thought to account for 90 percent of the mass of the universe, acting as a "cosmic glue" that holds together galaxies and clusters of galaxies.

democracy: A system of government that allows multiple political parties. Members of the parties are elected to various government offices by popular vote of the people.

détente: A relaxing of tensions between rival nations, marked by increased diplomatic, commercial, and cultural contact.

docking system: Mechanical and electronic devices that work jointly to bring together and physically link two spacecraft in space.

E

eclipse: The obscuring of one celestial object by another.

ecliptic: The imaginary plane of Earth's orbit around the Sun.

electromagnetic radiation: Radiation that transmits energy through the interaction of electricity and magnetism.

electromagnetic spectrum: The entire range of wavelengths of electromagnetic radiation.

epicycle: A small secondary orbit incorrectly added to the planetary orbits by early astronomers to account for periods in which the planets appeared to move backward with respect to Earth.

escape velocity: The minimum speed that an object, such as a rocket, must have in order to escape completely from the gravitational influence of a planet or a star.

exhaust velocity: The speed at which the exhaust material leaves the nozzle of a rocket engine.

F

flyby: A type of space mission in which the spacecraft passes close to its target but does not enter orbit around it or land on it.

focus: The position at which rays of light from a lens converge to form a sharp image.

force: A push or pull exerted on an object by an outside agent, producing an acceleration that changes the object's state of motion.

G

galaxy: A huge region of space that contains billions of stars, gas, dust, nebulae, and empty space all bound together by gravity.

gamma rays: Short-wavelength, high-energy radiation formed either by the decay of radioactive elements or by nuclear reactions.

geocentric model: The flawed theory that Earth is at the center of the solar system, with the Sun, the Moon, and the other planets revolving around it. Also known as the Ptolemaic model.

geosynchronous orbit: An orbit in which a satellite revolves around Earth at the same rate at which Earth rotates on its axis; thus, the satellite remains positioned over the same location on Earth.

gravity: The force of attraction between objects, the strength of which depends on the mass of each object and the distance between them.

gunpowder: An explosive mixture of charcoal, sulfur, and potassium nitrate.

H

hard landing: The deliberate, destructive impact of a space vehicle on a predetermined celestial object.

heliocentric model: The theory that the Sun is at the center of the solar system and all planets revolve around it. Also known as the Copernican model.

heliosphere: The vast region permeated by charged particles flowing out from the Sun that surrounds the Sun and extends throughout the solar system.

Hellenism: The culture, ideals, and pattern of life of ancient Greece.

hydrocarbon: A compound that contains only two elements, carbon and hydrogen.

hydrogen bomb: A bomb more powerful than the atomic bomb that derives its explosive energy from a nuclear fusion reaction.

hyperbaric chamber: A chamber where air pressure can be carefully controlled; used to acclimate divers, astronauts, and others gradually to changes in air pressure and air composition.

I

inflationary theory: The theory that the universe underwent a period of rapid expansion immediately following the big bang.

infrared radiation: Electromagnetic radiation with wavelengths slightly longer than that of visible light.

interferometer: A device that uses two or more telescopes to observe the same object at the same time in the same wavelength to increase angular resolution.

interplanetary: Between or among planets.

interplanetary medium: The space between planets including forms of energy and dust and gas.

interstellar: Between or among the stars.

interstellar medium: The gas and dust that exists in the space between stars.

ionosphere: That part of Earth's atmosphere that contains a high concentration of particles that have been ionized, or electrically charged, by solar radiation. These particles help reflect certain radio waves over great distances.

J

jettison: To eject or discard.

L

light-year: The distance light travels in the near vacuum of space in one year, about 5.88 trillion miles (9.46 trillion kilometers).

liquid-fuel rocket: A rocket in which both the fuel and the oxidizing agent are in a liquid state.

M

magnetic field: A field of force around the Sun and the planets generated by electrical charges.

magnetism: A natural attractive energy of iron-based materials for other iron-based materials.

magnetosphere: The region of space around a celestial object that is dominated by the object's magnetic field.

mass: The measure of the total amount of matter in an object.

meteorite: A fragment of extraterrestrial material that makes it to the surface of a planet without burning up in the planet's atmosphere.

microgravity: A state where gravity is reduced to almost negligible levels, such as during spaceflight; commonly called weightlessness.

micrometeorite: A very small meteorite or meteoritic particle with a diameter less than a 0.04 inch (1 millimeter).

microwaves: Electromagnetic radiation with a wavelength longer than infrared radiation but shorter than radio waves.

moonlet: A small artificial or natural satellite.

N

natural science: A science, such as biology, chemistry, or physics, that deals with the objects, occurrences, or laws of nature.

neutron star: The extremely dense, compact, neutron-filled remains of a star following a supernova.

nuclear fusion: The merging of two hydrogen nuclei into one helium nucleus, accompanied by a tremendous release of energy.

O

observatory: A structure designed and equipped to observe astronomical phenomena.

oxidizing agent: A substance that can readily burn or promote the burning of any flammable material.

ozone layer: An atmospheric layer that contains a high proportion of ozone molecules that absorb incoming ultraviolet radiation.

P

payload: Any cargo launched aboard a spacecraft, including astronauts, instruments, and equipment.

perigee: The point in the orbit of an artificial satellite or Moon that is nearest to Earth.

physical science: Any of the sciences—such as astronomy, chemistry, geology, and physics—that deal mainly with nonliving matter and energy.

precession: The small wobbling motion Earth makes about its axis as it spins.

probe: An unmanned spacecraft sent to explore the Moon, other celestial bodies, or outer space; some probes are programmed to return to Earth while others are not.

propellant: The chemical mixture burned to produce thrust in rockets.

pulsar: A rapidly spinning, blinking neutron star.

Q

quasars: Extremely bright, star-like sources of radio waves that are found in remote areas of space and that are the oldest known objects in the universe.

R

radiation: The emission and movement of waves of atomic particles through space or other media.

radio waves: The longest form of electromagnetic radiation, measuring up to 6 miles (9.7 kilometers) from peak to peak in the wave.

Red Scare: A great fear among U.S. citizens in the late 1940s and early 1950s that communist influences were infiltrating U.S. society and government and could eventually lead to the overthrow of the American democratic system.

redshift: The shift of an object's light spectrum toward the red end of the visible light range, which is an indication that the object is moving away from the observer.

reflector telescope: A telescope that directs light from an opening at one end to a concave mirror at the far end, which reflects the light back to a smaller mirror that directs it to an eyepiece on the side of the telescope.

refractor telescope: A telescope that directs light waves through a convex lens (the objective lens), which bends the waves and brings them to a focus at a concave lens (the eyepiece) that acts as a magnifying glass.

retrofire: The firing of a spacecraft's engine in the direction opposite to which the spacecraft is moving in order to cut its orbital speed.

rover: A remote-controlled robotic vehicle.

S

sidereal day: The time for one complete rotation of Earth on its axis relative to a particular star.

soft landing: The slow-speed landing of a space vehicle on a celestial object to avoid damage to or the destruction of the vehicle.

solar arrays: Groups of solar cells or other solar collectors arranged to capture energy from the Sun and use it to generate electrical power.

solar day: The average time span from one noon to the next.

solar flare: Temporary bright spot that explodes on the Sun's surface, releasing an incredible amount of energy.

solar prominence: A tongue-like cloud of flaming gas projecting outward from the Sun's surface.

solar wind: Electrically charged subatomic particles that flow out from the Sun.

solid-fuel rocket: A rocket in which the fuel and the oxidizing agent exist in a solid state.

solstice: Either of the two times during the year when the Sun, as seen from Earth, is farthest north or south of the equator; the solstices mark the beginning of the summer and winter seasons.

space motion sickness: A condition similar to ordinary travel sickness, with symptoms that include loss of appetite, nausea, vomiting, gastrointestinal disturbances, and fatigue. The precise cause of the condition is not fully understood, though most scientists agree the problem originates in the balance organs of the inner ear.

space shuttle: A reusable winged spacecraft that transports astronauts and equipment into space and back.

space station: A large orbiting structure designed for long-term human habitation in space.

spacewalk: Technically known as an EVA, or extravehicular activity, an excursion outside a spacecraft or space station by an astronaut or cosmonaut wearing only a pressurized spacesuit and, possibly, some sort of maneuvering device.

spectrograph: A device that separates light by wavelengths to produce a spectrum.

splashdown: The landing of a manned spacecraft in the ocean.

star: A hot, roughly spherical ball of gas that emits light and other forms of electromagnetic radiation as a result of nuclear fusion reactions in its core.

stellar scintillation: The apparent twinkling of a star caused by the refraction of the star's light as it passes through Earth's atmosphere.

stellar wind: Electrically charged subatomic particles that flow out from a star (like the solar wind, but from a star other than the Sun).

sunspot: A cool area of magnetic disturbance that forms a dark blemish on the surface of the Sun.

supernova: The massive explosion of a relatively large star at the end of its lifetime.

T

telescope: An instrument that gathers light or some other form of electromagnetic radiation emitted by distant sources, such as celestial bodies, and brings it to a focus.

thrust: The forward force generated by a rocket.

U

ultraviolet radiation: Electromagnetic radiation of a wavelength just shorter than the violet (shortest wavelength) end of the visible light spectrum.

United Nations: An international organization, composed of most of the nations of the world, created in 1945 to preserve world peace and security.

V

Van Allen belts: Two doughnut-shaped belts of high-energy charged particles trapped in Earth's magnetic field.

X

X rays: Electromagnetic radiation of a wavelength just shorter than ultraviolet radiation but longer than gamma rays that can penetrate solids and produce an electrical charge in gases.

Y

Yalta Conference: A 1944 meeting between Allied leaders Joseph Stalin, Winston Churchill, and Franklin D. Roosevelt in anticipation of an Allied victory in Europe over the Nazis during World War II (1939–45). The leaders discussed how to manage lands conquered by Germany, and Roosevelt and Churchill urged Stalin to enter the Soviet Union in the war against Japan.

Space Exploration
Biographies

Buzz Aldrin

Born January 20, 1930 (Montclair, New Jersey)

American astronaut, engineer, author

On July 20, 1969, American astronaut Buzz Aldrin made history as the second human to walk on the surface of the Moon. Climbing out of the hatch of the *Eagle* lunar landing module of the *Apollo 11* spacecraft, he followed **Neil Armstrong** (1930–; see entry) down to the surface. This historic first Moon landing came at an important time for the United States, which had been engaged with the former Soviet Union in a period of hostile relations known as the Cold War (1945–91). They were competing for military superiority as well as for dominance in space. In 1957, the Soviet Union launched Sputnik space satellites (objects that orbit in space) to study Earth's atmosphere, a development that alarmed many Americans. Now the *Apollo 11* mission had brought the United States to the forefront of space exploration. Although Armstrong is most closely identified with the first Moon landing, he has been reluctant to discuss his adventure. Aldrin went on to become a public figure, promoting commercial space travel and achieving success as a writer.

"There is no view quite like seeing our planet glowing blue and white from the distance of space."

Buzz Aldrin. *(AP/Wide World Photos)*

Wins war medal

Edwin Eugene Aldrin Jr. was born on January 20, 1930, in Montclair, New Jersey. Given the nickname "Buzz" by his sister, he changed his name legally from Edwin to Buzz after his Moon walk. Aldrin's upbringing had a direct influence on his decision to pursue a military career. His mother, Marion Moon, was the daughter of an army chaplain. His father, Edwin Eugene Aldrin Sr., was a U.S. Air Force officer and a former student of rocket scientist **Robert Goddard** (1882–1945; see entry).

Buzz Aldrin was a good student at Montclair High School, where he played center on the championship football team.

After high school, he entered the U.S. Military Academy at West Point, New York, graduating third in his class in 1951. A commissioned U.S. Air Force officer and fighter pilot, he was sent to Korea for combat duty the following year. He flew sixty-six missions during the Korean War (1950–53), earning the Distinguished Flying Cross (an award given to a person serving in the U.S. armed forces who performs an act of heroism or extraordinary achievement during an aerial flight). After the war, Aldrin was an air force flight instructor in Nevada, then an aide and flight instructor at the U.S. Air Force Academy in Colorado. In 1956, he served as a flight commander for a squadron in West Germany (now Germany).

Seeking a new career, Aldrin enrolled in an engineering program at the Massachusetts Institute of Technology (MIT) in 1960. Three years later, upon receiving a doctorate degree in orbital mechanics, he entered the National Aeronautics and Space Administration (NASA) astronaut training program. He was then selected to be in NASA's third group of fourteen astronauts, who would be trained for the Gemini and Apollo space missions. (The Gemini program was devoted to spacecraft docking and men making spacewalks; the goal of the Apollo program was to send astronauts to the Moon.) The first astronaut to hold a doctoral degree, Aldrin was also the only one who was not a test pilot.

Joins NASA

During eighteen months of intensive basic training, the astronauts participated in strenuous physical exercises, attended classes, and practiced in-flight exercises. Aldrin's first assignment was as the command pilot of *Gemini 12*. While completing an additional two thousand hours of specialized training for the mission, he pioneered the use of underwater training to simulate spacewalking. In November 1966, Aldrin and copilot James Lovell Jr. (1928–) were launched aboard *Gemini 12*. During the flight, Aldrin was the first to prove that astronauts could work outside an orbiting vehicle to make repairs. After *Gemini 12,* Aldrin began preparing for the Apollo spaceflights. He discovered ways to improve various technical processes, such as navigating according to the positions of stars. He also took geology field trips to Hawaii, Idaho, Oregon, and Iceland to study rock formations similar to those expected to be found on the Moon.

Walks on Moon

In 1968, Aldrin was named back-up command module pilot for *Apollo 8,* the first successful attempt to orbit a manned lunar spacecraft. The following year, he was selected to join Armstrong and Michael Collins (1930–; see box on page 5) on the crew of *Apollo 11,* the first lunar landing mission. On July 16, 1969, Aldrin, Armstrong, and Collins boarded *Apollo 11* and blasted off from Cape Kennedy (now Cape Canaveral) in Florida. The spacecraft consisted of three stages, or separate components—the *Saturn 5* booster rocket (used to propel the craft into space) was attached to the *Columbia* command module (all three astronauts rode aboard this spacecraft on the trip to and from the Moon) and the *Eagle* lunar landing module (the vehicle that would land on the Moon).

On July 19, *Saturn 5* propelled the craft into lunar orbit and circled the Moon twice. The next day, Aldrin and Armstrong transferred to the *Eagle.* After about five hours of tests, the *Eagle* and the *Columbia* separated successfully and the *Eagle* entered its own orbit. Within two hours, Aldrin and Armstrong began the 300-mile descent toward the Moon. At that point, a yellow caution light came on in the *Eagle,* signaling that the computer system had become overloaded. Under continuous instructions from the mission control center in Houston, Texas, the *Eagle* made a gradual descent toward touchdown on the Moon.

In *Apollo Expeditions to the Moon,* Aldrin later reflected upon those tense moments: "Back in Houston, not to mention on board the *Eagle,* hearts shot up into throats while we waited to learn what would happen. . . . We receive three or four more warnings but keep on going." The targeted computer-guided landing site was in an area called the Sea of Tranquility. A field of boulders was looming in front of the *Eagle,* so Armstrong landed without computer assistance about four miles away. At 4:18 P.M. on July 20, more than one-half billion people around the world heard Armstrong say: "Houston, Tranquility Base here. The *Eagle* has landed."

Seven hours after touchdown, at 10:56 P.M., Armstrong climbed down a nine-step ladder and became the first human

Michael Collins

Michael Collins piloted the command module *Columbia* during the *Apollo 11* lunar landing mission. A graduate of the U.S. Military Academy at West Point (1952), he joined NASA as an astronaut in 1963, along with Buzz Aldrin and Neil Armstrong. Three years later, Collins piloted the *Gemini 10* and became the third American to walk in space. (The first American to perform a space walk was Edward White (1930–1967; see *Apollo 1* entry) in June 1965 on the *Gemini 4* mission.)

In *Apollo Expeditions to the Moon,* Collins recalled the moment when Aldrin and Armstrong returned to the *Columbia* after becoming the first humans to walk on the Moon. "The first one through [the hatch] is Buzz, with a big smile on his face," Collins said. "I grab his head, a hand on each temple, and am about to give him a smooch on the forehead, as a parent might greet an errant child; but then, embarrassed, I think better of it and grab his hand, and then Neil's. We cavort about a little bit, all smiles and giggles over our success, and then it's back to work as usual."

Since leaving NASA, Collins has held various government positions, including di-

Michael Collins. *(© NASA/Roger Ressmeyer/Corbis)*

rector of the National Air and Space Museum (1971–78), and he holds the rank of lieutenant colonel in the U.S. Air Force Reserve. He has also published several books. Among them are *Carrying the Fire: An Astronaut's Journeys* (1974 and 1989), *Liftoff: The Story of America's Adventure in Space* (1988), *Mission to Mars* (1990), and *Flying to the Moon: An Astronaut's Story* (1994).

to set foot on the Moon. Aldrin joined him fifteen minutes later. Aldrin further elaborated on the experience in *Apollo Expeditions to the Moon:* "We opened the hatch [of the *Eagle*] and Neil, with me as his navigator, began backing out of the tiny opening. It seemed like a small eternity before I heard Neil say, 'That's one small step for man . . . one giant leap for mankind.' In less than fifteen minutes I was backing awkwardly out of

Open-Door Policy

As Aldrin descended down the ladder, he radioed to Armstrong: "Now I want to partially close the hatch, making sure not to lock it on my way out." Armstrong replied: "A good thought!"

the hatch and onto the surface to join Neil, who, in the tradition of all tourists, had his camera ready to photograph my arrival. I felt buoyant and full of goose pimples when I stepped down on the surface."

Aldrin and Armstrong quickly adjusted to the lighter gravity, finding they could walk easily on the lunar surface. They spent nearly twenty-one hours on the Moon. During their stay, they installed a television camera, conducted scientific experiments, took photographs, and collected rock and soil samples. They left an American flag, a mission patch, and medals commemorating American and Russian space explorers who had died in the line of duty. They also set up a plaque that read: "Here men from the planet Earth first set foot upon the Moon. We came in peace for all mankind." The astronauts' Moon walk was televised live on Earth, and President Richard M. Nixon (1913–1994; served 1969–74) made a telephone call to them from the White House. After returning to the *Eagle,* Aldrin and Armstrong rested for eight hours. Then they launched off the surface of the Moon and, two hours later, docked with Collins and the *Columbia.* After unloading their equipment onto *Columbia,* they abandoned the *Eagle.* The *Columbia* set out for Earth on its thirty-first orbit of the Moon. Sixty hours later, at 12:50 P.M. on July 24, the spacecraft splashed down in the sea some 950 miles (1,520 kilometers) southwest of Hawaii, only 2.7 miles (4.34 kilometers) from its destination point.

Aldrin, Armstrong, and Collins were picked up by Navy frogmen (divers) from the aircraft carrier *Hornet.* As the *Hornet* sailed for Hawaii, the astronauts remained aboard for eighteen days of quarantine (seclusion) to control any harmful bacteria they may have carried from the Moon. From Hawaii, the astronauts were flown to Houston, where they received a heroes' welcome. They were also honored in a parade in New York City, and they were greeted enthusiastically when they toured twenty-two foreign countries. They were awarded the Presidential Medal of Freedom, America's highest civilian honor.

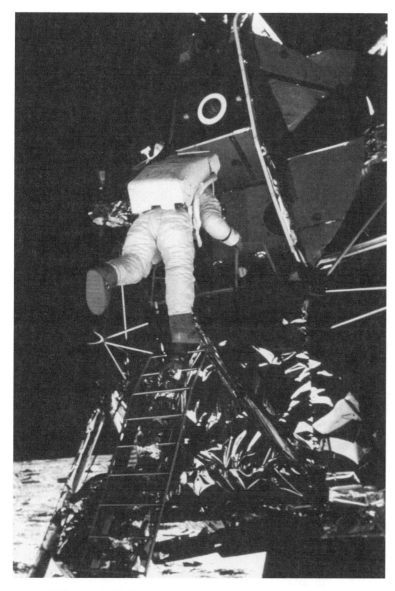

Buzz Aldrin steps off the *Eagle* lunar module onto the Moon, becoming the second human to walk on the Moon. *(NASA)*

Following the *Apollo 11* mission, the Air Force promoted Aldrin to commander of the test-pilot school at Edwards Air Force Base in California. He was unhappy in his new job, however, so he resigned from NASA in 1971. Soon thereafter, he underwent treatment for depression and retired from the Air

A Trip to Mars

In an interview published in *Odyssey* magazine, Buzz Aldrin described his vision of a future journey to Mars. The first leg of the trip would be made by a shuttle equipped with additional booster rockets that could propel it out of Earth's orbit. The shuttle would then dock with a large, reusable transfer ship, or space station, called the "Cycler." People would transfer from the shuttle to the Cycler, where they would live during the six-month trip to Mars. Assisted by the gravitational pull of the planets, the Cycler would be continuously moving on an oval path between Earth and Mars.

According to Aldrin, the safest, most efficient Mars transport system would involve two Cyclers, each operating in two phases—the "Go-Cycler" and the "Re-Cycler"—during a complete, eleven-month orbit between Mars and Earth. In the Go-Cycler phase, a Cycler would leave Mars without passengers, then pick up people coming from Earth aboard the shuttle and take them on the six-month trip back to Mars. In the Re-Cycler phase, the route would be the reverse: A Cycler would carry passengers on the six-month journey from Mars back to Earth, transfer them to the shuttle, then return empty to Mars.

Force. Aldrin then publicly acknowledged that he was a recovering alcoholic. This was a bold step because at the time celebrities were reluctant to talk about such a personal subject. In 1972, he was appointed chairman of the National Association of Mental Health and made appearances across the country describing his battle with depression.

Supports commercial space travel

In 1972, Aldrin founded his own company, now known as Starcraft Booster, Inc., to promote space tourism and travel to Mars. Aldrin has designed and patented several reusable spacecraft, which are part of a system he calls Starbooster. Aldrin elaborated on his ideas during an interview for *Odyssey* magazine in 2001. Asked why people would want to be space tourists, Aldrin replied, "Space travel is very pleasurable. . . . Floating around in zero-g [gravity] is fascinating and exhilarating! . . . There is no view quite like seeing our planet glowing blue and white from the distance of space." He said that today's young people can expect to be the scientists and explorers who prepare the way for civilian tourists, who could be traveling to orbital hotels by 2020.

Writes science fiction

Aldrin is also a successful writer. He has published an autobiography (*Return to Earth*, 1974) and an account of his Moon trip (*Men from Earth*, coauthored with Malcolm McConnell; 1989). With coauthor John Barnes, he wrote two

Former astronaut Buzz Aldrin holds his new science fiction novel *Encounter with Tiber* during an appearance in Las Vegas in August 1996. *(AP/Wide World Photos)*

science-fiction novels, *Encounter with Tiber* (1996) and *The Return* (2000). Aldrin has served as chairman of the board of the National Space Society and has been awarded fifty distinguished medals and citations from nations throughout the world. In 1996, he photographed the recovery of the wreckage *Titanic*, the famous ocean liner that sank in 1912 in the Atlantic Ocean 420 miles (676 kilometers) southeast of Newfoundland. The father of three children—James Michael, Janice Ross, and Andrew John—Aldrin lives in Southern California with his third wife, Lois Driggs Cannon. (His first two marriages ended in divorce.) Aldrin spends most of his time promoting commercial space travel, and he likes to joke about being the inspiration for Buzz Lightyear, a character in the popular *Toy Story* films.

For More Information

Books

Aldrin, Buzz, and John Barnes. *Encounter with Tiber.* New York: Warner Books, 1996.

Aldrin, Buzz, and John Barnes. *The Return.* New York: Forge, 2000.

Aldrin, Buzz, and Malcolm McConnell. *Men from Earth.* New York: Bantam Books, 1989.

Aldrin, Edwin Eugene Jr., and Wayne Warga. *Return to Earth.* New York: Random House, 1973.

Armstrong, Neil, Edwin Eugene Aldrin Jr., Michael Collins, Gene Farmer, and Jane Hamblin. *First on the Moon.* New York: Little, Brown, 1970.

Chaikin, Andrew. *A Man on the Moon.* New York: Time-Life, 1969.

Cole, Michael D. Apollo 11: *First Moon Landing.* Springfield, NJ: Enslow, 1995.

Cortright, Edgar M., ed. *Apollo Expeditions to the Moon.* Washington: Scientific and Technical Information Office, National Aeronautics and Space Administration, 1975.

Periodicals

Aldrin, Buzz. "America's Space Program: What We Should Do Next." *Popular Mechanics* (May 2003): pp. 110–13.

Eaglesham, Barbara. "Catch the Buzz: An Interview with Apollo Astronaut Buzz Aldrin." *Odyssey* (January 2001): p. 30.

Epstein, Robert. "Down to Earth Buzz Aldrin." *Psychology Today* (May 2001): p. 68.

Folger, Tim, Sarah Richardson, and Carl Zimmer. "Remembering Apollo." *Discover* (July 1994): p. 38.

Robbins, Gary. "Exploring the Titanic: Buzz Aldrin Goes from Astronaut to Argonaut." *Orange County Register* (Knight Ridder Tribune News Service; September 13, 1996).

Web Sites

"*Apollo 11* Transcripts." *Kennedy Space Center.* http://www-pao.ksc.nasa.gov/history/apollo/apollo-11/apollo11transcripts.htm (accessed on May 27, 2004).

Buzz Aldrin. http://www.buzzaldrin.com (accessed on May 27, 2004).

"Buzz Aldrin." *Lyndon B. Johnson Space Center, NASA.* http://www.jsc.nasa.gov/Bios/htmlbios/aldrin-b.html (accessed on May 27, 2004).

Apollo 1 Crew

Died January 27, 1967 (Cape Canaveral, Florida)

American astronauts

On January 27, 1967, the first step toward putting an American on the Moon ended in tragedy. That day, astronauts Roger Chaffee (1935–1967), Gus Grissom (1926–1967), and Edward White (1930–1967) died aboard their *Apollo 1* spacecraft. They had been conducting tests on the launch pad at Cape Kennedy (now Cape Canaveral) in Florida, when a fire broke out in their crew module. The accident was a severe blow to the National Aeronautics and Space Administration (NASA), which had given high priority to Project Apollo, the U.S. program that would send humans to the Moon. *Apollo 1* was to be the first in a series of manned Moon flights, but the accident forced a temporary halt to the program and NASA safety procedures underwent extensive review.

> "Fire in the cockpit."
>
> *Edward White*

Soviets triumph in space war

NASA initiated Project Apollo at a time when national pride was at stake. On May 25, 1961, President John F. Kennedy (1917–1963; served 1961–63) had vowed that the United States would put a man on the Moon within the next ten years. His vision captured the imagination of the Ameri-

Apollo 1 crew (left to right) Gus Grissom, Edward White, and Roger Chaffee. *(NASA)*

can people, and this spirit of adventure greatly expanded the mission of NASA. Kennedy's speech immediately followed the achievement of astronaut Alan Shepard (1923–1998), who had become the first American in space less than three weeks earlier. He piloted a Mercury space capsule 115 miles (185 kilometers) above Earth's surface and 302 miles (486 kilometers) across the Atlantic Ocean. Although the trip lasted for only about fifteen minutes, his journey was almost technically perfect. But Shepard was not the first human in space: On April 12, Soviet cosmonaut (astronaut) **Yuri Gagarin** (1934–1968;

see entry) had made a nearly complete orbit of Earth aboard the spacecraft *Vostok 1*. Gagarin's flight, which had been surrounded by intense secrecy, represented a technical triumph for the Soviet Union. Shepard had briefly flown in space, whereas Gagarin had virtually circled Earth.

Americans saw the Gagarin flight as yet another Soviet victory in the "space race." The space race was part of the Cold War (1945–91), a period of hostile relations between the former Soviet Union and the United States that began at the end of World War II (1939–45). Not only were the two superpowers involved in an arms race for military superiority, but they were also competing for dominance in space. The first major event in the space race had occurred in 1957, when the Soviet Union launched the *Sputnik 1* satellite (an object that orbits in space) to study the atmosphere of Earth. This achievement surprised the world and sent shock waves through American society. *Sputnik 1* was a sign that the Soviet Union was moving ahead in the Cold War. In 1958, the United States responded by creating NASA, which integrated U.S. space research agencies and established an astronaut training program.

The first stage of the NASA space program was Project Mercury. The goal was to develop the basic technology for manned space flight and investigate a human's ability to survive and perform in space. Shepard's flight was proof of Project Mercury's success, but Gagarin's effort showed that not enough progress was being made by the United States. Under pressure to match the Russian feat as soon as possible, NASA chose **John Glenn** (1921–; see entry) to be the first American to orbit Earth. On February 20, 1962, Glenn successfully made three orbits aboard the *Friendship 7*, another Mercury mission. In 1964, NASA initiated Project Gemini. This program provided astronauts with experience in returning to Earth from space as well as successfully linking space vehicles and "walking" in space. Gemini also involved the launching of a series of unmanned satellites, which would gain information about the Moon and its surface to determine whether humans could survive there.

The Apollo spacecraft

One major result of the U.S. space program was Project Apollo, named for the Greek god of the Sun. The first challenge was to design, develop, and test an Apollo spacecraft and related technology that would place a human on the Moon. With the support of NASA, **Werhner von Braun** (1912–1977; see entry) and his colleagues—who developed the V-2 rocket for Nazi Germany during World War II and afterward immigrated to the United States—developed the three-stage *Saturn 5* rocket to launch the spacecraft. The Saturn worked in stages (separate functions), a concept that was originated by Russian engineer **Konstantin Tsiolkovsky** (1857–1935; see entry) and tested by American physicist **Robert Goddard** (1882–1945; see entry). The rocket's first two stages propelled the spacecraft out of Earth's gravity into space and then dropped off. The third stage put the spacecraft into Earth orbit. The rocket then refired to send the spacecraft at a speed of 25,000 miles (40,225 kilometers) per hour toward the Moon, with the third stage dropping off along the way.

The spacecraft itself consisted of the command module (similar to the cockpit of an airplane), where the astronauts were stationed; the service module, which contained electrical power and fuel; and the lunar module, which, after entering the Moon's orbit, could separate from the rest of the spacecraft and carry the astronauts to the surface of the Moon. The lunar module, which stood 23 feet (7 meters) high and weighed 15 tons (13.6 metric tons), rested first on spiderlike legs used for landing and then on a launch platform for departure from the Moon's surface. The lunar module lacked heat shields (panels that protect against intense heat) and operated only in the vacuum of space. After launching itself from the Moon's surface, the lunar module would go into lunar orbit and dock with the command module, which would then readjust its course to head back to Earth. The service module powered the spacecraft on the return trip, falling away prior to reentry into Earth's atmosphere.

The *Apollo 1* crew

Once the Apollo spacecraft had been built, the next step was to choose a crew. Gus Grissom was the commander, Edward White was the command pilot, and Roger Chaffee was the pilot. Their mission was to be the first manned test in Earth orbit of the spacecraft that would eventually take people to the Moon.

Apollo 1 **commander Gus Grissom.** *(© Bettmann/Corbis)*

Gus Grissom

Virgil Ivan "Gus" Grissom was born on April 3, 1926, in Mitchell, Indiana. While growing up, he was fascinated by aviation, and he was determined to become a pilot. He enlisted in the Army Air Corps in 1944. After World War II, he enrolled at Purdue University in Indiana, earning a bachelor of science degree in mechanical engineering in 1950. He again enlisted in the military and was commissioned a second lieutenant in the air force. During the Korean War (1950–53), he flew combat missions, for which he won several medals. He was serving as a test pilot at Wright-Patterson Air Force Base in Ohio when NASA was seeking pilots to explore the problems of manned space flight for Project Mercury. Grissom volunteered for this project, and in 1959 he was one of seven military test pilots chosen to become the first American astronauts.

In 1961, Grissom participated in a test flight of the Mercury spacecraft *Liberty Bell 7*. The mission succeeded without incident until after the spacecraft landed, as planned, in the ocean. While helicopters approached to retrieve the capsule, the hatch blew off prematurely (an accident that was never satisfactorily explained), but Grissom managed to leave the spacecraft before it sank. He became the second American to fly in space when he was command pilot on the Gemini spacecraft *Molly Brown* in 1965. He and crewmate John W. Young (1930–) tested such objectives as how to control the craft's landing point. In March 1966, Grissom was named commander of *Apollo 1*.

Edward White

Edward Higgins White II was born on November 14, 1930, in San Antonio, Texas. His father, Edward H. White, was a career air force officer and pioneer army balloonist and aviator. The family was living in Washington, D.C., when White was in high school. Since the District of Columbia has no representative in the U.S. Congress, he won appointment to the U.S. Military Academy by making himself known to as many congressmen as possible. He graduated from the academy in 1952 with a commission as a second lieutenant in the air force. While serving as a fighter pilot in Germany, White followed with interest the development of the manned spaceflight program and set out to qualify as an astronaut. He earned a master's degree in aeronautical engineering from the University of Michigan in 1959. After completing a test pilot certification program, he was assigned to Wright-Patterson Air Force Base as a test pilot.

White applied for the astronaut program when NASA announced openings for a second group of trainees. He was accepted in 1962. Three years later, he was the pilot on *Gemini 4*, commanded by James A. McDivitt (1929–). *Gemini 4* was the first long-duration flight (sixty-two revolutions from June 3 through June 7) in the U.S. manned spaceflight program.

Apollo 1 **astronaut Edward White.** *(AP/Wide World Photos)*

During this mission, White became the first American to perform extravehicular activity, or "space walk," floating outside the spacecraft for twenty minutes over a distance of about 7,500 miles (12,068 kilometers). In 1966, White was named to the crew of *Apollo 1.*

Roger Chaffee

Roger Bruce Chaffee was born on February 15, 1935, in Grand Rapids, Michigan. After graduating from high school, he attended the Illinois Institute of Technology for one year and then transferred to Purdue University. He received a bach-

Apollo 1 **astronaut Roger Chaffee.** *(© Bettmann/Corbis)*

elor of science degree in aeronautical engineering from Purdue in 1957. Commissioned an ensign in the navy that same year, he went through flight training and was subsequently assigned to a photographic squadron in Florida. In January 1963, Chaffee entered the Air Force Institute of Technology to work toward a master's degree.

When NASA announced that it was recruiting a third group of astronaut trainees, he applied and was selected in 1963. By the time he had completed basic astronaut training, the Gemini program was well under way and Apollo flights were being planned. Chaffee was assigned to flight-control communications systems and spacecraft control systems. In March 1966, he was selected as a crew member of *Apollo 1*.

Crew dies in fire

On January 27, 1967, the Apollo spacecraft, then called *Apollo/Saturn 204,* was scheduled to go into space in less than a month. At 1:00 P.M. that day, Grissom, White, and Chaffee entered the crew module on the launchpad at Cape Kennedy. They began conducting a "plugs-out" test. This test is an exact simulation of launch activities, or count, but without fuel in the rocket. Almost immediately the crew encountered minor problems that delayed the process. The count was suspended at 5:40 P.M. after a communications failure. Then, at 6:31 P.M. technicians in the control room, who were monitoring radio communications with the module, heard someone (later determined to be Chaffee) say, "Fire, I smell fire." At 6:33 P.M., they heard White say, "Fire in the cockpit." The voices then became garbled, but the last moments of the crew were clearly audible in the control room until the transmission was cut off at 6:48 P.M.

In the meantime, rescuers had rushed to the spacecraft, but it took them five minutes to open the hatch (door to the module). The hatch was secured by several latches that had to be pried loose. The hatch swung inward, so pressure had to be released before it could be pushed open and the crew members pulled out of the module. Efforts were made to resuscitate Grissom, Chaffee, and White, but by that time they were all dead. The fire had spread with incredible speed, for the atmosphere in the vehicle was pure oxygen and the materials inside were highly flammable. Within thirty seconds, the three crewmen were unconscious and probably completely asphyxiated (made unable to breathe) by toxic gases. They thus became the first American astronauts to die in an accident directly related to space activity. An investigating board concluded that the fire was most likely started by a spark from an electrical short circuit that ignited the flammable materials.

As a result of the accident, the Apollo program was temporarily delayed. After an extensive investigation, NASA issued new safety precautions. In the future, spacecraft would contain self-extinguishing materials, and a nitrogen-oxygen mixture would replace pure oxygen. The hatch door was

The charred interior of the *Apollo 1* spacecraft, following the fire that killed astronauts Gus Grissom, Edward White, and Roger Chaffee. *(AP/ Wide World Photos)*

redesigned to swing outward, and an improved latch system allowed quick removal. In honor of Grissom, White, and Chafee, *Apollo/Saturn 204* was officially renamed *Apollo 1.*

Space program takes new direction

The next Project Apollo missions were unmanned flights that tested the safety of the equipment. The first manned flight was *Apollo 7* in October 1968. The most famous was *Apollo 11,* which successfully landed **Neil Armstrong** (1930–; see entry) and **Buzz Aldrin** (1930–; see entry) on the Moon. The last flight was *Apollo 17* in December 1972, which ended one of the most productive periods of exploration in U.S. history. After Project Apollo, NASA concentrated its efforts on space shuttle missions to space stations. (A space shuttle is a vehicle that transports people and cargo between Earth and space. A space station is a scientific research laboratory that orbits in space.) By 2004, U.S. shuttles had made several missions to the **International Space Station** (ISS; see entry), a space research endeavor that involves astronauts from nations throughout the world.

Tragedy struck NASA two more times. In 1986, the shuttle *Challenger* (see entry) exploded shortly after launch, killing seven astronauts. In 2003, seven other astronauts died when the shuttle *Columbia* (see box in *Challenger* **Crew** entry) broke up over the western United States. Since *Apollo 17,* there have been no other flights to the Moon, either by the United States or any other nation. In 2003, however, China sent its first person into space (see **Yang Liwei** [1965–] entry) and announced plans to go to the Moon. In 2004, President George W. Bush (1946–; served 2001–) renewed the U.S. commitment to a continuation of the Moon exploration program in the near future.

For More Information

Books

Brooks, Courtney G., James M. Grimwood, and Loyd S. Swenson, Jr. *Chariots for Apollo.* Washington, DC: National Aeronautics and Space Administration, 1979.

Brubaker, Paul. Apollo 1 *Tragedy: Fire in the Capsule.* Berkeley Heights, NJ: Enslow Publishers, 2002.

Carpenter, M. Scott, Virgil I. Grissom, and others. *We Seven, by the Astronauts Themselves.* New York: Simon & Schuster, 1962.

DeAngelis, Gina. *The* Apollo 1 *and* Challenger *Disasters.* Philadelphia: Chelsea House, 2001.

Greenberger, Robert. *Gus Grissom: The Tragedy of* Apollo 1. New York: Rosen Publishing Group, 2004.

Web Sites

"*Apollo 1* Fire." *AboutSpace.com.* http://www.space.about.com/astronautbios/a/apollo1 (accessed on May 28, 2004).

"*Apollo 1* Web site." *NASA.* http://www.hq.nasa.gov/office/pao/History/Apollo204/ (accessed on May 28, 2004).

Neil Armstrong

Born August 5, 1930 (Wapakoneta, Ohio)

American astronaut

"[The *Apollo 11* mission] was a culmination of the work of 300,000 to 400,000 people over a decade, and . . . the nation's hopes and outward appearance largely rested on how the results came out."

In 1957, the former Soviet Union launched the first *Sputnik* satellite (an object that orbits in space) to study the atmosphere of Earth, sending shock waves through American society. Since the end of World War II (1939–45), the United States and the Soviet Union had been engaged in a period of hostile relations known as the Cold War (1945–91). Not only were the two powers involved in an arms race for military superiority, but they were also competing for dominance in space. The *Sputnik* satellites were therefore a sign that the Soviet Union was moving ahead in the Cold War. In 1958 the United States responded by creating the National Aeronautics and Space Administration (NASA), which combined U.S. space research agencies and established an astronaut training program. Then, in the early 1960s, President John F. Kennedy (1917–1963; served 1961–63) made a pledge to put an American on the Moon by the end of the decade. On July 20, 1969, astronaut Neil Armstrong achieved that goal by stepping onto the surface of the Moon as millions of people throughout the world watched on television. Armstrong immediately became identified with human exploration of the Moon.

Neil Armstrong. *(NASA)*

Young pilot becomes war hero

Neil Alden Armstrong was born on August 5, 1930, on a farm near Wapakoneta, Ohio, the oldest of three children of Stephen Armstrong and Viola Engel Armstrong. Neil became fascinated with flying at an early age. Among his first memories was attending air races in Cleveland as a two-year-old with his father. Four years later he took his first airplane ride in the skies above his hometown. Pursuing his interest in flight throughout his childhood and teenage years, Armstrong subscribed to aviation magazines and built model airplanes. To test the durability of his models, he constructed a wind tunnel with a fan in the basement of the family home. When he was fourteen Armstrong decided he wanted to take flying lessons. The lessons were expensive—nine dollars an hour—so he got a job at a local drugstore to earn the money. Paid forty cents an hour, he swept floors and stacked boxes. He rode his bicycle 3 miles to the Wapak Flying Service to take lessons. Within a year he flew solo, then earned his pilot's wings on his sixteenth birthday, even before he had gotten a driver's license.

A good student throughout his school years, Armstrong skipped first grade and did especially well in science and mathematics. He also enjoyed reading books on astronomy. While in high school he formed a small jazz band and played baritone horn; music continued to be his hobby during adulthood. Armstrong was active in Boy Scouts, and at age seventeen he became an Eagle Scout. After graduating from high school in 1947 he was awarded a U.S. Navy scholarship at Purdue University in West Lafayette, Indiana. Majoring in aeronautical engineering, he joined the Naval Air Cadet program.

Armstrong's college studies were interrupted two years later when he was called to active duty at the beginning of the Korean War (1950–53). Trained to fly fighter jets at Pensacola Naval Air Station in Florida, the twenty-year-old was the youngest pilot in his squadron. During his service in Korea, Armstrong flew seventy-eight combat missions in F9F-2 fighter jets, winning three air medals. When the war was over he returned to Purdue and, in 1955, completed a degree in aeronautical engineering. After graduation he took a job with the Lewis Flight Propulsion Laboratory of the National Advisory Committee for Aeronautics (NACA) in Cleveland. In 1956 Armstrong married Janet Shearon, whom he had met at Purdue. The couple later had two sons, Mark and Eric; their daughter, Karen, died at age three.

Sets records as test pilot

Armstrong soon transferred to the NACA High Speed Flight Station at Edwards Air Force Base in California, where he became a test pilot. He flew numerous experimental aircraft, including the B-29, a "drop plane" used for launching rocket-propelled planes. He also piloted the X-1B rocket plane,

The Astronaut and the Boy Scout

When Neil Armstrong was a freshman in college, he became an Eagle Scout, the highest rank in the Boy Scout program. Years later, after he had gained fame as an astronaut hero, Armstrong helped another young Scout earn a merit badge. The Scout was Ken Drayton, who recalled the experience in an *American Heritage* magazine article in 1999.

In 1973, four years after Armstrong's walk on the Moon, Drayton was seventeen years old and living in Marietta, Ohio. He wanted to work on a space-exploration badge, which he needed to advance to Star rank in the Boy Scouts. This badge had only recently been added to the scouting program, so there were no counselors in Marietta who could help Drayton meet the requirements. After doing some research, he found that Armstrong was a professor of aeronautical engineering at the University of Cincinnati and lived on a farm near Lebanon, Ohio. Drayton decided to make the 150-mile drive to Armstrong's farm, hoping to meet the former astronaut and request his assistance. When Drayton arrived, he caught sight of Armstrong, who was dressed in jeans and a work shirt, remodeling the old farmhouse. Much to Drayton's surprise, Armstrong was open to the idea of assisting with the badge. He outlined a list of items he wanted Drayton to complete for the space-exploration badge.

An elated Drayton drove back home and set to work. After finishing the assignment, he waited anxiously for word from Armstrong. Finally, Armstrong sent a letter to Drayton's scoutmaster, stating, "In my opinion, [Drayton] has completed all requirements satisfactorily." On the thirtieth anniversary of Armstrong's walk on the Moon, Drayton wrote his article to pay tribute to the "former Eagle Scout [who] took the time to help another Scout achieve a goal."

a version of the first plane that had earlier broken the sound barrier (a sudden increase of air pressure on an airplane as it approaches the speed of sound). Armstrong was one of the first three NACA pilots to fly the X-15 rocket plane, an experimental spacecraft on which he made seven flights. Once, he set a record altitude of 207,500 feet (63,246 meters) and a speed of 3,989 miles (6,418 kilometers) per hour aboard the X-15. While at Edwards he was invited to join the NASA astronaut program, but he declined. He was now a civilian pilot (at that time all astronauts were in the military). Moreover, he believed the X-15, which had wings, had greater potential for space travel than the Mercury capsule (small pressurized compartment or vehicle) being used by NASA. His experience with the X-15 led to his assignment by NACA to test the Dynasoar, an experimental craft that could leave the atmosphere (the whole mass of air surrounding Earth), orbit Earth, reenter the atmosphere, and land like a conventional airplane.

When it became apparent that the Dynasoar project was destined for cancellation, in 1962—the year American astronaut **John Glenn** (1921–; see entry) successfully orbited Earth—Armstrong decided to apply to the NASA program. Upon acceptance with the second group of U.S. astronauts, he became America's first civilian astronaut and began training on the *Gemini* mission in Houston, Texas. Four years later he made his first space flight as a command pilot: On March 16, 1966, Armstrong and his copilot, David Scott (1932–), were launched aboard *Gemini 8* from Cape Kennedy (now Cape Canaveral) in Florida. Successfully entering orbit, they flew 105,000 miles (168,945 kilometers) and docked (connected) as planned with an unmanned orbiting spacecraft, the *Agena*. The docking of two orbiting spacecraft was a historic first.

Armstrong's job was to hook the nose of *Gemini 8* onto a docking collar on the *Agena*. One-half hour after the linkup, however, the two vehicles started spinning out of control. Armstrong thought the *Agena* was causing the problem, so he disconnected the *Gemini 8*. But then the *Gemini 8* began spinning wildly—one revolution per second—and lost contact with the ground control facility at the Manned Spacecraft Center in Houston. The ground control crew thought *Gemini 8* was lost in space. Armstrong then brought the spacecraft down in the Pacific Ocean, only 1.1 nautical miles (measurement of distance at sea; one nautical mile is equal to 6076 feet or 1852 meters) from the targeted landing point. Armstrong's handling of the near disaster earned him a reputation as a brave, cool pilot.

Known for coolness under pressure

Although Armstrong continued training on *Gemini* spacecraft, he did not fly another *Gemini* mission. In January 1969 he was named commander of the *Apollo 11* mission, which was to be the first attempt to land a human on the Moon. Training in laboratories that simulated the Moon environment, Armstrong and his fellow astronauts studied Moon maps and practiced walking in their space suits, which were

Neil Armstrong and pilot David R. Scott in the *Gemini 8* spacecraft after an emergency landing in the Pacific Ocean. The landing came after a historic mission that docked two orbiting crafts in space.
(AP/Wide World Photos)

sturdy enough to resist small meteoroids (a small meteor in orbit around the Sun). Risk could not be completely eliminated, but every possible precaution was taken. Once, during a routine training flight, Armstrong's lunar landing research vehicle went out of control. (A lunar landing research vehicle permits astronauts to practice landing on the Moon.) Armstrong ejected himself and landed by parachute only yards away from the training vehicle, which had crashed in flames.

He calmly walked away and made his report, again showing an ability to remain cool under pressure.

On July 16, 1969, Armstrong and pilots **Buzz Aldrin** (1930–; see entry) and Michael Collins (1930–) blasted off from Cape Kennedy aboard *Apollo 11*. The spacecraft consisted of three stages, or separate components—the *Saturn 5* rocket (the booster that propelled the craft into space), the *Eagle* lunar module (the vehicle that would land on the Moon), and the *Columbia* command module (the craft that would remain in orbit during the Moon landing). Armstrong and his crew took with them small sections of the wing and propeller of the plane that aviation pioneers Orville (1871–1948) and Wilbur (1867–1912) Wright flew on their first successful flight in 1903 at Kitty Hawk, North Carolina.

On July 19, *Saturn 5* entered lunar orbit and circled the Moon twice. The next day Armstrong and Aldrin transferred to the *Eagle,* which would later separate from the *Columbia.* Armstrong would be the commander, with Aldrin as the copilot, while Collins would pilot the *Columbia.* After about five hours of tests, the crafts separated successfully and the *Eagle* entered its own orbit. Within two hours Armstrong and Aldrin began the 300-mile descent toward the Moon. At that point the computer system suddenly became overloaded, but under continuous instructions from the mission control center in Houston, Texas, Armstrong continued the gradual touchdown. The targeted computer-guided landing site was in an area called the Sea of Tranquility. When Armstrong looked out the window, however, he saw a field of boulders looming in front of the *Eagle.* Realizing he would have to land without computer assistance, he quickly switched to manual control and searched for a new site. He guided the *Eagle* over the boulders to a smooth landing about 4 miles (6.44 kilometers) away, with only ten seconds of fuel left. At 4:17:40 P.M. EDT on July 20, 1969, people around the world heard Armstrong send an important radio message: "Houston, Tranquility Base here. The *Eagle* has landed."

Walks on the Moon

Seven hours after touchdown, Armstrong and Aldrin opened the *Eagle*'s hatch. Climbing down a nine-step ladder at 10:56 P.M., Armstrong became the first human to set foot

Neil Armstrong stands near the lunar module *Eagle* during the historic *Apollo 11* mission, the first manned mission to land on the moon. *(NASA)*

on the Moon. His words, "That's one small step for man, one giant leap for mankind," were transmitted around the world. (Later, he stated that he had intended to say, "That's one small step for *a* man, one giant leap for mankind.") Aldrin joined him shortly thereafter. Armstrong and Aldrin spent nearly twenty-one hours on the Moon. During this time they installed a television camera, conducted scientific experiments, took photographs, and collected rock and soil samples. They left an American flag, a mission patch, and medals commemorating American and Russian space explorers who had died in the line of duty. They also set up a plaque that read: "Here men from the planet Earth first set foot upon the Moon. We came in peace for all mankind." The astronauts' Moon walk was televised live on Earth, and President Richard M. Nixon (1913–1994; served 1969–74) made a telephone call to them from the White House.

After returning to the *Eagle,* Armstrong and Aldrin rested for eight hours. Then they launched off the surface of the Moon and, two hours later, docked with the *Columbia,* in which Collins had been circling the Moon. Armstrong and Aldrin unloaded their equipment onto *Columbia* and abandoned the *Eagle.* The *Columbia* set out for Earth on its thirty-first orbit of the Moon. Sixty hours later, at 12:50 PM EDT on July 24, the spacecraft splashed down in the sea some 950 miles (1,526 kilometers) southwest of Hawaii, only 2.7 miles (4.34 kilometers) from its destination point. The astronauts were picked up by Navy frogmen (divers) from the aircraft carrier *Hornet.* As the *Hornet* sailed for Hawaii, Armstrong, Aldrin, and Collins remained aboard for eighteen days of quarantine (isolated from others) to control any microorganisms they may have carried from the Moon. From Hawaii the astronauts were flown to Houston, where they received a heroes' welcome. They were also honored in a parade in New York City, and they were greeted enthusiastically when they toured twenty-two foreign countries. They were awarded the Presidential Medal of Freedom, America's highest civilian honor.

Gains worldwide fame

Armstrong was regarded as a hero. He addressed a joint session of the U.S. Congress on September 16, 1969, about his adventures on the Moon. In his hometown of Wapakoneta, the local airport and the street where his parents lived were named after him. A Neil Armstrong Museum was also built in the city. The Moon mission brought him numerous other honors, including the Harmon International Aviation Trophy, the Royal Geographic Society's Hubbard Gold Medal, and praise and awards from many nations. He became a Fellow of the Society of Experimental Test Pilots, the American Astronautical Society, and the American Institute of Aeronautics and Astronautics, and he earned the Wright Award from the National Aeronautic Association.

Apollo 11 was Armstrong's final space mission. After the Moon voyage he joined the NASA Office of Advanced Research and Technology as deputy associate administrator for aeronautics. One of his main responsibilities was to conduct research into controlling high-performance aircraft by computer. In 1970 he earned a master's degree in aerospace

Lunar Laser Ranging Experiment

At the end of the twentieth century, scientists were still receiving results from the Lunar Laser Ranging Experiment, which Neil Armstrong and Buzz Aldrin started during the *Apollo 11* mission. The experiment consists of four reflectors set in different locations on the surface of the Moon. Armstrong and Aldrin positioned the first reflector, *Apollo 14* and *Apollo 15* astronauts placed the second and third, and a Russian lander installed the fourth. Resembling flat computer screens, the reflectors are composed of silica cubes attached to tilted aluminum panels. The cubes function as prisms that reflect laser beams sent from optical telescopes at observatories in Texas and France. The beams bounce back from the Moon to Earth within 2.3 to 2.6 seconds. Scientists then multiply laser beam return time by the speed of light to calculate the distance between Earth and the Moon at a particular moment.

The Lunar Laser Ranging Experiment has enabled astrophysicists to study the Moon's orbit and movement. They have discovered, for instance, that the force of gravity has not changed with time. They have also measured the distance—239,000 miles (384,551 kilometers)—from the center of the Moon to the center of Earth, using this data to observe the effects of tides on the interaction between the Moon and Earth. In 1999 Jim Williams (1944–), a lunar ranging researcher at the NASA Jet Propulsion Laboratory, caused a stir when he announced that the Moon has a liquid core.

engineering from the University of Southern California. Armstrong left NASA the following year, moving back to Ohio with his family and settling on a dairy farm near the town of Lebanon. From 1971 until 1980 Armstrong was a professor of aeronautical engineering at the University of Cincinnati. He took special interest in the application of space technology to such challenges as improving medical devices and providing data on the environment. In 1978 Armstrong was among the first six astronauts who were awarded the congressional Space Medal of Honor.

Since leaving NASA, Armstrong has served on the boards of directors of numerous corporations, and he chaired the board of trustees of the Cincinnati Museum of Natural History. While he was on the board of Gates Learjet Corporation, in 1979, he piloted the company's new business jet to five world-altitude records and time-to-climb records for that class of aircraft. In 1979 he also founded a computer systems firm.

Armstrong accepted two further government appointments. In 1984 he was named to the National Commission on Space, which two years later completed a report outlining an ambitious future for American space programs. In 1986 Armstrong was appointed deputy chair of the Rogers Commission to investigate the explosion of the space shuttle *Challenger* (see entry). The commission's work resulted in major changes in NASA's management structure and safety practices.

Reflects on Moon mission

An intensely private man, Armstrong rejected most opportunities to profit from his fame, and he was noted for his reluctance to speak publicly about his achievements. In 2001, however, he agreed to conduct a rare, seven-hour interview with two historians at the Johnson Space Center in Houston. Details from the interview were reported a year later in an article in the *Chicago Tribune* newspaper. During the conversation, the historians noted that other astronauts have said Earth seems very fragile when viewed from space. Armstrong agreed: "And I think everybody shares that observation. And I don't know why you have that impression, but it's so small, it's very colorful . . . you see an ocean and a gaseous layer, a little bit, just a tiny bit, of atmosphere around it. And, compared with all the other celestial objects—which, in many cases, are much more massive, more terrifying—it looks like it couldn't put up a very good defense against a celestial onslaught."

When asked how he felt about being the first human to walk on the Moon, Armstrong responded with typical modesty. "I was certainly aware," he said, "that this was a culmination of the work of 300,000 to 400,000 people over a decade, and that the nation's hopes and outward appearance largely rested on how the results came out. With those pressures, it seemed the most important thing to do was focus on our job as best we were able to try to allow nothing to distract us from doing the very best job we could." He attributed the low rate of equipment failure during the Moon mission "to the fact that every guy in the project, every guy at the bench building something, every assembler, every inspector, every guy that's setting up the tests, cranking the torque wrench, and so on, is saying, man or woman, 'If anything goes wrong here, it's not going to be my fault because my part is going to be better than I have to make it.'"

For More Information

Books

Armstrong, Neil, Michael Collins, and Edwin Aldrin. *The First Lunar Landing: 20th Anniversary*. Washington, DC: National Aeronautics and Space Administration, 1989.

Armstrong, Neil, Michael Collins, and Malcolm McConnell. *First on the Moon*. New York: Little, Brown, 1970.

Chaikin, Andrew. *A Man on the Moon: One Giant Leap*. New York: Time-Life, *1999*.

Dunham, Montrew. *Neil Armstrong: Young Pilot*. New York: Simon & Schuster Children's, 1995.

Periodicals

Drayton, Ken. "My Moon Shot." *American Heritage* (July 1999): p. 26.

Gaffney, Timothy R. "'The *Eagle* Has Landed.'" *Boys' Life* (July 1999): p. 18.

Reardon, Patrick T. "A Quiet Hero Speaks: Neil Armstrong Finally Opens Up—A Little Bit." *Chicago Tribune* (October 2, 2002).

Web Sites

Lloyd, Robin. "*Apollo 11* Experiment Still Returning Results." *CNN*. July 21, 1999. http://www.cnn.com/TECH/space/9907/21/apollo.experiment/index.html (accessed on June 17, 2004).

"Neil Armstrong." *Johnson Space Center, NASA*. www.jsc.nasa.gov/Bios/htmlbios/armstrong-na.html (accessed on July 9, 2004).

Guy Bluford

Born November 22, 1942 (Philadelphia, Pennsylvania)

American astronaut, engineer, pilot

"Flying in space is well worth the risks in order to help all of us improve our way of life."

In the 1950s and 1960s, the early years of the U.S. space program, all astronauts were white males (see **Buzz Aldrin** [1930–], **Neil Armstrong** [1930–], and **John Glenn** [1921–] entries). This situation changed during the late 1960s and 1970s when the National Aeronautic and Space Administration (NASA) recognized that many talented scientists were being overlooked by the astronaut training program. Consequently, NASA began opening the application process to minorities and women. Since then, astronauts from these groups have made contributions to space exploration (see **Franklin Chang-Diaz** [1950–], **Mae Jemison** [1956–], **Shannon Lucid** [1943–], **Mercury 13, Ellen Ochoa** [1958–], and **Sally Ride** [1951–] entries; also see box on page 37). Among them was Guy Bluford, an aerospace engineer who was one of the first African Americans in space and a pilot on four U.S. space shuttle missions.

Bluford is frequently hailed as a pioneer, but he has rejected this label. He told an interviewer for the *Philadelphia Inquirer* that he was only one member of a hard-working team: "I felt an awesome responsibility," he said, "and I took the responsibility very seriously, of being a role model and open-

Guy Bluford. *(NASA)*

ing another door to black Americans. But the important thing is not that I am black, but that I did a good job as a scientist and an astronaut. There will be black astronauts flying in later missions . . . and they, too, will be people who excel, not simply who are black . . . who can ably represent their people, their communities, their country."

Determination pays off

Guion S. (Guy) Bluford Jr. was born in Philadelphia, one of three sons of Guion and Lolita Bluford. Nicknamed

"Bunny" as a child, he grew up in a well-educated family in a racially mixed neighborhood. His father, a mechanical engineer, was forced into early retirement by epilepsy (a neurological condition that causes seizures). His mother worked as a special-education teacher in the Philadelphia public schools. Lolita was also related to Carol Brice Carey, a noted singer and voice coach, and Guion Sr. was the brother of the editor of the *Kansas City Call* newspaper. During his school years Bluford preferred to spend his spare time building model airplanes and working crossword puzzles. Inspired by his father's struggle with ill health, he was determined to become an aeronautics engineer. Although Bluford devoted himself to his studies at Overbrook, a mostly white high school, a guidance counselor once suggested that he might not be college material. Nevertheless, he maintained a C-plus average in difficult math and science courses before graduating in 1960.

In 1960 Bluford was admitted to Pennsylvania State University, where he was the only black student in the engineering school. During his senior year he married Linda Tull, who had also grown up in Philadelphia. After graduating with a bachelor of science degree he enrolled in the Reserve Officers Training Corps (ROTC) in the U.S. Air Force and attended flight school. He earned his pilot's wings in 1966. By this time the United States had become deeply involved in the Vietnam War (1954–75; a conflict in South Vietnam between government forces aided by the United States and rebel forces aided by North Vietnam). Bluford was assigned to active duty with the 557th Tactical Fighter Squadron at Cam Ram Bay in Vietnam, where he eventually flew 144 combat missions, 65 of them over North Vietnam. During his one-year tour in Vietnam he earned numerous medals and citations, including an air force commendation medal. After returning home as a lieutenant colonel, he was a flight instructor and a test pilot at Sheppard Air Force Base in Texas for five years.

"The cloak of prejudice was raised"

A turning point in Bluford's career came when he was chosen to be one of only a few candidates to attend the Air Force Institute of Technology (AFIT), a graduate-education program, near Dayton, Ohio. In 1974 he received a master of science degree in aerospace engineering, and in 1978 he earned a doc-

Women and Minority Astronaut Firsts

In the late 1960s and 1970s NASA opened the astronaut training program to women and minorities. The following astronauts from these groups achieved significant "firsts."

Robert Henry Lawrence Jr. (1935–1967) was the first African American to be selected for astronaut training. An air force officer and a test pilot, he was killed during a training flight in 1967. Had Lawrence lived, he probably would have traveled to space in a *Gemini* B spacecraft.

Sally Ride (1951–) entered the astronaut program in 1978. Five years later she became the first American woman to fly in space, aboard the shuttle *Challenger*.

Ellison S. Onizuka (1946–1986) was the first Asian American in space. Joining the astronaut corps in 1978, he was a mission specialist on the *Discovery* space shuttle in 1985. Onizuka died during his second shuttle mission, aboard the *Challenger* shuttle, which exploded shortly after takeoff in 1986.

California native Ellen Ochoa (1958–) became the first Latina in space in 1993, when she served as the sole female crew member of the *Discovery* space shuttle. She followed the first Latino astronaut, Mexico native Rodolfo Neri (1952–), who flew his first space shuttle mission in 1985.

Mae Jemison (1956–) was the first African American woman to be admitted to the astronaut training program. Her eight-day flight aboard the shuttle *Endeavor* in 1992 established her as the first female African American space traveler.

John Bennett Herrington (1958–) made history as the first Native American to walk in space. The flight engineer on the shuttle *Endeavor* in 2002, he traveled to the International Space Station and installed equipment on the outside of the spacecraft. In honor of his Native American heritage, Herrington carried a Chickasaw Nation flag during the trip.

---

toral degree in aerospace engineering with a minor in laser physics. During his years at AFIT he ranked consistently among the top 10 percent of his class. He also continued to work as a test pilot and an instructor for military aviators.

After receiving his doctorate Bluford applied to the space shuttle program. (A space shuttle is a craft that transports people and cargo between Earth and space.) As one of nearly eight thousand other military personnel competing for only thirty-five openings, he assumed he had little chance of being accepted. He was therefore surprised when he received the call informing him that he was chosen for astronaut training.

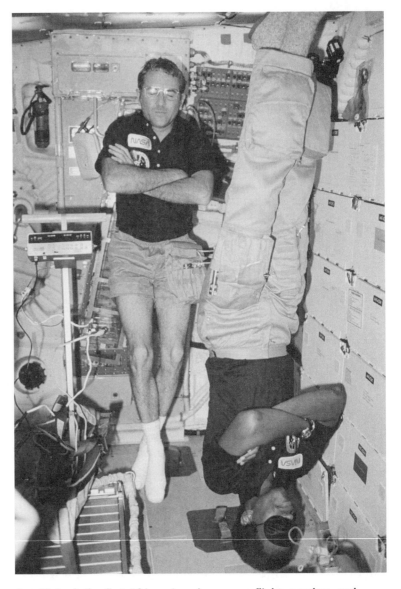

Guy Bluford, the first African-American space flight member, and mission commander Richard Truly in their sleeping positions aboard the space shuttle *Challenger.* *(© NASA/Roger Ressmeyer/Corbis)*

Bluford quietly celebrated the news with his wife and two sons. He later told the *Philadelphia Inquirer* that it was an important moment: He and several other black aviators who are now astronauts "had to be ready in 1977 and 1978, when the doors of opportunity were opened to us and the cloak of prejudice was raised. As black scientists and engineers and aviators, we had to prove that black people could excel."

Bluford completed the training program and was named to the eighth mission of the space shuttle, aboard the *Challenger*. He was neither the first African American astronaut nor the first black man in space: Robert Lawrence (1935–1967) was the first African American astronaut (see box on page 37), and Cuban astronaut Arnaldo Tamayo-Méndez (1942–) had flown with the Soviet Union's space program. Nevertheless, Bluford was the first African American to be a member of a space flight. After launching from Cape Canaveral in Florida on August 30, 1983, the *Challenger* crew conducted a variety of experiments during the week-long mission.

Setting a record for the first nighttime shuttle launch and landing, the *Challenger* touched down at Edwards Air Force Base in California on September 5. Upon returning to Earth, Bluford discovered that he was a national celebrity. He was greeted in a number of America's biggest cities, especially Philadelphia, and was in great demand as a public speaker. Bluford accepted this role reluctantly, protesting that he was simply another member of the space shuttle team.

Involvement in space continues

In 1986 the ***Challenger*** (see entry) exploded shortly after takeoff. Aboard the shuttle was Ronald E. McNair (1950–1986), the second black American in space. Only months earlier Bluford had completed a *Challenger* mission, yet the disaster did little to dampen his enthusiasm for space travel. In 1991 he participated in a *Discovery* flight that was launched to observe Earth's atmosphere and such phenomena as the Northern Lights (aurora borealis; streamers or arcs of light that occur in polar regions) and cirrus (wispy white) clouds.

Before retiring from NASA and the air force in 1993, Bluford clocked about 314 hours in space. Once asked by a *Philadelphia Inquirer* interviewer to describe how it feels to rocket into space, Bluford replied: "Imagine driving down the street, and you look out the window, and all you see are flames. And your car is being driven by remote control, and you're saying to yourself, 'I hope this thing doesn't blow up.'" In 2003 he reflected on his career in a NASA Web site article.

Commenting on his role as one of the first African Americans in space, he said, "I wanted to set the standard, do the best job possible so that other people would be comfortable with African Americans flying in space and African Americans would be proud of being participants in the space program."

Bluford has retained his ties to the space program. In 1993 he became vice president and general manager of the engineering and computer software company NYMA, Inc., based in Cleveland, Ohio. Later renamed Logicon Federal Data Corporation (FDC), it was purchased by Northrop Grumman in 1997. Bluford was responsible for overseeing FDC's programs related to aerospace engineering and research. He has also served on the board of directors of such organizations as the American Institute of Aeronautics and Astronautics and the Board of the Space Foundation. In 2001 Bluford became a speaker with The Space Agency, a public relations firm that represents former astronauts and space pioneers. The following year he was featured in a cameo role in the music video by Will Smith (1968–) for "Black Suits Comin', Nod Ya Head," from the *Men in Black II* movie soundtrack.

Bluford has received numerous awards and honors, including two Defense Meritorious Service Medals, four NASA Space Flight Medals, the NASA Distinguished Service Medal, and the Air Force Legion of Merit. He was inducted into the International Space Hall of Fame in 1997. On that occasion Bluford observed, "Flying in space is well worth the risks in order to help all of us improve our way of life."

For More Information

Books

Beck, Isabel, et al. *Guion Bluford: A Space Biography*. New York: Harcourt, 2003.

Haskins, James S. *Space Challenger: The Story of Guion Bluford: An Authorized Biography*. Minneapolis: Lerner, 1988.

Periodicals

"Profiles in African American History: Guion Bluford Jr." *Time for Kids* (February 14, 2003): p. 2.

Web Sites

"Col. Guion S. Bluford Jr." *Military.com*. http://www.military.com/Content/MoreContent?file=ML_bluford_bkp (accessed on June 29, 2004).

"Guion 'Guy' Bluford—NASA Astronaut." *About Space/Astronomy.*
http://space.about.com/cs/formerastronauts/a/guionbluford.htm
(accessed on June 29, 2004).

"Guy Bluford Remembered Twenty Years Later." *NASA.* http://www.
nasa.gov/news/highlights/Bluford_feature.html (accessed on June
29, 2004).

Challenger Crew

Date of mission January 28, 1986

American astronauts

On January 28, 1986, seven astronauts died in the midair explosion of the U.S. space shuttle *Challenger*. (A space shuttle is a craft that transports people and cargo between Earth and space.) Other American astronauts have lost their lives—in 1967 the three crewmembers of *Apollo 1* (see entry) were killed in an accident on the ground, and in 2003 the shuttle *Columbia* broke apart over the western United States, killing the entire crew (see box on page 44). The *Challenger* mission, however, was the first to come to a fatal end while a vehicle was in space. Mourned by the nation, the loss of the crew and the shuttle resulted in an official investigation that called for far-ranging reforms in the National Aeronautics and Space Administration (NASA).

The *Challenger* crew

The seven-person *Challenger* crew was commanded by Francis Scobee (1939–1986), and the pilot was Michael Smith (1945–1986). Mission specialists were Ellison Onizuka (1946–1986), Ronald McNair (1950–1986), and Judith Resnick (1949–1986), who were responsible for deploying satellites (objects

The *Challenger* shuttle crew. *(AP/Wide World Photos)*

that orbit in space) and conducting experiments. Payload specialist Gregory Jarvis (1944–1986) was in charge of a Tracking and Data-Relay Satellite (TDRS), and schoolteacher Christa McAuliffe (1948–1986) was to be the first civilian in space.

Francis R. Scobee

Commanding officer Francis R. Scobee was born in 1939 in Elum, Washington. The son of a railroad engineer, he grew up south of Seattle. At age eighteen, after graduating from Auburn High School, he enrolled in the U.S. Air Force. While working as an air force mechanic, he was able to attend night school and earn a bachelor's degree in aerospace engineering from the University of Arizona. He later became an air force pilot, flying thousands of hours in many different types of aircraft. He also flew missions in the Vietnam War. Scobee was selected as an astronaut in 1978. He had piloted the *Challenger* into space once before, in 1984, to retrieve and repair a damaged satellite.

The *Columbia* Accident

On February 1, 2003, the space shuttle *Columbia* broke apart over the western United States while returning to Earth from a sixteen-day mission. All seven crew members were killed, as pieces of the descending craft fell from the sky. The day after the accident NASA administrator Sean O'Keefe (1956–) organized the Columbia Accident Investigation Board (CAIB). On August 26 the CAIB issued a final report.

The most immediate cause of the crash was a piece of insulating foam that had separated from the shuttle's left wing during takeoff. This piece left a hole near a reinforced carbon panel. When the *Columbia* started on its descent to Earth, superheated air penetrated the hole and began melting the wing. Soon the spacecraft was becoming increasingly disabled, and as it entered the atmosphere over Dallas–Fort Worth, Texas, the damaged wing caused it to spin completely out of control.

Among the other CAIB findings was that the *Columbia* was not properly equipped for its final mission, a trip to the **International Space Station** (ISS; see entry). Built earlier than other existing shuttles—the *Columbia* was the first shuttle to leave Earth orbit— the vehicle had been used primarily for sci-

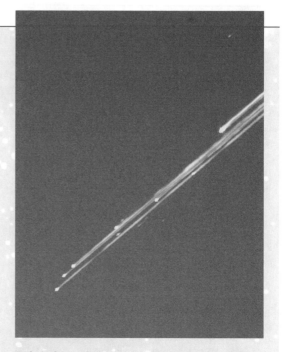

Debris from the space shuttle *Columbia* as it streaked across the sky over Texas. *(AP/Wide World Photos)*

entific missions and for servicing the **Hubble Space Telescope** (see entry). On the flight to the ISS it was required to carry larger cargo, which the crew had difficulty handling because the *Columbia* did not have a space station docking system. The CAIB report concluded that the *Columbia* accident was caused in large part by deficiencies within NASA and by a lack of government oversight.

Michael J. Smith

The *Challenger* pilot, Michael J. Smith, was born in 1945 in Beaufort, North Carolina, and grew up on a fourteen-acre farm in that state. He attended Beaufort High School, where he was a quarterback on the football team and an honors student. He began piloting an airplane while still a teenager. Smith attended the U.S. Naval Academy in Annapolis, Maryland, and became a pilot. During the Vietnam War, he flew 225 combat missions. He was selected by NASA to become an astronaut in 1980, but he had never flown in space.

Ellison S. Onizuka

Mission specialist Ellison S. Onizuka was born in 1946 in Kealakekua, Hawaii, and grew up on the Kona Coast of Hawaii. The grandson of Japanese immigrants, he was the first Hawaiian and first person of Japanese descent to fly in space. He was an honors student in high school and an Eagle Scout. He later attended the University of Colorado and received undergraduate and graduate degrees in aerospace engineering. After completing his education he spent eight years in the air force as a test pilot. He was selected to become an astronaut in 1978. In 1985 he rode aboard the space shuttle *Discovery*, performing various tasks such as the filming of Halley's comet.

Ronald McNair

Mission specialist Ronald McNair was born in 1950 in Lake City, South Carolina. He attended North Carolina A & T University in Greensboro and went on to earn a Ph.D. in physics from the Massachusetts Institute of Technology. After receiving his doctorate, he worked at Hughes Research Laboratories in California. In the late 1970s, NASA began looking for a new breed of astronaut, a "scientist-astronaut" whose background was in science training rather than test piloting. In 1977 McNair applied for admission to the space program as a scientist-astronaut and was accepted to the program in 1978. In 1984 McNair became the second African American man in space (the first was **Guy Bluford** [1942–]; see entry). On that mission he flew aboard *Challenger* and helped to launch a communications satellite.

Judith A. Resnik

Judith A. Resnik, the third mission specialist, was born in 1949 in Akron, Ohio. She attended Firestone High School in Akron, and excelled in mathematics and at playing the piano. She later attended Carnegie-Mellon University in Pittsburgh, and received a Ph.D. in electrical engineering from the University of Maryland. After earning her doctorate, Resnik went to work for Xerox Corporation. In 1978 she was selected from thousands of applicants as one of the first six female astronauts. (Also in that group was **Sally Ride** [1951–], the first American woman in space; see entry.) Resnik became the second American woman in space in 1984, when she rode aboard the shuttle *Discovery*. Her duties aboard that flight included operating the *Discovery*'s remote-control arm.

Gregory Jarvis

Payload specialist Gregory Jarvis was born in 1944 in Detroit, Michigan, and grew up in Mohawk, New York. After graduating from Mohawk High School, he attended the State University of New York at Buffalo and received a bachelor's degree in electrical engineering. He then earned a master's degree in engineering from Northeastern University. Joining the U.S. Air Force in 1969, he became a specialist in tactical communications satellites. In 1973 he went to work for the Hughes Aircraft Corporation and continued to work on satellite design. The *Columbia* mission was Jarvis's first trip in space.

Christa McAuliffe

Christa McAuliffe was born on September 2, 1948, in Framingham, Massachusetts, the daughter of an accountant. She attended high school in Framingham and later graduated from Framingham State College in 1970. In the early 1970s McAuliffe and her husband moved to Washington, D.C., where she earned a master's degree in education from Bowie State College while her husband earned a law degree. They later moved to Concord, New Hampshire, where she became a high-school social studies teacher. McAuliffe was selected from among eleven thousand applicants to be the first "Teacher in Space." She was an instant media celebrity and promoted as a role model for American women.

Setbacks plague mission

The *Challenger* crew was embarking on a routine mission when they entered the spacecraft at Cape Canaveral. By that time there had already been a series of setbacks. NASA had scrambled to meet an ambitious schedule for 1986: In January the space agency announced that it would launch fifteen missions, using all four of its shuttles—*Columbia, Challenger,*

Atlantis, and *Discovery*—during the next twelve months. The year did not get off to a good start. During the month of January, NASA had to postpone at least seven missions of various shuttles and to abort yet another.

In the days that followed, everyone worked feverishly to prepare the *Challenger* for a January mission. *Challenger* had completed its ninth flight in November 1985, slightly more than two months earlier. NASA was under pressure because this mission would involve the much-publicized "Teacher in Space" program. McAuliffe would be broadcasting live satellite reports about space travel to students throughout the world. NASA was also launching the TDRS and the high-priority Spartan-Halley comet research observatory into space. The flight was scheduled to last six days, during which time the Spartan observatory would be recovered from orbit. Because of tight schedule requirements, the Spartan could be orbited no later than January 31.

The *Challenger* launch was set for January 22, but it was delayed. Additional postponements followed on January 24 and January 25. Then a forecast of bad weather on the 26th held up the flight until Monday the 27th. On this date a further delay was caused by a problem with a hatch bolt. During the night of January 27, the temperature at Cape Canaveral dropped as low as 19°F (-7.2°C). This prompted a late-night meeting of NASA managers and engineers with managers from Morton Thiokol, the government contractor that manufactured the O-rings on the booster rockets. (A booster rocket is fired to propel the spacecraft into space. The booster rocket is built in sections and then strapped onto the shuttle. The rubber O-rings are required to seal the sections together.) The Thiokol engineers were concerned that the O-rings would stiffen in the cold, causing the seal to fail. Since the O-rings had never been tested at low temperatures, the Thiokol managers overruled the engineers. They signed a statement claiming that the boosters were safe for launch at a temperature lower than 53°F (11.6°C).

Commission investigates disaster

Other problems arose on the morning of January 28 because a thin layer of ice had formed on the shuttle and the launch pad. Liftoff was delayed twice because officials at the

The space shuttle *Challenger* exploded shortly after lifting off from the Kennedy Space Center in Florida. *(AP/Wide World Photos)*

site were concerned about icicles potentially breaking off during launch and damaging insulation tiles that protected the shuttle from intense heat as it reentered Earth's atmosphere. Inspection teams examined the *Challenger* and reported no abnormalities. Countdown proceeded, and at 11:38 A.M. the *Challenger* lifted off into the blue sky. After two explosions—the first at fifty-four seconds into launch and the second at seventy-three seconds—the shuttle disintegrated, vanishing in a trail of smoke as a crowd on the ground and millions of television viewers throughout the world watched in disbelief. Among the spectators on the ground were McAuliffe's husband and two children and a group of her students.

A few days after the disaster, President Ronald Reagan (1911–2004; served 1981–89) praised the *Challenger* crew during a televised memorial ceremony at the Johnson Space Center in Houston, Texas. On February 3, 1986, he established a presidential commission to investigate the accident, appointing former secretary of state William B. Rogers (1913–2001) as head. Six weeks after the crash the shuttle's crew module was recovered from the floor of the Atlantic Ocean. The crew members were subsequently buried with full honors. There was considerable speculation about whether they had survived the initial explosion. Evidence gathered later by NASA indicated that they had survived the breakup and separation of the boosters from the shuttle. They had also begun to take emergency action inside the crew cabin. Whether all seven astronauts remained conscious throughout the two-minute, forty-five-second fall into the ocean remains unknown. NASA investigators determined that at least two were breathing from emergency air packs they had activated.

On June 6, 1986, the Rogers Commission released a 256-page report stating that the explosion was caused by destruction of the O-rings. After checking into the history and performance of the sealing system, the commission discovered that the O-rings had failed regularly, though only partially, on previous shuttle flights. Both NASA and Thiokol were concerned about weaknesses in the seals, but they had chosen not to undertake a time-consuming redesign of the system. They regarded O-ring erosion as an "acceptable risk" because the seal had never failed completely. But when the *Challenger* flew in the dead of winter, frigid temperatures made the O-rings so brittle that they never sealed the joint. Even before the shuttle had cleared the launch tower, hot gas was already seeping through the rings. Investigators blamed NASA and Thiokol management procedures for not allowing critical information to reach the right people. The U.S. House of Representatives Committee on Science and Technology then conducted hearings on the matter. The committee determined that NASA and Thiokol had sufficient time to correct the O-ring problem, but the space agency and the manufacturer had sacrificed safety to meet flight schedules and cut costs.

NASA suffers setbacks

The charges had a grave impact on NASA. Public confidence was shaken, and the astronaut corps was highly concerned. Astronauts had never been consulted or informed about the dangers posed by the O-ring sealing system. The Rogers Commission made nine recommendations to NASA, among them allowing astronauts and engineers a greater role in approving launches. The other recommendations included a complete redesign of the rocket booster joints, a review of astronaut escape systems, regulation of scheduling of shuttle flights to assure safety, and sweeping reform of the shuttle program management structure.

Following these decisions, several top officials left NASA. A number of experienced astronauts also resigned as a result of disillusionment with NASA and frustration over the long redesign process that delayed their chances to fly in space. An American shuttle was not launched again until September 29, 1988. NASA eventually built the *Endeavour* to replace the *Challenger,* and it flew for the first time in 1992.

For More Information

Books

Lewis, Richard S. *Challenger: The Final Voyage.* New York: Columbia University Press, 1988.

McConnell, Malcolm. *Challenger: A Major Malfunction.* New York: Doubleday, 1987.

Periodicals

"Looking for What Went Wrong." *Time* (February 10, 1986): pp. 36–38.

"NASA Faces Wide Probe." *U.S. News and World Report* (February 17, 1986): pp. 18–19.

"Out of Challenger's Ashes—Full Speed Ahead." *U.S. News and World Report* (February 10, 1986): pp. 16–19.

"Seven Who Flew for All of Us." *Time* (February 10, 1986): pp. 32–35.

"What Happened?" *Newsweek* (February 17, 1986): pp. 32–33.

Web Sites

"Information on the STS–51L/Challenger Accident." *NASA.* http://www.hq.nasa.gov/office/pao/History/sts51l.html (accessed on June 29, 2004).

"Jan. 28, 1986: The *Challenger* Disaster." http://www.chron.com/content/interactive/special/challenger (accessed on June 29, 2004).

"Space Shuttle *Columbia* and Her Crew." *NASA.* http://www.nasa.gov/columbia (accessed on June 29, 2004).

Franklin Chang-Díaz

Born April 5, 1950 (San José, Costa Rica)

Costa Rican-born American astronaut, physicist

While growing up in Costa Rica and Venezuela, Franklin R. Chang-Díaz dreamed of exploring space. He achieved his goal when he became an astronaut in the United States, eventually completing seven space shuttle missions in 2002 and tying the world record for the most trips in space. As the director of the Advanced Space Propulsion Laboratory at the National Aeronautics and Space Administration (NASA) Johnson Space Center, he conducts research on conquering the next space frontier: human flights to Mars. Chang-Díaz is a national hero in his native Costa Rica.

> "Humans began exploring space the day they chose to walk out of their caves in search of food. Space exploration is nothing less than human survival."

Inspired by "Atoms for Peace"

Franklin R. Chang-Díaz was born on April 5, 1950, in San José, Costa Rica, the son of Maria Eugenia Díaz and Ramón Chang Morales, an oil worker of Costa Rican-Chinese descent. When Franklin was about one year old, the family moved to Venezuela. In 1957, while they were living in Venezuela, his mother told him about the launch of the *Sputnik 1* Soviet satellite. The first man-made craft to orbit Earth, the satellite captured the imagination of six-year-old

Franklin Chang-Díaz. *(NASA)*

Franklin. Climbing a mango tree, he gazed at the sky for hours in search of *Sputnik*.

By the time the family returned to Costa Rica, Chang-Díaz was already interested in science. When he was in grade school he had an experience that shaped his life. In 2003 he recalled this experience in a speech on rocket research that he gave to the U.S. House of Representatives Subcommittee on Energy: "A traveling scientific exhibition, sponsored by the United States, was set up in a large inflatable dome at the national airport in San José," Chang-Díaz told his audience. "It was entitled 'Atoms for Peace' and was sent throughout Latin America to inform and educate the public about atomic energy. The exhibition spent several days in the country and, while it was there, every day after school I delighted myself in examining the new universe of atomic particles, their magical and amazing power for converting their mass into energy."

An equally important event took place when Chang-Díaz was in high school and found a NASA brochure titled "Should You Be a Rocket Scientist?" It was written by **Wernher von Braun** (1912–1977; see entry), the leading rocket researcher of the time. The scientist was then living in the United States after an earlier career developing the V-2 rocket for Nazi Germany. Chang-Díaz told the energy subcommittee members, "I immediately sent [von Braun] a letter with a resounding 'yes.' The NASA form letter response . . . came months later and had a simple message: to pursue such a career I would have to come to the United States."

After completing high school in Costa Rica, Chang-Díaz decided to earn some money so he could travel to the United States and attend college. Taking a job at the National Bank of Costa Rica, he saved fifty dollars in eight weeks.

Chang-Díaz moved to Hartford, Connecticut, where he lived with an uncle and cousins. He spoke no English, however, and he lacked sufficient academic credits to enter an American university. In order to learn English he enrolled in transitional classes as a senior at Hartford High School. Chang-Díaz impressed his teachers with his performance in mathematics and science, so they urged him to apply for a scholarship at the University of Connecticut. Admissions officials granted the scholarship because they thought Chang-Díaz was from Puerto Rico and therefore a U.S. citizen. Upon learning that he was from Costa Rica, they withdrew the offer. Finally his Hartford teachers persuaded the university to accept him.

Chang-Díaz entered the University of Connecticut in 1969 and obtained a bachelor of science degree in mechanical engineering four years later. In 1977 he earned a doctorate in plasma physics (science that deals with the structure and interaction of plasma, a collection of charged particles that resembles some gases) at the Massachusetts Institute of Technology (MIT). He immediately applied to the NASA astronaut program, but he was not accepted. Chang-Díaz then joined the Charles Stark Draper Laboratory, where he conducted research on a fusion reactor (a device that converts the nucleus of an atom to usable energy) technology. During this time he married his first wife, the former Canoce Buker; after their divorce, he later married Peggy Doncaster. He is the father of four children.

Ties space-flight record

In 1980 Chang-Díaz reapplied to the astronaut corps and was accepted as one of only nineteen candidates from three thousand applicants. During his astronaut training he worked at the Shuttle Avionics Integration Laboratory, and he contributed to early design studies for the **International Space Station** (ISS; see entry). (A space station is a large artificial satellite, or a body that orbits in space; it is designed to be occupied for long periods and to serve as a base for conducting research. The International Space Station, completed in 1998, is used by various nations for research.) In 1982 he was named to the support crew (astronauts who assist the pilot and copilot) for the first Space Lab mission (a research laboratory in space). He went on to fly seven space shuttle missions between 1986 and 2002. (A space shuttle, also called a shuttle orbiter, is a space plane that transports cargo and passengers between Earth and space. NASA has operated five space shuttles: *Discovery, Challenger, Columbia, Atlantis,* and *Endeavour. Enterprise* was the first shuttle to be built; however, it never went into orbit and was used primarily for "captured flights" involving takeoff and re-entry exercises.)

Chang-Díaz's first flight, in 1986, was a six-day mission aboard the *Columbia*. The space shuttle completed ninety-six orbits of Earth and launched the SATCOM KU (a satellite used to make observations pertaining to astronomy, the ionosphere [the part of Earth's atmosphere in which radiation waves are converted into ions, or positive and negative electrons], Earth's atmosphere, the Sun, and other scientific areas). His next flight was in 1989 on the space shuttle *Atlantis*. He and fellow crewmembers deployed (launched in space) the *Galileo*, an unmanned satellite programmed to explore the planet Jupiter. Completing seventy-nine orbits, the *Atlantis* crew also operated the Shuttle Solar Backscatter Ultraviolet Instrument, which mapped ozone (a gas that produces air

The space shuttle *Discovery,* on which Franklin Chang-Díaz served during the first joint U.S.-Russian space program. *(© Corbis)*

pollution) in Earth's atmosphere. Again aboard the *Atlantis,* Chang-Díaz helped to launch the European Retrievable Carrier satellite and test the first Tethered Satellite System. (The European Retrievable Carrier satellite contained experiments for studying microgravity [the virtual absence of gravity], the Sun, and matter. The Tethered Satellite System consists of a small satellite attached to the space shuttle with a tether, or connecting cable; it is a tool for research in space plasma physics.) Lasting eight days in 1992, this mission involved 126 orbits of Earth.

Chang-Díaz's fourth mission, in 1994, was on the space shuttle *Discovery,* which completed 130 orbits of Earth. The first joint U.S.-Russian space shuttle mission to include a Russian cosmonaut (astronaut) as a crew member, it was also the first flight of the Wake Shield Facility (a disc-shaped

Franklin Chang-Díaz on one of three spacewalks during his record-setting mission to the Alpha Magnetic Spectrometer. *(AP/Wide World Photos)*

platform for the development of space-based manufacturing of film materials) and the second flight of the Space Habitation Module-2 (Spacelab 2; used to carry equipment for the International Space Station). During the mission Chang-Díaz participated in several experiments involving biological materials, Earth observation, and life science. His next flight was aboard the *Columbia,* which completed 252 orbits of Earth in 1996. On this fifteen-day mission the shuttle crew conducted additional Tethered Satellite System experiments. In addition, they conducted research with the U.S. Microgravity Payload, which provided information that helps improve the production of medicines, metal alloys (combinations of metals), and semiconductors (solids that act both as conductors and as insulators of electrical energy).

In 1998 Chang-Díaz flew on the *Discovery*. It was the ninth and final mission for the U.S. space shuttle and the Russian space station *Mir* in the first phase of the joint U.S.-Russian space shuttle program. Chang-Díaz and other *Discovery* crewmembers brought supplies and equipment to *Mir*. They also ran experiments on the Alpha Magnetic Spectrometer, the first research project of its kind on antimatter (matter composed of subatomic particles) in space. Chang-Díaz took his seventh flight, on the *Endeavor,* in June 2002. He tied a record for the number of space flights set by U.S. astronaut Jerry Ross (1948–; see box on this page) the previous month. During the twelve-day mission, Chang-Díaz participated in three space walks.

Conducts pioneering research

In 1993, at the height of his astronaut career, Chang-Díaz was appointed director of the Advanced Space Propulsion Laboratory at the NASA Johnson Space Center in Houston, Texas. He supervises research on plasma rocket engines. Advanced Space Propulsion Laboratory research could lead to technology that would significantly reduce the amount of time required to travel from Earth to Mars. Rockets using chemical-based propulsion can achieve a speed of only ten thousand miles per hour. At this rate, a trip to Mars would take at least ten months each way. Higher rocket speeds could be reached if a spacecraft's propellant (the substance used to power the craft into space) were superheated, but the extreme heat would melt the rocket. After more than twenty years of research and experimentation, Chang-Díaz may have found a solution—the variable specific impulse magnetic resonance

Jerry Lynn Ross

In June 2002 Franklin R. Chang-Díaz tied the world record of seven space flights set by U.S. astronaut Jerry Lynn Ross (1948–) the previous month.

Ross is a Crown Point, Indiana, native and Purdue University graduate who joined the astronaut corps in 1980. From 1985 through 2002 he flew seven missions aboard the space shuttles *Atlantis, Columbia,* and *Endeavor.* During an *Atlantis* flight in 1991 he helped deploy the 35,000-pound Gamma Ray Observatory (an orbiting telescope that observes high-energy radiation) and to test prototype space station *Freedom* hardware. In 1993 he flew aboard the *Columbia* on a German-sponsored Space Lab mission. Ross and the crew conducted nearly ninety experiments in areas such as physics, robotics, astronomy, and Earth and its atmosphere. Two years later he flew on the *Atlantis* during the second U.S. space shuttle mission to rendezvous and dock with the Russian space station *Mir.* In 1998 Ross was involved in assembling the International Space Station. By 2002 he had spent 58 days in space.

(VASIMR) propulsion system. Chang-Díaz and his team discovered that the VASIMR prevents a rocket from melting by using magnetic fields (portions of space where magnetic forces can be detected) to contain and guide propellant gases. The VASIMR can be compared the process to that of a microwave oven.

With a VASIMR engine, rockets could achieve speeds of 650,000 miles (1,045,850 kilometers) per hour. At the same time, VASIMR's superior fuel efficiency would significantly reduce the weight of the spacecraft and decrease the high cost of space missions. Chang-Díaz calculated that a VASIMR-powered mission to Mars, including one spacecraft for astronauts and another for supplies, would weigh only about four hundred tons (362.8 metric tons), half the weight of an earlier spacecraft design for a Mars mission. VASIMR technology could cut the time of a mission from Earth to Mars from ten months to only ninety-three days. Chang-Díaz has predicted that the VASIMR could be ready for a Mars flight in 2018. This achievement would fulfill the dream of **Robert Goddard** (1882–1945; see entry), the American physicist who launched the first liquid-propellant rocket in 1926. Goddard's inspiration for conducting his rocket experiments was sending a person to Mars.

Chang-Díaz works in other areas of space-related research as well. He travels widely in the United States, Mexico, and Latin America, speaking on the importance of sharing space-age technologies with developing nations. In 1991, while visiting Costa Rica, he became interested in finding a cure for Chagas's disease. It is caused by a parasite (an organism that lives within another organism) called Trypanosoma and kills some 45,000 people a year, mostly in Latin America. Because the microgravity (virtual absence of gravity) of space creates ideal conditions for the production of crystals (the basic structure of some drugs), Chang-Díaz theorized that the space shuttle could become an important laboratory for studying Chagas's disease. On the *Columbia* flight in 1996 he and NASA biochemist Lawrence J. DeLucas (1950–) started a study of proteins (complex substances in plants and animals) made by the Chagas parasite, but they did not have time to complete the experiment. Astronauts on four later flights, however, made crystal forms of an enzyme (a complex protein that produces a chemical reaction in the body) produced in the disease and researched compounds that could be used in treatment. Chang-Díaz predicted that the Chagas project could lead to other innovations, such as new agricultural techniques based on study of the interconnection of rain forests (tropical woodlands with rainfall of at least 100 inches annually), biodiversity (an environment that contains numerous plants and animals), and space.

Chang-Díaz has been active in community service throughout his career. In 1987 he founded the Astronaut Science Colloquium Program to build closer relationships between astronauts and scientists. The following year he helped organize the Astronaut Science Support Group to utilize the expertise of astronauts who have flown space shuttle missions. The group advised the National Space Transportation System and the Space Station programs on science and technology issues. For two and one-half years he was a house manager in an experimental residence for people with severe mental illness who were being released from institutionalized care. He has also been an instructor and advisor in a Massachusetts rehabilitation program for Hispanic drug abusers.

Promotes space education

Along with fellow team members at the Johnson Research Center, Chang-Díaz introduced a space-education program at Odyssey Academy, a predominantly Hispanic middle school in Galveston, Texas. Twenty students from the sixth, seventh, and eighth grades were chosen for participation in eleven weeks of classes on plasma rockets. Each class was taught by two members of the team. As Chang-Díaz reported to the House Subcommittee on Energy in 2003, the project was so successful that the Johnson Space Center is planning to expand the program to other schools in the area.

A strong advocate of space education for the younger generation, Chang-Díaz closed his statement with these words: "Humans began exploring space the day they chose to walk out of their caves in search of food. Space exploration is nothing less than human survival. You probably have heard us say that the first human being to set foot on Mars is alive now somewhere on planet Earth, a young girl or boy sitting in one of our classrooms at this very moment. Will they be discouraged or encouraged by their elders? I was blessed with the best parents anyone could ever have and perhaps fortunate to find a traveling display on atomic power and a NASA brochure on rocket science to keep nudging me on."

The recipient of numerous honors and awards—including two NASA Distinguished Service Medals (1995, 1997), the Liberty Medal (1986), and the Medal of Excellence from the Congressional Hispanic Caucus (1987) in the United States—Chang-Díaz was named "Honorary Citizen" by the government of Costa Rica in 1995. This is the highest award given by Costa Rica to a foreign citizen, and since the astronaut came from that country he became the first honoree who was born there. In addition to his work at Johnson Space Center, Chang-Díaz is a part-time professor of physics at Rice University in Houston, Texas, and the University of Houston. He has also presented papers at technical conferences and published articles in scientific journals.

For More Information

Periodicals

"2000 Hispanic Achievement Award." *Hispanic Magazine* (July 2000): p. 80.

Chang, Kenneth. "Novel rockets speed dreams of sending people to Mars." *The New York Times* (June 20, 2000): p. D5.

Eng, Dinah. "From Jungle to Space in Pursuit of New Drugs." *The New York Times* (November 28, 2000): p. F8.

Web Sites

"Astronaut Statistics." *Encyclopedia Astronautica*. http://www.astronautix.com/articles/aststics.htm (accessed on June 29, 2004).

"Franklin Chang-Díaz (Astronaut)." *infoCostaRica.com*. http://www.info-costarica.com/people/franklin.html (accessed on June 29, 2004).

"Jerry Lynn Ross." *Encyclopedia Astronautica*. http://www.astronautix.com/astros/ross.htm (accessed on June 30, 2004).

"Statement of Franklin Chang-Díaz before the Subcommittee on Energy, Committee on Science, House of Representatives." *House Committee on Science*. http://www.house.gov/science/hearings/energy03/dec04/changdiaz.htm (accessed on June 29, 2004).

Yuri Gagarin

Born March 9, 1934 (Klushino, Russia)
Died March 27, 1968 (Near Moscow, Russia)

Russian cosmonaut

In 1957 the former Soviet Union launched *Sputnik,* the first man-made space satellite (an object that orbits in space). Four years later, on April 12, 1961, Soviet cosmonaut (astronaut) Yuri Gagarin made a successful orbit of Earth aboard the spacecraft *Vostok*. As the first human to fly in space, Gagarin represented a technical triumph for the Soviet Union. Since the end of World War II (1939–45) the Soviet Union had been engaged in the Cold War (1945–91), a period of hostile relations, with the United States. The two world powers were not only competing for military superiority but also racing to be the first to explore space. Gagarin's achievement, therefore, signaled that the Soviet Union was moving ahead in the Cold War. Although Gagarin did not make another space flight, he remained a national hero and a leader in Russia's cosmonaut training program. His death during a training mission in 1968 was mourned throughout the Soviet Union.

"He invited us all into space."

Neil Armstrong, Aviation Week and Space Technology

Prepares for aviation career

Yuri Alekseevich Gagarin was born on March 9, 1934, the third of four children of Aleksey Ivanovich and Anna Gagarin.

Yuri Gagarin. *(Getty Images)*

The family lived on a collective farm in Klushino, Russia, where his father was a carpenter and his mother was a dairymaid. Gagarin grew up helping them with their work. Lacking extensive formal education themselves, his parents encouraged him to stay in school in the nearby town of Gzhatsk. Gagarin's education was interrupted in 1941, however, when Germany invaded the Soviet Union during World War II. German troops evicted the Gagarins from their home, forcing them to live in a dug-out shelter. When the Germans retreated they took two of Gagarin's sisters with them as slave laborers. The sisters were able to return home after the war.

When the war was over, Gagarin completed school in Gzhatsk and moved to a suburb of Moscow to work in a steel factory. Apprenticing as a foundryman (a skilled steel worker), he attended a vocational college in Moscow. After a year he was accepted into a technical college in the town of Saratov. Prior to graduation in 1955 he began attending night courses in aviation at a nearby flying school, where he took his first airplane ride and made a parachute jump. This introduction to flying, Gagarin later wrote in *Road to the Stars,* "gave meaning to [his] whole life." He graduated from college with honors and also earned a diploma from the aviation school. The following summer he went to an aviation camp and learned how to fly. Gagarin was then accepted at the Orenburg Flight Training School, graduating two years later. In the town of Orenburg, Gagarin met Valentina Ivanova Goryacheva, a nursing student and his future wife. After graduation he joined the Soviet Air Force and volunteered for a difficult assignment in the Russian Arctic while Valentina finished nurse's training in Moscow. Yuri and Valentina were married in 1957; they later had two children, a daughter and a son.

In 1958 Gagarin joined the Communist Party, the political organization that controlled Soviet government and society. Since the first *Sputnik* flight the previous year, Gagarin had been closely following news of other *Sputnik* launches. He knew that manned space flights would be the next challenge, so he volunteered for the secret cosmonaut training program in 1959. The following year, just before his twenty-sixth birthday, he completed physical examinations and testing. After being accepted as a member of the first group of twelve cosmonauts, he could not tell even his wife that he was training to go into space. Finally, in 1961, he was allowed to reveal the truth when his family was settled into the new space-program complex called Zvezdniy Gorodok (Star Town), 40 miles (64 kilometers) from Moscow.

Pioneers human space flight

By the time Gagarin entered the cosmonaut program, the Soviets had been preparing for the first manned space flight for a year. In May 1960 they launched a series of *Vostok* test rockets. ("Vostok" is the Russian word for east.) Although the first two rockets failed, the third launched two dogs into space

Laika: First Animal in Space

In 1961 Yuri Gagarin made history as the first human to travel in space. The distinction of being the first living creature to orbit in space, however, is held by a Russian dog named Laika (Barker). A perky three-year-old mixed breed with pointy ears, Laika was launched from Earth on November 3, 1957, aboard *Sputnik 2.* Wearing a special harness, she traveled in a padded capsule equipped with life-support instruments. Electrodes had been attached to her body before take-off so her reactions could be monitored by the ground control crew. Even though she was weightless during the flight, Laika was able to eat food and drink water. She also barked, and she could move around within the confines of her harness.

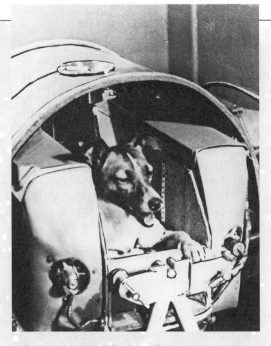

Laika, the dog inside *Sputnik 2.* *(© Bettmann/Corbis)*

Sputnik 2 circled Earth for 163 days, completing 2,370 orbits. Laika was not alive when the spacecraft touched down on April 15, 1958. Soviet officials never released details of the flight, so it is not known how long she lived—estimates range from twenty-four hours to one week—or how she died. According to some theories, she was deliberately poisoned or gassed to prevent her from suffering, but Russian scientists believe she died from extreme heat the day after the launch. In 1997 a plaque was placed at the Institute of Aviation and Space Medicine at Star City, in honor of Laika and other animals used for space experimentation. Laika's image has also appeared on postage stamps issued by many countries around the world.

and brought them safely back to Earth. The program was shut down for three months, however, after two rockets crashed with dogs on board in December 1960. The *Vostok* was then redesigned. After *Sputnik 9* and *Sputnik 10* were successfully launched in March 1961, the Soviets decided to go ahead with a *Vostok* manned flight. The final phase of the rocket was secretly assembled at the space center in Tyuratam in Kazakhstan, which was then a republic of the Soviet Union.

On April 8, 1961, Gagarin was selected to be the first human to go into space. Gherman Titov (1935–2000) was named as his backup, or the person who would take Gagarin's place if necessary. Two days later plans were finalized for a launch on April 12. At 5:00 A.M. on April 11 *Vostok* was towed to the launch pad, and at 1:00 P.M. Gagarin was driven to the site, accompanied by Sergei Korolev (1907–1966), the chief architect of the Soviet space program. After Gagarin was presented to the workers who had assembled the rocket, he and Korolev made final preparations for the launch.

Gagarin and Titov were awakened at 5:30 A.M. on April 12. Sensors were attached to their bodies to monitor pulse, blood pressure, and other functions. Two hours later Gagarin boarded *Vostok,* then waited ninety minutes for the final countdown. The spacecraft blasted off at 9:07 A.M., reaching a maximum pressure of six g's (six times the weight of gravity) in nine minutes. At 10:00 A.M. the manned *Vostok* mission was announced on Moscow radio.

Vostok was operated by a ground control crew. In the event of a malfunction, Gagarin would use a secret code that would allow him to operate the controls manually. *Vostok* reached an altitude of 327 kilometers and the flight proceeded smoothly. Gagarin was therefore free to make observations of Earth and to record his own reactions to being weightless. He proved that people can perform physical tasks, eat food, and drink liquids in space. Gagarin frequently commenting on the beauty of Earth from space—he was the first human to observe that Earth has a spherical shape. He also reported that weightlessness was a pleasant feeling. During the 108-minute flight *Vostok* made nearly one complete orbit of Earth. At 10:25 A.M., while passing over West Africa, the spacecraft reentered Earth's atmosphere. At an altitude of 26,247 feet (8,000 meters) the hatch of *Vostok* blew off and Gagarin parachuted to Earth, landing safely near the village of Smelovka in Russia.

Hailed as a hero

Although ejecting from a spacecraft was standard procedure for *Vostok* pilots, Soviet officials reported that Gagarin had remained aboard all the way to the ground. This was required for international certification of the *Vostok* flight as a record. Gagarin never revealed the truth, and for many

Yuri Gagarin became the first human in space when he flew inside the *Vostok*, pictured here. *(© Roger Ressmeyer/Corbis)*

decades the Soviets concealed the actual facts of the landing. On April 14 Gagarin was presented to the public in Moscow as a hero. Greeted by Nikita Khrushchev (1894–1971), the leader of the Soviet Union, he appeared before an enormous crowd. Gagarin's mother and father also came from their village to greet him. The event was broadcast live throughout the world—another technological first.

Gagarin was instantly promoted to the rank of major and he made appearances around the world. In addition to being named a Hero of the Soviet Union and a Hero of Socialist Labor, he became an honorary citizen of fourteen cities in six countries. He received the Tsiolkovsky Gold Medal of the Soviet Academy of Sciences, the Gold Medal of the British Interplanetary Society, and two awards from the International Aeronautical Federation. Gagarin became commander of the cosmonaut team. In 1964 he was made deputy director of the cosmonaut training center at the space program headquarters complex, where he oversaw the selection and training of the first women cosmonauts. He served as capsule communicator (the link between cosmonauts and ground controllers) for four later space flights in the *Vostok* and *Voskhod* programs. He also held various political posts.

Dies in training crash

Gagarin always wanted to venture back into space. In 1966 he was returned to active status to serve as back-up cosmonaut for Vladimir Komarov (1927–1967) in the first flight of the new Soyuz spacecraft. *Soyuz 1* was launched on April 23, 1967, but Komarov died as the result of a parachute malfunction on reentry. Gagarin was then assigned to command the upcoming *Soyuz 3,* but he would not fly the mission. On March 27, 1968, he took off for a routine proficiency flight in a two-seat MiG-15 training jet with his flight instructor. (A MiG jet is a Russian-made jet fighter designed to fly at an altitude of 80,000 feet [24,384 meters] and three times the speed of sound.) During low-level maneuvers with two other jets, Gagarin's plane crossed close behind another jet and was caught in its wind path. He lost control and the jet crashed into the tundra at high speed, instantly killing both Gagarin and the instructor. Gagarin was given a hero's funeral. At the time it was said that his ashes were buried in the wall of the Kremlin (the Soviet capitol building in Moscow). In 1984 it was revealed that his body was never found.

The cosmonaut training center was renamed in Gagarin's honor, as were his former hometown, a space tracking ship, and a lunar crater. His office at the center was preserved as a museum, and a huge statue of him was erected in Moscow. His book *Survival in Space* was published after his death. Written with space-program physician Vladimir Lebedev, the work outlines Gagarin's views on the problems and requirements for successful long-term space flights. On April 12, 1991, thirty years after Gagarin's flight, his cosmonaut successors, along with eighteen American astronauts, gathered in Russia to salute his achievements.

For More Information

Books

Gagarin, Yuri. *Road to the Stars*. Translated by G. Hanna and D. Myshne. Moscow: Foreign Languages Publishing House, 1962.

Gagarin, Yuri, and Vladimir Lebedev. *Psychology and Space*. Translated by Boris Belitsky. Moscow: Mir Publishers, 1970.

Gagarin, Yuri, and Vladimir Lebedev. *Survival in Space*. Translated by Gabriella Azrael. New York: Bantam Books, 1969.

Oberg, James E. *Red Star in Orbit*. New York: Random House, 1981.

Periodicals

Oberg, James E. *Aviation Week and Space Technology* (April 8, 1991): p. 7.

Web Sites

Memorial to Laika. http://www.novareinna.com/bridge/laika.html (accessed on June 30, 2004).

"Yuri Gagarin." *Guardian Unlimited*. http://www.guardian.co.uk/netnotes/article/0,6729,470879,00.html (accessed on June 29, 2004).

"Yuri Gagarin." *Starchild*. http://starchild.gsfc.nasa.gov/docs/StarChild/whos_who_level1/gagarin.html (accessed on June 29, 2004).

The Yuri Gagarin Cosmonauts Training Center. http://howe.iki.rssi.ru/GCTC/gctc_e.htm (accessed on June 29, 2004).

John Glenn

Born July 18, 1921 (Cambridge, Ohio)

American astronaut, senator, businessman

John Glenn was the first American to orbit Earth. He achieved this feat in 1962, at a time when the United States and the Soviet Union were engaged in a space race. Five years earlier the Soviets had stunned the world by launching unmanned *Sputnik* space satellites (objects that orbit in space). Then, in 1961, Soviet cosmonaut (astronaut) **Yuri Gagarin** (1934–1968; see entry) became the first human to orbit Earth. The ultimate goal for both the United States and the Soviet Union was to land a person on the Moon, so Gagarin's flight had clearly pulled the Soviet Union ahead in the race. Yet Glenn's three complete orbits paved the way for the U.S. victory scored by **Neil Armstrong** (1930–; see entry) and **Buzz Aldrin** (1930–; see entry) when, in 1969, they became the first humans to walk on the Moon. In 1998 Glenn made history again as the oldest American to travel in space. During his long career he has also been a U.S. senator and a successful businessman.

"I say you should live life based on how you feel and not by the calendar."

Pilots war planes

John Herschel Glenn Jr. was born on July 18, 1921, in Cambridge, Ohio. His parents, John Herschel Glenn, a plumb-

John Glenn. *(© Bettmann/Corbis)*

ing contractor, and Clara Sproat Glenn, had two other children who died in infancy. The Glenns later adopted a daughter, Jean. Glenn grew up in nearby New Concord, where he attended high school. A serious student, he earned top grades and he excelled in athletics. After graduating in 1939 he entered Muskingum College in New Concord to study chemical engineering. His high school sweetheart, Anna (Annie) Castor, also attended the college. When the United States entered World War II (1939–45) in 1941, Glenn enrolled in a civilian pilot training program and learned to fly aircraft. He then left college to enter the naval aviation cadet program, graduating in March 1943 with a commission in the Marine Corps Reserve. The following April, before he went on to advanced training and combat duty, he and Annie were married. The couple later had two children, John David and Carolyn Ann.

Glenn was assigned to squadron VMO-155, which was based on Majuro in the Marshall Islands in the Pacific Ocean. During the war he flew F4U Corsair fighter-bombers on fifty-nine missions. When the war ended in 1945, Glenn remained in the marine reserves as a fighter pilot and then as a flight instructor. Promoted to captain the following year, he entered the regular marine corps. In 1952 he was assigned to combat duty as a pilot in the Korean War (1950–53). Initially he flew ground-support missions, often returning in planes riddled with bullet holes and shrapnel (shell-fragment) holes. Just before the end of the war, Glenn transferred to a U.S. Air Force squadron through an exchange program. Flying F-86 Sabre jets, he shot down three North Korean MiG fighters (Russian-made jet fighters designed to fly at an altitude of 80,000 feet [24,384 meters] and three times the speed of sound) in nine days. He flew a total of ninety missions and was promoted to the rank of major in 1953. During his service in the wars he was awarded four Distinguished Flying Crosses and numerous other medals.

Upon returning from Korea, Glenn entered the Patuxent River naval test pilot school in Maryland. After graduation he spent two years evaluating new aircraft. He then moved to the Navy Bureau of Aeronautics in Washington, D.C., where he continued to oversee development of new fighters, including the F8U Crusader. Glenn made this plane famous in Project Bullet, an effort to break the non-stop transcontinental supersonic flight record, refueling in midair three times. On July 16, 1957, he flew a Crusader from Los Angeles to New York in three hours and twenty-three minutes, earning a fifth Distinguished Flying Cross.

Orbits Earth

In 1958, in response to Soviet progress in space exploration, the United States created the National Aeronautics and Space Administration (NASA). This new government agency integrated U.S. space research agencies and established Project Mercury, an astronaut training program. The goal of Project

Mercury was to place a human in orbit around Earth. When Glenn learned about the astronaut program, he immediately began to prepare for application. He began to strengthen his qualifications by improving his physical condition and volunteering for centrifuge tests and other research projects. He also took courses at the University of Maryland to work on his college degree. (Glenn received a bachelor's degree in mathematics from Muskingum College in Ohio in 1962, after he had flown in space.) In April 1959 Glenn, now a lieutenant colonel, was selected as one of America's seven Mercury astronauts.

Glenn was involved in designing the cockpit layout and the control instruments for the Mercury space capsule. He became the unofficial spokesperson for the Mercury team, so he was disappointed when fellow astronaut Alan Shepard (1923–1998; see box on page 74) was chosen to make the first U.S. spaceflight. It took place in 1961, shortly followed by a second flight piloted by Virgil "Gus" Grissom (1926–1967). Like Shepard, Grissom made a suborbital flight (a flight lasting less than one orbit) in the Mercury craft, which was launched by a Redstone rocket. Glenn was back-up pilot (one who will take the place of the command pilot if necessary) for both Shepard and Grissom. These efforts were overshadowed by Soviet cosmonaut Gagarin's successful orbit around Earth. Under pressure to match the Russian feat as soon as possible, NASA chose Glenn to make the first U.S. Earth orbit, officially known as Mercury-Atlas 6.

The launch of Glenn's space capsule, the *Friendship 7,* was postponed several times by unsuitable weather and technical problems. It finally roared into orbit on February 20, 1962, from Cape Canaveral (renamed Cape Kennedy after President John F. Kennedy's assasination in 1963) in Florida. Glenn performed many experiments, constantly giving observations and physiological reports to NASA ground controllers in Houston, Texas. Among the experiments was pulling on an elastic cord to determine the effects of physical work in weightlessness. Unlike the secrecy surrounding the Soviet space program, Glenn's flight received extensive publicity. One incident not revealed at the time, however, was that the ground control crew had received a signal that the heat shield might not be secured to the *Friendship 7.* The heat shield is a panel that protects the

John Glenn next to the Mercury-Atlas 6 spacecraft known as *Friendship 7*. On February 20, 1962, Glenn orbited Earth in *Friendship 7*, becoming the first American to complete a full orbit. *(© Bettmann/Corbis)*

capsule from intense heat produced by flames from the rockets that propel the craft into space and back to Earth. The heat shield was therefore vital for Glenn's safe reentry to Earth's atmosphere.

First American in Space

On May 5, 1961, Alan B. Shepard became the first American in space. He piloted the Mercury space capsule 115 miles (185 kilometers) above Earth's surface and 302 miles (486 kilometers) across the Atlantic Ocean. Although the trip lasted for only about fifteen minutes, his journey was almost technically perfect, paving the way for many more flights by U.S. astronauts. In 1963 Shepard was diagnosed as having Ménière's syndrome, a disease of the inner ear. NASA removed him from active flight duty and reassigned him to the NASA center in Houston, Texas, where he became chief of the astronaut office.

In 1968 Shepard underwent a successful operation in which a small drain tube was implanted in his inner ear. He then applied for readmission to active duty, and the following year NASA chose him to command the *Apollo 14* flight to the Moon. On January 31, 1971, *Apollo 14* blasted off from Cape Kennedy (Cape Canaveral), nearly ten years after Shepard's first space flight. Five days later Shepard and fellow astronaut Edgar Mitchell (1930–) landed on the Moon's surface. From their lunar module, the two astronauts stepped out into the Fra Mauro Highlands as the world watched on television. (The Fra Mauro Highlands are a widespread hilly geological area covering large portions of the lunar surface, with an eighty-kilometer-diameter crater, the Fra Mauro crater, located within it. The Fra

Alan Shepard, the first American in space. *(AP/ Wide World Photos)*

Mauro crater and surrounding formation take their names from a 15th century Italian monk and mapmaker.)

The astronauts had brought a lunar cart with them, and during two trips outside the lunar module they conducted experiments and gathered rock specimens. On one excursion Shepard hit a golf ball across the Moon's surface. In addition, the astronauts left behind a miniature scientific station that would continue to send messages to scientists on Earth. The story of the flight was immortalized in a book by author Tom Wolfe (1931–) and in a movie, both titled *The Right Stuff.*

Ground controllers told Glenn to change the original plan of releasing the retro-rocket apparatus, a rocket attached to the capsule that is used to slow its descent to Earth. Instead, the rocket would be kept in place, strapped over the heat shield, to keep the shield from coming loose. When Glenn was informed about the problem, he left the rocket on the capsule as directed and then began operating the *Friendship 7* manually. After three orbits of Earth he guided the spacecraft to a perfectly safe reentry. It was later determined that the signal had been a false alarm, but the incident proved to Glenn that astronauts must be prepared to respond to unexpected events.

Pursues new careers

Glenn became an instant hero after his successful flight. Awarded the NASA Distinguished Service Medal by President John F. Kennedy (1917–1963; served 1963–61), he addressed a joint session of Congress. This honor is normally reserved for top officials and visiting heads of state. He received hundreds of thousands of letters, some of which he collected in a book, *Letters to John Glenn*. He also befriended President Kennedy and the president's brother, Robert Kennedy (1925–1968), who was the U.S. attorney general. The president urged Glenn to enter politics and, without Glenn's knowledge, directed that the famous astronaut's life not be risked by another spaceflight. Glenn left NASA after working on preliminary designs for Project Apollo, which had the goal of putting a man on the Moon.

Glenn applied for military retirement to enter the Ohio senate race in 1964, but he had to withdraw after suffering a serious head injury in a bathroom fall. He retired from the marines in January 1965, having logged over 5,400 hours of flying time. His space adventures brought numerous civilian honors, including induction into the Aviation Hall of Fame and the National Space Hall of Fame, and the award of the Congressional Space Medal of Honor. He was granted honorary doctorates in engineering by four universities. After retirement Glenn went into business, first with the Royal Crown cola company and later with a management group that operated Holiday Inn hotels.

Although Glenn became a successful businessman, he was still interested in a political career. In 1970 he again declared

"Pretty Good for a 40-year-old Guy"

During his second flight in space, at age seventy-seven, John Glenn participated in numerous tests that monitored the effects of space travel on older people. The tests focused primarily on problems associated with weightlessness. When NASA released the results, however, there were some surprising findings. At a conference sponsored by NASA and the National Institute on Aging in 1999, researchers revealed that stress had more impact than weightlessness, and that age was not necessarily a factor. Instead, the tests—which were conducted on the younger *Discovery* astronauts along with Glenn—showed that further study was needed on stress-producing hormone changes in the digestive and immune systems.

The researchers reported that Glenn endured the flight with few aftereffects, mainly because he was in good physical shape. A healthy lifestyle proved to be the best preparation for space travel, regardless of age. Another consideration was that the *Discovery* flight was so short that there was no significant difference between test results for Glenn and those for men and women half his age. Dr. John Charles (1955–), the NASA senior life scientist for the mission, was referring to Glenn's excellent physical condition when he joked in "Aging in Space" in the magazine titled *Simply Family:* "Basically, he [Glenn] did pretty good for a 40-year-old guy."

his candidacy for the U.S. Senate, narrowly losing in the Democratic primary (a contest to choose a political party's candidate) to Howard Metzenbaum (1917–). When another Senate seat opened in 1974, Glenn ran a more effective campaign and won the election. He went on to serve four terms, or twenty-four years, in the Senate, earning respect among colleagues and the public for his honesty and hard work. Glenn supported increased funding for education, space exploration, and basic scientific research. He was a strong advocate of the **International Space Station** (ISS; see entry), a research facility maintained in space by nations throughout the world. In 1984 he ran unsuccessfully as the Democratic nominee for the presidency. He retired from the senate in 1999.

Test space travel for older people

Glenn enjoyed his work in politics, but he longed to return to space. In 1998, at age seventy-seven, he asked NASA if he could fly again. Glenn later told *National Geographic* magazine interviewer William R. Newcott that he had a specific reason for making the request: While doing research for the ISS he became interested in studying the effects of space travel on young people and older people. "Over the years," Glenn noted, "NASA has observed more than fifty changes that occur in the human body in space. And nine or ten of these are very similar to things that happen in the process of aging. Things like loss of muscle strength. Bone density loss. Cardiovascular changes. Changes in balance and coordination. . . . My idea was to send an older person up and study the body's reaction to space flight—see if there were differences between younger and older people."

In January 1998, NASA announced that Glenn, who had made history thirty-six years earlier as the first American to orbit Earth, would fly in space again. As a payload specialist aboard the space shuttle *Discovery,* mission STS-95, he would test the effects of weightlessness on older space travelers. Amid excited media coverage, the *Discovery* lifted off from Kennedy Space Center on October 29 and returned to Earth on November 7. Having endured the flight surprisingly well, Glenn was a hero once again. He was also an inspiration to older Americans. Reflecting on their reaction to his flight, Glenn remarked to Newcott, "I've noticed that because of all this, people are seeing themselves in a way they hadn't before. They're realizing that older people have the same ambitions, hopes, and dreams as anybody else. I say you should live life based on how you feel and not by the calendar."

Glenn's second flight inspired the idea behind *Space Cowboys* (2000) a high-tech space adventure film about aging former astronauts who try to prevent a satellite from slamming into Earth. *Space Cowboys* was made in cooperation with NASA.

For More Information

Books

Glenn, John H. *Letters to John Glenn: With Comments by J. H. Glenn, Jr.* New York: World Book Encyclopedia Science Service, 1964.

Montgomery, Scott, and Timothy R. Gaffney. *Back in Orbit.* Atlanta, GA: Longstreet, 1998.

Pierce, Philip N., and Karl Schuon. *John H. Glenn: Astronaut.* New York: Franklin Watts, 1962.

Wolfe, Tom. *The Right Stuff.* New York: Farrar, Straus, 1979.

Periodicals

Newcott, William R. "John Glenn: Man with a Mission." *National Geographic* (June 1999): p. 60+.

"Space Cowboys." *Astronomy* (September 2000): p. 107.

"Victory Lap." *Time* (November 9, 1998): p. 64.

Web Sites

"Astronaut Bio: John H. Glenn. NASA. http://www.grc.nasa.gov/WWW/PAO/html/glennbio.htm (accessed on June 29, 2004).

Bowman, Lee. "Aging in Space." *Simply Family.* http://www.simplyfamily.com/display.cfm?articleID=000207_John_Glenn.cfm (accessed on June 29, 2004).

The John Glenn Institute at Ohio State University. www.glenninstitute.org (accessed on June 29, 2004).

Robert H. Goddard

Born October 5, 1882 (Worcester, Massachusetts)
Died August 10, 1945 (Annapolis, Maryland)

American physicist, rocket pioneer

Robert Goddard is credited with launching the world's first liquid-propellant rocket. (A liquid-propellant rocket is fired with liquid fuel. Prior to the twentieth century rockets were fired with gun powder, known as solid fuel.) For centuries, scientists had realized that rockets were the only way to reach distant space. Among the important modern theorists was **Konstantin Tsiolkovsky** (1857–1935; see entry), a Russian teacher who promoted spaceflight and wrote books on the subject. Goddard was the first to succeed in firing a rocket a significant distance, however, and his research produced a technological revolution. By the end of his life he held more than two hundred patents for such inventions as turbo-fed rockets powered by gas generators, automatic rocket launching and guidance controls, and optical-telescope tracking methods.

At the end of World War II (1939–45) German scientists, headed by **Wernher von Braun** (1912–1977; see entry), used Goddard's innovations to build V-2 rockets. Germany used the V-2 against the Allies (the military forces of Great Britain, the United States, and several other countries) but with limited

"I was a different boy when I descended the tree from when I ascended, for existence at last seemed very purposive."

Robert Goddard. *(Library of Congress)*

effectiveness. After the war Goddard's innovations formed the basis of missile and space programs in the United States and in the former Soviet Union. Goddard's influence on rocket science may have been even greater if he had not worked alone and if he had been more willing to publish the results of his research.

Climbs cherry tree, dreams about Mars

Robert Hutchings Goddard was born on October 5, 1882, in Worcester, Massachusetts. During his early childhood his family moved to Boston, where his father, Nahum Danford Goddard, became part-owner of a machine shop. Robert's mother, Fannie Louise Hoyt Goddard, suffered from tuberculosis, a severe lung disease that kept her bedridden. Nahum and Fannie Goddard had a second son who died in infancy. Thin and frail as a boy, Robert was frequently ill and he missed school so often that he fell years behind in his education. Spending most of his days at home alone, he entertained himself by playing with kites, slingshots, and rifles. Thus began his lifelong interest in flying projectiles, objects that are shot into the air by force.

In 1898, after Fannie Goddard was diagnosed with tuberculosis, the family moved back to Worcester. Around this time Goddard, who was now sixteen years old, discovered science fiction when he read *War of the Worlds* by **H.G. Wells** (1866–1946; see entry). This classic tale describes an invasion of Earth by aliens from the planet Mars. The following year Goddard had a life-changing experience. According to biographical accounts, he was doing yardwork one day and needed to trim a cherry tree behind his house. Climbing the tree, he gazed out into a nearby meadow and began daydreaming about a spaceship that could go to Mars. This moment gave him such a sense of purpose that he never forgot the date—October 19, 1899. He later wrote in his autobiography, "I was a different boy when I descended the tree from when I ascended, for existence at last seemed very purposive." For the rest of his life he recorded October 19 as "anniversary day" in his diary, and he revisited the tree on that date whenever he was in Worcester.

Goddard's experience in the cherry tree compelled him to excel in math and physics. Up to this point, however, his formal education had been deficient, especially in algebra, because of his illnesses. So in 1899, at age seventeen, Goddard entered Worcester South High as a sophomore. When he graduated in 1904, he ranked at the top of his class and, at twenty-one, had the distinction of being the oldest graduate in the history of the school. A few months later he enrolled at Worcester Polytechnic Institute, a small college where he majored in physics. By his senior year he was experimenting with rockets in the small basement laboratory at the college. At that time the only rockets available were fired with powder ignited by a flame, so they were little more than fireworks. Goddard envisioned developing a manned rocket (one that carries a person). After testing the amount of energy released by a powder rocket, he concluded that he needed to find a more powerful source of propulsion (a force that causes forward motion).

In 1908 Goddard earned a bachelor's degree from Worcester Polytechnic. Shortly after being hired as a physics instructor at the college, he began graduate studies at nearby Clark University. He received a doctorate from Clark in 1911, then became a research instructor in physics at Princeton University in Princeton, New Jersey. When Goddard fell dangerously ill in 1913 he was, like his mother, diagnosed with tuberculosis. Initially given only two weeks to live, he recovered sufficiently the following year to return to Clark as a physics instructor. Promoted to assistant professor in 1915, he would remain at Clark throughout most of his academic career, except for leaves of absence to pursue rocket research. Goddard was eventually named head of the physics department and director of the physical laboratories, becoming a full professor in 1934. In 1924 he married Esther Christine Kisk, the secretary to the president of Clark. Although the couple had no children, they were devoted to one another and to Goddard's rocket research. Esther became his assistant, keeping notes and photographic records of his work.

Invents two-stage rocket

In 1914 Goddard obtained a patent for a two-stage powder rocket. A two-stage rocket fires twice—first to begin motion and again to keep moving or to move faster. He later received a patent for a rocket that burned a mixture of gasoline and liquid nitrous oxide (a colorless gas; also called laughing gas). Although Goddard knew that liquid propellants were more effective, they were difficult to obtain. He therefore continued experiments with smokeless powder. Goddard eventually achieved higher rates of energy efficiency and exhaust power than previous rockets had exhibited. In 1917, after the United States had entered World War I (1914–18), Goddard wrote to the Smithsonian Institution, suggesting the possible military application of his rocket. Convinced of Goddard's vision, the Smithsonian asked the U.S. Department of War to contribute up to fifty thousand dollars—a considerable amount of money in those days—toward his research. Soon he had his own well-equipped laboratory and shop at Clark, with seven men working for him full-time.

When Goddard relocated his shop to Pasadena, California, in 1918 he and his team had already developed two military rocket launchers. The same year, at the Aberdeen Proving Ground in Maryland, Goddard demonstrated his launcher, which could propel a rocket through a hand-held tube. Intended as a portable weapon for foot soldiers, it was the first bazooka (a light weapon that launches armor-piercing rockets and is fired from the shoulder). Military observers were impressed with Goddard's invention, and they requested immediate production. The launcher was never used in World War I combat, however, because hostilities ended five days after the demonstration.

After the war Goddard returned to Clark, where he taught physics and continued his research on high-altitude rockets. Meanwhile, the Smithsonian published "A Method of Reaching Extreme Altitudes," his paper on sending rockets into space. Unfortunately, reaction to the paper was shaped by a Smithsonian press release that emphasized a point Goddard had not intended to be the focus of his work. Specifically, the press release concentrated on his method of proving that a rocket had reached a high altitude. To do so, Goddard suggested sending a small quantity of flash powder on a rocket to the dark side of the Moon. He theorized that once the rocket had arrived at its destination, the powder would be ignited and the flash of light could be viewed from Earth through telescopes. Playing up the idea of a "Moon rocket," the press completely ignored the rest of his theory. In fact, some even called Goddard "Moon Man." He had always been reluctant to publicize his work—in fact, the chairman of the Clark physics department had pressured him into publishing the paper—so he became even more secretive about his theories in the future.

Starts rocket-science center

Goddard continued his rocket research, switching to liquid propellants in 1921. Five years later, on March 16, 1926, he launched the world's first liquid-propellant rocket from a hill in Auburn, Massachusetts. The rocket traveled 184 feet (56 meters) in 2.5 seconds. Still wary of publicity, he did not

Robert Goddard teaching a physics class at Clark University in Worcester, Massachusetts, in 1924. At Clark Goddard developed many of his ideas for liquid rocket propellants. *(AP/Wide World Photos)*

announce his success for several months. In 1930 Goddard received a fifty-thousand-dollar grant from philanthropist Daniel Guggenheim (1856–1930). (A philanthropist donates money to help others.) Taking a leave of absence from Clark University, he moved with his wife and a few technical assistants to a rented farmhouse near Roswell, New Mexico. Goddard's laboratory eventually became the world center of rocket science.

Hundreds of tests were performed and forty-eight launches were attempted at a site in the desert. The rockets grew progressively larger and more sophisticated, approaching 22 feet (6.7 meters) in length and weighing up to one-quarter ton. Goddard invented and patented a large number of innovations, including a guidance system controlled by a gyroscope (a wheel or disk that spins and rotates at the same time), which permitted a rocket to "correct" its path during flight. The greatest height one of his rockets reached was estimated at 8,000 to 9,000 feet (2,438 to 2,743 meters) on March 26, 1937. This was considerably short of the 100 to 200 miles (161 to 322 kilometers) of altitude he had originally expected to achieve.

In 1941 Goddard returned to defense-related rocket research. The following year he moved his crew of assistants to the Naval Engineering Experimental Station in Annapolis, Maryland. They worked on various devices, including a rocket motor that became the basis for the first aircraft in America to use an engine operated with a throttle. Like the bazooka, this was an important advance. Despite his technical achievements, Goddard's career remained somewhat flawed by his failure to reach the extreme altitudes he sought, and by his secretive nature. In 1936 he did publish another paper, titled "Liquid-Propellant Rocket Development," but it provided little useful information to other scientists.

Honored for achievements

Goddard died on August 10, 1945, of throat cancer, which had been diagnosed only two months earlier. His importance to the United States is shown by the numerous memorials to his work. Many streets, buildings, and awards were named in his honor, perhaps the most significant being the National Aeronautical and Space Administration (NASA) Goddard Space Flight Center. It was dedicated on March 16, 1961, the thirty-fifth anniversary of the first flight of Goddard's liquid-propellant rocket. On that occasion Esther Goddard accepted a Congressional Gold Medal on behalf of her deceased husband. Nine years later Clark University named

WAC Corporal Surpasses Goddard Rockets

Robert Goddard was extremely reluctant to publicize the results of his experiments. This unwillingness to share information eventually damaged his career, because scientific progress depends to a great degree on the free exchange of ideas and achievement. In 1936 Goddard published a paper titled "Liquid-Propellant Rocket Development"—only the second, and last, paper he published in his lifetime—but it did not provide useful information to other scientists. For the most part, rocket researchers had to develop their own models of Goddard's innovations because they lacked a detailed knowledge of his pioneering inventions. This was notably the case with Frank J. Malina (1912–1981) and his rocket team, who worked at a laboratory, which eventually would become the Jet Propulsion Laboratory, in southern California. This group developed solid-propellant rocket technology that was important for later missile technology. On October 11, 1945, the Malina team succeeded in launching a rocket, named the WAC Corporal, to an altitude of some 230,000 feet (7,010 meters)—far higher than any of Goddard's rockets had ever reached.

its new library after Goddard. Since 1958, the National Space Club in Washington, D.C., has awarded a Goddard Memorial Trophy for achievement in missiles, rocketry, and space flight. In 1960 Goddard became the ninth recipient of the Langley Gold Medal, an honor awarded only a few times since 1910 by the Smithsonian Institution for excellence in aviation.

For More Information

Books

Goddard, Robert H. *The Autobiography of Robert Hutchings Goddard, Father of the Space Age; Early Years to 1927.* Worcester, MA: A. J. St. Onge, 1966.

Goddard, Robert H. *Rockets.* Mineola, NY: Dover Publications, 2002.

Lehman, Milton. *Robert H. Goddard: Pioneer of Space Research.* New York: Da Capo, 1988.

Winter, Frank H. *Rockets into Space.* Cambridge, MA: Harvard University Press, 1990.

Periodicals

Crouch, Tom D. "Reaching Toward Space: His 1935 Rocket Was a Technological Tour de Force, But Robert H. Goddard Hid It from History." *Smithsonian* (February 2001): p. 38.

Goddard, Robert H. "Liquid-Propellant Rocket Development." *Smithsonian* (1936).

Goddard, Robert H. "A Method of Reaching Extreme Altitudes." *Smithsonian* (1919).

Web Sites

"Robert Goddard (1882–1945)." *About.com.* http://inventors.about.com/library/inventors/blgoddard.htm (accessed on July 21, 2004).

"Robert Goddard and His Rockets." *NASA.* http://www-istp.gsfc.nasa.gov/stargaze/Sgoddard.htm (accessed on June 29, 2004).

"Robert H. Goddard: American Rocket Pioneer." *NASA.* http://www.gsfc.nasa.gov/gsfc/service/gallery/fact_sheets/general/goddard/goddard.htm (accessed on June 29, 2004).

Claudie Haigneré

Born May 13, 1957 (Le Creusot, France)

French astronaut

Claudie Haigneré grew up during the dawn of the space age. In October 1957, slightly more than five months after her birth, the former Soviet Union surprised the world by launching *Sputnik 1*. The first artificial satellite (an object that orbits in space), it was followed four years later by the flight of Soviet cosmonaut **Yuri Gagarin** (1934–1968; see entry), the first human to orbit in space. In 1969, when Haigneré was twelve years old, American astronaut **Neil Armstrong** (1930–; see entry) became the first human to walk on the Moon. By 2001 Haigneré herself had made space exploration history: She was the first European woman astronaut to visit the **International Space Station** (ISS; see entry). She had the further distinction of being only the second European Space Agency (ESA) astronaut to make the trip. After her flight to the ISS, Haigneré was appointed minister of research and new technologies in the French government.

"Men and women are different but complementary. . . . When we explore the planets, it will be a huge step forward for the entire human race. And the human race has two sexes."

Inspired by Armstrong

Claudie André-Deshays Haigneré (pronounced cloh-dee ahn-DRAY day-shay heh-nyair-AY) was born on May 13, 1957,

Claudie Haigneré. *(AP/Wide World Photos)*

in Le Creusot, France, where she grew up. (She married fellow astronaut Jean-Pierre Haigneré in 2001. For most of her career she was known as Claudie André-Deshays, but in most recent publications she is generally called Claudie Haigneré.) In an interview published on the ESA website, she said that Armstrong's moon walk inspired her fascination with space. "For me, it was a kind of revelation," Haigneré recalled. "I was watching a dream turn into reality. A door was open. I didn't immediately imagine that it was open for me, but the lunar landing gave me a taste for space." As a space exploration enthusiast, she read books and watched television documentaries on the subject. Before becoming an astronaut, however, she pursued a career in medicine. Graduating from high school at age fifteen, she went on to earn degrees in biology (the study of plant and animal life), sports medicine, and rheumatology (the study of inflammation and pain in joints of the body).

In 1985, while practicing as a doctor at a hospital in Paris, Haigneré happened to see a National Center for Space Studies (CNES) notice on a bulletin board: The agency was seeking applications from scientists to work in its microgravity research program (research on the virtual absence of gravity). She leaped at the chance, knowing this was an opportunity to become involved in space exploration. After a lengthy selection process she was chosen as one of only seven candidates—and the only woman—from one thousand applicants. While waiting for her first flight she continued her scientific career. In 1986 she received a diploma in the biomechanics and physiology of movement (the study of biological and physical processes of the body), then six years later she completed a Ph.D. in neuroscience (the study of the nervous system). During this time she was involved in studying human reactions to weightlessness. Her experiments were part of preparations for the French-Soviet *Aragatz* mission to the Russian space station *Mir,* which took place in 1988. (A space station is a research laboratory that orbits in space.) Since France does not maintain its own space vehicles, French astronauts participated in missions sponsored by the Russian Aviation and Space Agency (Rosoviakosmos). They prepared for flights at Star City, the Russian cosmonaut (astronaut) training center near Moscow.

Beginning in 1989, Haigneré coordinated preflight scientific experiments for the French-Russian *Antarès* mission, which took place in 1992. She also headed space physiology and medical programs in the Life Sciences Division of CNES in Paris. In 1992 she was chosen as a backup crew member for Jean-Pierre Haigneré on the French-Russian *Altair* mission. (A backup crew member is an astronaut trained to take the place of a main-crew astronaut who is not approved to go on a flight.) Jean-Pierre completed the flight—the *Altair* was launched on July 1, 1993, and returned to Earth on July 22— so Claudie remained on the ground at the mission control center in Kaliningrad, Russia. She monitored biological and medical experiments that were being conducted in space by

Jean-Pierre Haigneré

Jean-Pierre Haigneré (1948–) became an astronaut with the French National Space Agency in 1985. He made two trips to the Russian space station *Mir*. The first was a three-week stay in 1992; the second was a historic six-month visit launched on February 20, 1999. Traveling on the Soyuz craft *Perseus,* Haigneré was the first non-Russian to serve as onboard engineer both for a Soyuz flight and for the *Mir*. During his stay on the space station he participated in life science, physics, and biology experiments. He also took a spacewalk to perform biological and comet dust experiments outside the station. When the *Perseus* landed in Kazakhstan nearly 189 days later, on August 28, Haigneré had made the longest flight by a non-Russian astronaut. The record was previously held by American astronaut **Shannon Lucid** (1943–; see entry), whose *Mir* mission had lasted 188 days, 4 hours, and 14 seconds.

The *Perseus* crew members were the last people to stay on *Mir*. Before returning to Earth they left the space station in a "standby" mode, with no occupants onboard. (Russia took *Mir* out of service in

Jean-Pierre Haigneré returns to Earth after six months aboard *Mir*. *(© Reuters/Corbis)*

2004, crashing it in the Pacific Ocean.) Upon returning from the *Mir* mission, Haigneré was appointed head of the Astronaut Division of the European Astronaut Corps (EAC). In 2003 he became senior advisor to the director of launchers, a position in which he oversees the Soyuz human spaceflight program at the EAC spaceport in French Guiana.

the *Altair* crew. The following year she supervised French experiments for the ESA *Euromir 94* space station mission.

Makes two space flights

Haigneré was finally selected for her first flight in 1994. As a scientific research consultant and main crew member on the Soyuz vehicle *Cassiopeé,* she started training in January

1995 at Star City. (Soyuz is the name of a Russian manned space capsule. A name such as *Cassiopeé* refers to a specific mission of a Soyuz capsule.) The *Cassiopeé* was launched into space on August 17, 1996, returning safely to Earth sixteen days later, on September 2. Haigneré then remained in Moscow as the French representative of Starsem, a French-Russian space technology firm. In 1998 she was again selected as the backup for Jean-Pierre, this time on the French-Russian *Perseus* mission to *Mir*. During training she qualified as a cosmonaut engineer for a Soyuz spacecraft and for the *Mir* space station. She thus became the first woman to achieve the rank of Soyuz return commander, a position in which she was responsible for the reentry of a three-person Soyuz capsule from space. Jean-Pierre participated in the *Perseus* flight, which took place in February 1999, while Claudie was stationed at the ground control center in Korolev, Russia. She coordinated communication between the *Perseus* crew and ground control.

In 1998 Claudie Haigneré was selected for the European Astronaut Corps (EAC), which had been formed by the ESA. The ESA had participated in manned spaceflight prior to that time, but it did not have a formal astronaut program. The ESA first recruited astronauts in 1978 for flights to *Skylab,* a U.S. space station. The ESA selected its next group of astronauts in 1992 for the ESA Hermes and Columbus programs. The ESA created the EAC, which is based in Cologne, Germany, to train astronauts for the ISS program. The EAC constitution established a permanent corps of sixteen astronauts: four from Germany, four from France, four from Italy, and four from member states of the European Union. Claudie Haigneré and Jean-Pierre Haigneré were among the first seven EAC astronauts chosen in 1998.

After joining the EAC, Claudie Haigneré was involved in microgravity and medical projects for the European space program. In 2001, after three months of training at Star City for her second flight, she went into space with a Russian crew onboard the Soyuz vehicle *Andromede*. On this flight she became the first woman to visit the ISS and the first non-Russian woman to be a Soyuz flight engineer. The goal of the mission, called a "taxi flight," was to replace the old Soyuz capsule presently on the ISS with a new one. This meant that the astronauts would leave the capsule they arrived in at the space station and then return to Earth in the old capsule. After

Claudie Haigneré and her husband Jean-Pierre Haigneré. Both served as astronauts for the European Astronaut Corps. *(© Alain Nogues/Corbis Sygma)*

completing the eight-day mission, Haigneré and the two other members of her crew returned to Earth, landing in Kazakhstan, where Russian support crews pulled them out of the capsule, wrapped them in double fur bags, and put them in special chairs to ease their readjustment to Earth's gravity.

Takes government post

Claudie and Jean-Pierre were married in 2001. The following year she was appointed to the post of minister for research and new technologies in the French government. She was also awarded the French Legion of Honor. Haigneré sees part of her mission as educational: showing young Europeans that Europe has a strong space program and that careers in science and technology can be fulfilling. She also would like to see more women involved in the European Astronaut

Corps. Only one in sixteen European astronauts, or 6 percent, is female, and Haigneré believes this number could be higher. As she commented to an ESA interviewer, however, she also realizes that it is difficult for women to have "100 percent commitment and 100 percent availability" for the program. Women are usually more constrained than men by work and family responsibilities. Yet, she added, "I am confident that the new generation will be in better shape to choose its own future without any constraints of inequality." Haigneré also noted that women do well in space, and that teams that included both men and women have been shown to perform better than all-male teams. "Men and women are different but complementary," she concluded. "When we explore the planets, it will be a huge step forward for the entire human race. And the human race has two sexes."

For More Information

Periodicals

Balter, Michael. "France's Highflier Comes Down to Earth." *Science* (August 16, 2002): pp. 1112–13.

Web Sites

"Claudie Haigneré." *WorldSpaceFlight.com.* http://www.worldspaceflight. com/bios/h/haignere-c.htm (accessed on June 29, 2004).

"ESA Astronaut Claudie Haigneré Appointed Minister." *ESA* (June 18, 2002). http://www.esa.int/export/esaCP/ESAU80OED2D_Life_0.html (accessed on June 29, 2004).

"First European Woman Heads for Space Station Alpha." *Spaceflight Now* (October 20, 2001). http://www.spaceflightnow.com/news/n0110/ 20haignere/ (accessed on June 29, 2004).

"An Interview with Claudie Haigneré." *ESA.* http://www.esa.int/ export/esaHS/ESA2CU0VMOC_astronauts_0.html (accessed on June 29, 2004).

"Jean-Pierre Haigneré." *Encyclopedia Astronomica.* http://www.astronautix. com/astros/haignere.htm (accessed on June 29, 2004).

Hubble Space Telescope

April 25, 1990

"We do not know why we are born into the world, but we can try to find out what sort of a world it is at least in its physical aspects."

Edwin P. Hubble

The Hubble Space Telescope (HST) is the most significant advance in astronomy since Italian astronomer Galileo Galilei (1564–1642) perfected the telescope in the seventeenth century. (An astronomer is a scientist who studies bodies in space.) Named for twentieth-century astronomer Edwin P. Hubble (1889–1953), the HST orbits Earth in outer space, taking pictures of stars, galaxies, planets, and vast regions previously unknown to humans. (A galaxy is a large group of stars and associated matter.) Since it is positioned beyond Earth's atmosphere, the space observatory receives images that are brighter and more detailed than those captured by telescopes based on land. Launched by the National Aeronautics and Space Administration (NASA) in 1990, the HST has taken spectacular pictures of the universe. In 2004, a year after the *Columbia* space shuttle disaster (see box in *Challenger* **Crew** entry), NASA canceled the final service mission to the HST. Supporters of the orbiting observatory began seeking ways to prolong the life of the largest, most successful astronomy project in history.

The Hubble Space Telescope. *(© Corbis)*

How the HST works

The HST is an observatory (a structure that houses a telescope for astronomical viewing) approximately the size of a school bus that orbits Earth at a speed of 5 miles (about 8 kilometers) per second. The cylinder-shaped body of the spacecraft holds a reflecting telescope and scientific instruments. The telescope contains a primary mirror and a secondary mirror, which operate in conjunction with five main recording instruments: a faint-object camera, a wide-field planetary camera, a faint-object spectrograph (an instrument that sends out radiation), a high-resolution (rendering of detail) spectrograph, and a high-speed photometer (an instrument that measures light intensity). The reflecting telescope collects light from objects in space. The primary mirror, which measures 94 inches (2.4 meters), and the smaller secondary mirror then direct the light into the two cameras and the two spectrographs.

The wide-field planetary camera can record images with a resolution that is ten times greater than that of any telescope based on Earth. It can take pictures of wide expanses of space, or it can take more focused pictures of objects such as planets and bodies inside and outside of galaxies. The faint-object camera can detect objects that are fifty times fainter than those that can be observed by any telescope on Earth. The high-resolution spectrograph receives ultraviolet light (light at the violet end of the light spectrum) that cannot reach Earth because it is absorbed by the atmospheric layer. The faint-object spectrograph records data about the chemical composition of an object.

The telescope is pointed in the right direction by six gyroscopes (wheels or disks that spin horizontally and perpendicularly), which also keep it stable. Attached to the HST are two solar arrays (panels that capture light from the Sun) that resemble wings. Each measuring 8 feet (2.4 meters) wide and 40 feet (12 meters) long, the arrays supply the spacecraft with electrical power. A solar cell blanket (layer) on each array converts sunlight into energy and charges six nickel-hydrogen batteries during the sunlit part of orbit. The batteries then provide power when the HST is in Earth's shadow.

Telescopes make revolutionary discoveries

Since ancient times, astronomers have been developing theories about the universe. Prior to the invention of the telescope, they had to depend entirely on the naked eye to make their observations. Although they produced knowledge about stars and planets, their theories about the relation of Earth to other celestial bodies were wrong. By the third century B.C.E. astronomers were asserting that Earth was a sphere at rest at the center of the universe, with twenty-seven concentric (having a common center) spheres rotating around it. This theory was not questioned until the late sixteenth century C.E., when Polish astronomer Nicolaus Copernicus (1473–1543) published an opposite view.

Using the naked-eye method and complex mathematical formulas, Copernicus proposed that the Sun is at the center of the solar system and that the planets—including Earth—orbit around the Sun. He also came to believe that Earth is a relatively small and unimportant component of the universe.

Copernicus's theory was proven in the early seventeenth century by Galileo, when he perfected his telescope. Made with two lenses (pieces of glass ground and polished to magnify objects), the telescope magnified objects thirty-two times their original size and was strong enough for astronomical viewing.

From Galileo's time onward, astronomers all over the world developed larger and more powerful telescopes. They were able to collect records of stars, planets, and other bodies that previously could not be seen by the naked eye. Although the Sun-centered universe was now an accepted theory, astronomers still believed that there was only one galaxy—the Milky Way, which contains Earth and its known solar system. According to this theory, nothing existed outside the Milky Way except a vast, empty space.

In 1924 Edwin Hubble (see box on page 98) made a revolutionary discovery: Using the 100-inch (254 centimeters) telescope at Mount Wilson near Los Angeles, California, he observed billions of other galaxies. Moreover, Hubble found that the galaxies were moving away from one another, an indication that the universe is expanding. As a result of Hubble's discovery, astronomers engaged in speculation about the beginning and end of the universe, producing such ideas as the big-bang theory. The big-bang theory states that the universe was formed ten to twenty billion years ago when a highly condensed form of energy and matter exploded. According to this view, effects of the huge explosion are still taking place with the expansion of the universe.

History of the HST

Despite the benefits of advanced technology, modern astronomers were unable to receive precise images from their telescopes. Like the naked-eye observers before them, they encountered a limitation—in this case Earth's atmosphere (air surrounding Earth). Even the most powerful telescopes situated atop the highest mountains could not penetrate the thick layer of dust and gases that make up the atmosphere. As early as 1923 the German rocket scientist **Hermann Oberth** (1894–1989; see entry) had come upon a solution to the problem. He envisioned attaching a telescope to a rocket and sending it into Earth orbit. In 1946 American astrophysicist Lyman

Edwin P. Hubble

The Hubble Space Telescope was named for astronomer Edwin P. Hubble (1889–1953), who added important basic knowledge to the field of astronomy. Among his contributions was the discovery of other galaxies, which proves that the universe is constantly expanding. In simplified terms, he basically discovered the universe.

At a time when scientists did not believe any other galaxies existed outside the Milky Way, Hubble proved otherwise. He also showed that the universe is expanding, and he developed a mathematical model known as Hubble's law for observing this expansion. Although he was not the first to suggest that the universe is expanding, he was the first to recognize the existence of other galaxies and to form a clear theory along with a law to prove it. Generally speaking, Hubble's law states that the farther away a galaxy exists from Earth's galaxy (the Milky Way), the faster it is moving away from Earth. This concept later became part of the big-bang the-

Edwin P. Hubble. *(Library of Congress)*

ory of the creation of the universe. In 1990 NASA launched the Hubble Space Telescope in honor of the astronomer. Orbiting 370 miles (595 kilometers) above Earth's surface, the device was designed to collect data that would build upon Hubble's earlier findings.

Spitzer Jr. (1914–1997) expanded this idea, proposing a space-based observatory that would orbit above Earth's atmosphere.

In the late 1950s NASA launched two Orbital Astronomical Observatories (OAOs) into Earth orbit. The OAOs led to the construction of the HST over twenty-five years later. The first step was the Large Space Telescope (LST) project, which was initiated in 1969. An immediate result of the LST was the introduction of the space shuttle, a reusable vehicle that would launch the LST into orbit. Five space shuttles—*Columbia, Challenger, Atlantis, Discovery,* and *Endeavour*—have been built since establishment of the program. (*Enterprise* was the first shuttle to be built; however, it never went into orbit and was used primarily for "captured flights" involving takeoff and re-entry exercises.) The space shuttle represented a major shift in direction for the U.S. manned space flight program. During the 1960s NASA had concentrated its efforts on reaching the Moon by developing Project Mercury, Project Gemini, and Project Apollo (see **Buzz Aldrin** [1930–], **Neil Armstrong** [1930–], **John Glenn** [1921–], and **Christopher Kraft** [1924–] entries). Interest in further Moon exploration had steadily declined in the early 1970s, and NASA's attention was refocused on space research that could be conducted by the LST.

Technical issues and lack of funding caused a series of delays before the LST project was finally approved by the U.S. Congress in 1977. Collaborating with the European Space Agency, NASA began building the telescope, which was first renamed the Space Telescope and then the Hubble Space Telescope. The Hubble was assembled and ready for launch in 1985, but the *Challenger* (see entry) disaster forced a two-year delay. During that time NASA improved the solar panels, made modifications for easier instrument replacement and servicing, and upgraded computer systems. On April 24, 1990, the HST was lifted into space during a five-day mission by the space shuttle *Discovery*. The five crew members were commander Loren J. Shriver (1944–), pilot Charles F. Bolden Jr. (1946–), and mission specialists Steven A. Hawley (1951–), Bruce McCandless II (1937–), and Kathryn D. Sullivan (1951–). They released the HST into orbit on April 25.

HST fulfills mission

The HST had been orbiting for about a month when NASA scientists became concerned about fuzzy images it was sending back to Earth. The scientists determined that the primary mirror had a defect called spherical aberration. This means the manufacturer had made the mirror the wrong shape, which prevented it from reflecting sharp, clear images. In addition, there were problems with the gyroscopes and solar panels. On December 2, 1993, NASA launched the space shuttle *Endeavour* on an eleven-day mission to the HST. (The *Endeavour* was the newest shuttle in the NASA fleet, having been built to replace the *Challenger*.) The five crew members were commander Kenneth D. Cameron (1949–), pilot Stephen S. Oswald

(1951–), and mission specialists C. Michael Foale (1957–), Kenneth D. Cockrell (1950–), and **Ellen Ochoa** (1958–; see entry), who was the first Hispanic woman to travel in space.

To correct the problem with the primary mirror, the crew installed a device containing ten small mirrors that redirect the light paths from the primary mirror to the spectrographs and the photometer. Making a total of five spacewalks, the crew also replaced the wide-field planetary camera and changed a bent solar panel. (The panel could not be taken back to Earth, so it was released into space. It reentered Earth's atmosphere nearly five years later, in October 1998.)

The HST worked perfectly after the repair mission, capturing spectacular images and making many astronomical advances and discoveries. The orbiting observatory has provided the sharpest view of Mars ever obtained by a telescope, showing icy white clouds and orange dust storms that swirl above the rust-red planet. The HST also confirmed the existence of black holes. (A black hole is a region with intense gravitational force caused by the collapse of a star.) The HST revealed black holes to be at the center of most galaxies. Moreover, it proved that quasars (bright, distant objects that resemble stars) are nuclei (centers) of galaxies and that they are powered by black holes. Another important discovery is that gamma rays (photons emitted by a radioactive substance) originated from distant galaxies in the early universe. Other observations include the expansion of the universe by an unknown force, the birth and death of stars, and the collisions of comets. Images sent back to Earth by the HST reveal a vast blue-black space full of dazzling light, brilliant colors, swirling clouds and dust, and endless galaxies. The telescope is still making new discoveries about the universe, which astronomers once thought to be nothing but a deep, dark void beyond the Milky Way.

The future of the HST

Although the HST has reached expectations, it was designed to have a limited life span. After the observatory was launched in 1990, astronauts were to make periodic visits to do maintenance work and install new equipment. By 2003 three service missions were completed, and the fourth and final mission was scheduled for 2006. It was canceled after the *Columbia* disaster (see box in **Challenger Crew** entry). In

View of the planet Mars taken from the Hubble Telescope, showing
clouds and dust storms not viewable with previous technology.

(Photograph by David Crisp and the WFPC2 Science Team [JPL/Caltech]. NASA Photoplanetary
Journal)

February 2003 the *Columbia* broke apart over the western United States while returning to Earth from a mission to the **International Space Station** (ISS; see entry). All seven crew members were killed. Built earlier than other existing shuttles, the *Columbia* had been used primarily for scientific missions and for servicing the HST. The day after the accident NASA administrator Sean O'Keefe (1956–) appointed the Columbia Accident Investigation Board (CAIB). In August the CAIB issued a final report, which stated that shuttle flights were becoming increasingly dangerous and that NASA should fly a minimum number only when necessary. The following January, as a result of new safety guidelines stated in the report, O'Keefe canceled the final service mission to the HST. In April of that year, O'Keefe reported to a House subcommittee that preliminary experiments indicated that robots (devices designed to perform human activities) possibly could be used to service the HST.

The HST continued to operate normally, but it could not be expected to last indefinitely. Its original mission was expected to last fifteen years, and that had been extended to twenty years, or until 2010. Without servicing and repair, the components of the observatory will eventually wear out. The HST was built to dock with a space shuttle, so another type of spacecraft could not be used for a service mission. Concern over the fate of the HST prompted O'Keefe to ask the National Academy of Science (NAS) to study possible ways to prolong its life. In 2004 NAS appointed a committee of former astronauts, professors, scientists, and engineers to explore alternatives.

For More Information

Books

Goodwin, Simon. *Hubble's Universe: A Portrait of Our Cosmos.* New York: Viking Penguin, 1997.

Kerrod, Robin. *Hubble: The Mirror on the Universe.* Buffalo, NY: Firefly Books, 2003.

Periodicals

"HST, Keck Find a Galaxy from the 'Dark Ages.'" (May 2004): p. 30.

"Hubble's Gifts." *Kids Discover* (May 2004): pp. 10–11.

Muir, Hazel. "I Spy with My Little Eye." *New Scientist* (April 3, 2004): pp. 40+.

Reddy, Francis. "Swirling Echoes of Light." *Astronomy* (June 2004): p. 22.

Reichhardt, Tony. "NASA Seeks Robotic Rescuers to Give Hubble Extra Lease on Life." *Nature* (March 25, 2004): p. 353.

Web Sites

"The Hubble Project." *NASA*. http://hubble.nasa.gov (accessed on June 25, 2004).

HubbleSite. http://hubblesite.org (accessed on June 25, 2004).

Other Sources

The Big Bang. World Almanac Video, 1999.

Exploding Stars and Black Holes. PBS Home Video, 1997.

International Space Station

November 20, 1998

The International Space Station (ISS), under construction since 1998, is the largest international scientific partnership in history. The project involves seventeen countries: the United States, the eleven member nations of the European Space Agency, Canada, Japan, Russia, Italy, and Brazil. When the ISS is completed, astronauts will have assembled a total of one hundred separate parts during forty-five missions while the station orbits 240 miles (384 kilometers) above Earth. The ISS will eventually consist of several modules, and as many as seven crew members will live on board, conducting scientific experiments and space research. By 2004 eight crews had already stayed on the ISS for months at a time. Construction had been postponed in 2003, however, as a result of the *Columbia* space shuttle disaster, and the future of the ISS remained uncertain. (A space shuttle is a craft that transports people and cargo between Earth and space.)

Soviets launch first space stations

Although the former Soviet Union built the first space stations, which ultimately led to the development of the ISS, the

International Space Station (ISS). *(NASA)*

actual concept has roots in the nineteenth century. The idea of a space station has been traced back to "The Brick Moon: From the Papers of Captain Frederic Ingham," a story by author Edward Everett Hale (1822–1909) published in the *Atlantic Monthly* magazine (1869–70). "The Brick Moon" describes how Captain Frederic Ingham and his former college friends build an artificial Moon made of brick. According to Elizabeth Paulhaus, writer of the online article "Brick Moon Rising."

The first known mention of the term "space station" was made by the German rocket engineer **Hermann Oberth** (1894–1989; see entry) in 1923. He envisioned a wheel-like vehicle that would orbit Earth and provide a launching place for trips to the Moon and Mars. About two decades later the German-born American rocket engineer **Wernher von Braun** (1912–1977; see entry) proposed a more detailed concept of a space station in a series of articles in *Collier's* magazine. He described a giant vehicle, 250 feet (762 meters) in diameter, that would spin to create its own gravity as it orbited 1,000 miles (1,609 kilometers) above Earth.

The Soviets launched the world's first space station, *Salyut 1,* in 1971, during a time of intense competition between the Soviet Union and the United States. Since World War II (1939–45) the two superpowers had been engaged in a period of hostile relations known as the Cold War (1945–91), which involved not only a race for military superiority but also a race for dominance in space. In 1957 the Soviets had launched *Sputnik 1,* the first artificial satellite (an object that orbits in space), sending shock waves through American society. *Sputnik 1* was a sign that the Soviet Union was moving ahead in the Cold War. The next year the United States responded by creating the National Aeronautics and Space Administration (NASA)—and the space race began.

In April 1961 the Soviets stunned the world again by achieving the first manned space flight when cosmonaut (astronaut) **Yuri Gagarin** (1934–1968; see entry) made a nearly complete orbit of Earth. The following month U.S. astronaut Alan Shepard (1923–1998; see box in **John Glenn** entry) made a brief but successful trip into orbit. Two years later Soviet cosmonaut **Valentina Tereshkova** (1937–; see entry) became the first woman in space. Then, in the early 1960s, President John

F. Kennedy (1917–1963; served 1961–63) publicly pledged to put an American on the Moon by the end of the decade (see **Christopher Kraft** [1924–] entry). In 1969, U.S. astronauts **Neil Armstrong** (1930–; see entry) and **Buzz Aldrin** (1930–; see entry) accomplished that goal by stepping onto the surface of the Moon.

Mir: first permanent space station

By the 1970s the United States lacked funding for further Moon exploration. The Soviet Union was in a similar situation and therefore never attempted a Moon flight. Instead the Soviets focused on the Salyut program, launching seven Salyut space stations between 1971 and 1982. The United States put the *Skylab* space station into orbit in 1973, but it remained in space for only one year and was visited by three crews of astronauts. Soviet cosmonauts regularly traveled to the Salyuts, but they did not stay for long periods of time because the space stations did not have adequate living accommodations. Improving upon the Salyut design, the Soviets built *Mir*, the first permanent residence in space, which was launched in 1986.

Mir provided valuable information about building, maintaining, and living on a space station. Remaining in orbit for more than fifteen years, until 2001, it was officially taken out of service in 1999. During that time astronauts conducted nearly 16,500 experiments, primarily on how humans adapt to long-term space flight. From 1986 until 1999 the space station was almost continually occupied by a total of one hundred cosmonauts and astronauts. Among them were seven NASA astronauts, a Japanese journalist, a British candy maker, and visitors from other countries that did not have their own space programs. In 1995 Russian cosmonaut Valery Polyakov (1942–) set the record for the longest mission aboard *Mir,* having stayed 438 days. The same year American astronaut **Shannon Lucid** (1943–; see entry) set the record for a non-Russian, on a mission that lasted 188 days, 4 hours and 14 seconds.

Lucid's record was broken in 1999 by French astronaut Jean-Pierre Haigneré (see box in **Claudie Haigneré** entry), when he stayed nearly 189 complete days. Haigneré was also a member of the last crew to visit *Mir.* Before returning to Earth the crew left the space station in a standby mode, with no occupants onboard. When Russia took *Mir* out of service in 2001, most of the spacecraft burned up over the Pacific Ocean. The remaining remnants of the space station crashed into the Pacific in 2004.

United States and Russia strike a deal

Mir became an international effort, eventually providing a model for the ISS. Before the first two components of the ISS were launched in 1998, however, the United States had attempted to develop its own space station. In 1984 President Ronald Reagan (1911–2004; served 1981–89) provided funding to NASA for development of a space station to be named *Freedom*. By 1990 cost overruns and poor management had forced NASA to scale back its plans and to design a new space station, the *Alpha*. Confronted with continuing financial problems, NASA approached Russian officials in 1993 about collaborating on a space station that would merge the *Alpha* with a second version of *Mir*. Russia was running out of money to build a *Mir 2* that would replace the retired *Mir,* so a deal was struck. Thus the idea for an international space station was born, and initial on-ground construction began the following year.

ISS is built in space

The ISS is being assembled in three phases, which involve shuttle missions with specific goals, such as delivering and assembling parts, transporting crews, delivering cargo and supplies, and maintaining and servicing the station. A total of twenty-eight missions had been completed by 2004. Selected highlights of the three construction phases are described below.

Phase 1 (1994–98). During the first phase the first two modules and various other elements were constructed for assembly in space. A total of seven U.S. astronauts also gained experience with living in space by spending twenty-seven months aboard the *Mir*.

Phase 2 (1999–2000). The second phase involved initial in-orbit construction by crews from Russia and the United States. On November 20, 1998, Russia lifted the first component, the cargo block Zarya (Sunrise), into orbit on a Proton

Working on the ISS

Upon completion the ISS will weigh one million pounds and consist of several modules, which astronauts assemble while walking in space. The main components are a port for a Soyuz rescue craft (Soyuz is a Russian space shuttle), a Russian service module, a cargo block, a NASA docking module, a U.S. habitat (living space) module, a U.S. laboratory module, European and Japanese modules for scientific experiments, and a docking port for a U.S. space shuttle. Attached to the modules are trusses (leg-like structures), which will be as long as a football field. The trusses support solar panels (devices for capturing radiation from the Sun), which provide energy for powering the station and scientific experiments. The energy is stored in radiators mounted on the trusses. Communications equipment is also installed on the trusses.

Astronauts receive extensive training in performing extravehicular activities (activities outside a space vehicle). More commonly known as spacewalks, extravehicular trips allow astronauts to work on the ISS. During a spacewalk an astronaut remains connected to the station by means of a device on his or her spacesuit, which is attached to a joint airlock module. The joint airlock module consists of two sections—a crew lock and an equipment lock. An astronaut hooks the device on the spacesuit to the crew lock when exiting the station or while spending extended periods of time outside the station. The equipment lock is used for storing gear.

A spacesuit is adjustable so it will fit different crew members. It is equipped with special features such as gloves that allow free movement of the hands, a radio that permits five people to talk with one another at the same time, and heating and cooling systems. Floodlights and spotlights are mounted on the astronaut's helmet, and the astronaut carries a jet-pack life jacket to be used if he or she is accidentally disconnected from the space station. Astronauts also work with robotic arms to assist them in maneuvering large components and in moving around work areas. While living and working on the ISS, crews must keep track of more than fifty thousand items. To facilitate this process, an electronic tag—roughly one-fourth the size of a postage stamp—is attached to each item. Astronauts read the tags with a solar-powered infrared transmitter, which can scan fifteen thousand tags per minute at a distance of up to 40 feet (12 meters).

rocket. On December 4, 1998, the U.S. space shuttle *Endeavour* transported the second component, the Unity node, which is a docking hub where major sections of the ISS are locked together. During this mission the *Endeavour* crew, which included American astronaut **Ellen Ochoa** (1958–; see entry),

Astronauts work on the construction of an antenna on the Russian-made space station module Zarya, the first of three modules that were constructed in space that would make up the International Space Station. *(AP/Wide World Photos)*

conducted spacewalks and attached the Unity to the Zarya. The third component, the Russian-built service module Zvedza (Star), was launched on July 12, 2000. It provided initial living quarters and life support systems.

The first ISS expeditionary crew (astronauts and cosmonauts who live on the space station) was launched aboard a Soyuz capsule on October 31, 2000. The expedition commander was U.S. astronaut William M. "Bill" Shepherd (1949–); the Soyuz commander was Russian cosmonaut Yuri Gidzenko (1962–); and the flight engineer was Russian cosmonaut Sergei Krikalev (1958–). With their four-month mission the crew began living aboard the ISS. An *Endeavour* crew visited the ISS in December 2000 to attach a truss structure, on which they installed solar panels, radiators, and communications systems. When the solar panels were installed, the ISS became the third-brightest object in the night sky.

Phase 3 (2001–06). According to the original plan, construction of the ISS is to be completed during the third phase. A considerable amount of work was accomplished from February 2001 until October 2003. Seven more expeditionary crews lived on the station, assembling main modules and other elements. The U.S. Destiny laboratory was attached to the Unity, adding facilities for scientific research on near-zero gravity conditions in space. The Italian-made Leonardo multipurpose module was installed to provide "moving vans" that carry equipment, supplies, and experiments between the station and a shuttle. The Russian Pirs (Pier) docking port was added, a Canadian-made robotic arm was installed for use in future construction projects, and work continued on the complex truss system.

During this period three Soyuz "taxi flights" visited the ISS to exchange the old Soyuz with a new one. This means that the taxi crew left the capsule they arrived in at the space station, then returned to Earth in the old capsule. In October 2001, French astronaut **Claudie Haigneré** (1957–; see entry) arrived with the third taxi crew aboard the Soyuz vehicle *Andromede*. On this flight she became the first woman to visit the ISS and the first non-Russian woman to serve as a Soyuz flight engineer.

Columbia tragedy causes delay

Further construction on the ISS was delayed after the space shuttle *Columbia* accident. On February 1, 2003, the *Columbia* broke apart over the western United States while returning to Earth from a visit to the ISS (see ***Challenger* Crew** entry). All seven crew members were killed as pieces of the descending craft fell from the sky. The day after the incident NASA administrator Sean O'Keefe (1956–) organized the Columbia Accident Investigation Board (CAIB). On August 26 the CAIB issued a final report. The most immediate cause of the disintegration was a piece of insulating foam that had separated from the shuttle's left wing during takeoff. The missing foam left a hole through which leaking gas was ignited by the intense heat of the rocket that propelled the *Columbia*.

The board also found that the *Columbia* was not properly equipped for its mission to the ISS. Built earlier than other U.S. shuttles—the *Columbia* was the first shuttle to leave Earth orbit—the vehicle had been used primarily for scientific missions and for servicing the **Hubble Space Telescope** (see entry). On the flight to the ISS it was required to carry larger cargo, which the crew had difficulty handling because the *Columbia* did not have a space station docking system. The CAIB report concluded that the *Columbia* accident was caused in large part by deficiencies within NASA and by a lack of government oversight. The report stated that shuttle flights were becoming increasingly dangerous and that a minimum number should be flown only when necessary. Completion of the ISS was consequently postponed while NASA studied space shuttle safety issues.

For More Information

Books

Bond, Peter. *The Continuing Story of the International Space Station.* New York: Springer-Verlag, 2002.

Launius, Roger D. D. *Space Stations: Base Camps to the Stars.* Washington, DC: Smithsonian Institution Press, 2003.

Periodicals

Hanson, Torbjorn. "Deep Space 1999." *Boys' Life* (June 1999): p. 28.

Scott, Phil. "Eye on the Junk: Space Station Noises Renew Worry about Orbital Debris." *Scientific American* (May 3, 2004): p. 27.

Sietzen, Frank Jr. "A New Vision for Space." *Astronomy* (May 2004): pp. 48+.

Web Sites

"Human Spaceflight." *NASA.* http://www.spaceflight.nasa.gov/station/ (accessed on June 25, 2004).

"International Space Station." *Discovery.com.* http://www.discovery.com/ stories/science/iss/iss.html (accessed on June 24, 2004).

Paulhus, Elizabeth. "Brick Moon Rising." *International Space Station Challenge.* http://voyager.cet.edu/iss/cafe/articles/brickmoonrising.asp (accessed on June 25, 2004).

"Where Is the International Space Station?" *NASA*. http://www.science.
nasa.gov/temp/StationLoc.html (accessed on June 25, 2004).

Other Sources

Super Structures of the World: International Space Station—Cities in Space.
Unapix/Ardustry, 2000 (Video).

Mae Jemison

Born October 17, 1956 (Decatur, Alabama)

American astronaut, physician

"I felt like I belonged right there in space. I realized I would feel comfortable anywhere in the universe—because I belonged to and was a part of it, as much as any star, planet, asteroid, comet, or nebula."

Mae Jemison went into space in 1992 aboard the space shuttle *Endeavour*. (A space shuttle is a craft that transports people and cargo between Earth and space.) Having been a physician before she became an astronaut, she performed scientific experiments during the eight-day voyage. The first science mission specialist sent into orbit by the National Aeronautics and Space Administration (NASA), she was also the first woman of African descent to travel in space. After leaving NASA, Jemison founded her own advanced technology companies and has been active in the field of education. Her goal is to use her knowledge and experience to solve problems faced by people on Earth.

Inspired by science fiction

Mae Carol Jemison was born on October 17, 1956, in Decatur, Alabama. She was the youngest of three children of Charlie Jemison, a custodian and contractor, and Dorothy Jemison, a teacher. The family moved to Chicago, Illinois, when Mae was a small child. By the time she entered kindergarten in 1961 she knew how to read, and she had already

Mae Jemison. *(NASA)*

decided to be a scientist when she grew up. She enjoyed reading about science, becoming a science-fiction enthusiast. Jemison told a *SuperScience* magazine writer that, in sixth grade,
two of her favorite books were *A Wrinkle in Time* and *Arm of
the Starfish* by author Madeline L'Engle (1918–). "Those books
stand out," Jemison said, "because they had women scientists
and heroines."

In 1968, at age twelve, Jemison had a disturbing experience. Near her predominantly African American neighborhood civil rights demonstrations were being held prior to a
major political event. Seeking to prevent disorder, the Chicago

mayor sent in the National Guard. As Mae watched the guardsmen march through the streets carrying rifles, she felt both frightened and defiant. Recalling the event almost twenty-five years later, she told *SuperScience,* "I reminded myself that I was as much a part of the United States as the guardsmen."

During high school Jemison concentrated on science, studied dance and art, and participated in student government. After graduation she entered Stanford University in California, where she majored in chemical engineering and African studies and learned the Russian and Swahili (an African dialect) languages. After earning a bachelor's degree from Stanford in 1977, Jemison studied medicine for four years at Cornell University in New York. While at Cornell she traveled to Thailand and Kenya to provide primary medical care services. Upon completing her medical internship (supervision by a certified doctor) at Los Angeles/USC Medical Center in 1982, Jemison joined the Peace Corps in West Africa. (The Peace Corps is a volunteer organization for service in developing countries sponsored by the U.S. government.) She served as a staff physician until 1985, when she returned to Los Angeles to practice general medicine.

Flies in space

Jemison applied to the NASA astronaut training program in October 1985. Three months later, in January 1986, the space shuttle *Challenger* (see entry) exploded shortly after takeoff. Seven astronauts died in the disaster, and NASA postponed the application process. After reapplying later in the year, Jemison became one of only fifteen candidates selected from a field of nearly two thousand aspiring astronauts. Trained for the position of mission specialist (scientist astronaut), she awaited a shuttle assignment and worked as a liaison between the Johnson Space Center in Houston, Texas, and NASA crew members in Cape Canaveral, Florida. On her first assignment Jemison was a mission specialist with the ground crew in Houston for the space shuttle *Discovery,* or Spacelab-J. (Spacelab is a research laboratory that orbits in space.) Launched in June 1991 at Cape Canaveral, Spacelab-J was a joint venture with Japan. The purpose of the flight was to conduct experiments in space to help scientists better understand Earth's environment. Jemison learned the procedures involved in operating a shuttle, conducting experiments in orbit, launching payloads (equipment and supplies) or satellites (orbiting spacecraft), and performing space walks.

On September 12, 1992, over five years after joining NASA, Jemison served as a science mission specialist during an eight-day voyage aboard the space shuttle *Endeavour*. Although Patricia Cowings (1948–; see box on page 119) was the first African American woman to be trained as an astronaut, Jemison became the first female of African descent to go into space. Her job was to study the effects of weightlessness and motion sickness on the seven-person crew. She also conducted an experiment with tadpoles. "We wanted to know how the tadpoles would develop in space with no gravity," she explained in an interview with *Essence* magazine. "When we got back to Earth," she continued, "the tadpoles were right on track, and they have [sic] turned into frogs." Jemison commented to the *SuperScience* reporter that while she was still aboard the *Endeavour* she looked down and saw her hometown of Chicago. At that moment she thought about her student days and then, she said, "I felt like I belonged right there in space. I realized I would feel comfortable anywhere in the universe—because I belonged to and was a part of it, as much as any star, planet, asteroid, comet, or nebula."

Mae Jemison in her flight suit prepares for a shuttle mission. *(AP/Wide World Photos)*

Starts her own companies

Soon after Jemison resigned from NASA in 1992 she started The Jemison Group to use advanced technology to improve the quality of life in developing countries. For instance, she envisioned using satellite mapping to survey a country's topography (details of the surface of the land) in order to locate resources and to build roads. As Jemison observed to a reporter for the *Christian Science Monitor* newspaper, drawing a map on the ground is too time consuming. But "From space, you can take one picture and get incredible amounts of data, even though one picture may cost $5,000." Another possible use of technology, she added, is to make fuels from plants to replace fossil fuels such as coal. In 1999 Jemison founded BioSentient Corporation to explore the commercial applications of Autogenic Feedback Training Exercise (AFTE), a technology developed by Patricia Cowings for NASA in 1979. A research psychologist at Ames Research Center in California, Cowings originally designed AFTE, which monitors biofeedback (biological processes of the body), to ease the effects of space adaptation syndrome in astronauts. (Space adaptation syndrome is similar to motion sickness.) After extensive testing, in 2003 BioSentient was preparing to offer AFTE as a drug-free treatment for stress-related disorders such as anxiety and nausea. The plan was to market the equipment to psychiatrists, neurologists, and other health care professionals.

Promotes science education

Since leaving NASA Jemison has made significant contributions in science education. In 1993 she joined the faculty at Dartmouth College in Hanover, New Hampshire, where she became director of The Jemison Institute for Advancing Technology in Developing Countries. Jemison has cosponsored an annual International Science Camp for students age twelve to sixteen. The month-long summer camp is free to qualified applicants and focuses on critical thinking (a way of thinking about a topic or problem by using careful analysis and judgment) and experiential learning (learning by experience: by doing, as opposed to reading or listening). She also promoted science for children by serving as the National School Literacy Advocate for the Bayer Corporation's program "Making Science Make Sense." In 2001 Jemison published a memoir, *Find Where the Wind Goes: Moments from My Life,* for readers in grades seven through twelve.

Jemison has received extensive recognition for her achievements. In 1988 she was presented the Essence Award, two years later she was named the Gamma Sigma Gamma

Patricia Cowings, Pioneering Scientist

In 1977 Patricia S. Cowings (1948–) became the first female scientist, as well as the first African American woman, to be trained as an astronaut. A research psychologist at the Ames Research Center (ARC) in California, Cowings studied the physical effects of flying in space. She developed the Autogenic Feedback Training Exercise (AFTE) to ease the effects of space adaptation syndrome, which is similar to motion sickness.

Cowings described her early career in the following excerpts from an essay she wrote for the NASA website:

*I was the first female scientist trained to be an astronaut. This was way before [first U.S. female astronaut in space] Sally Ride's day [see **Sally Ride** (1951–) entry] and they didn't even have a uniform for me. I was the alternate and never got a chance to fly but that experience is something I will never forget. The event was Spacelab Mission Development-3, a joint effort between Johnson Space Center (JSC) and ARC and was the first simulation of a life-sciences-dedicated space shuttle mission. . . . There were two years of fairly intense science development and crew training—half of the time at Ames and the other half at JSC. There was also training at university sites. It was a good two years in which "much ado" was made about my inclusion. . . .*

In 1979, my own flight experiment [AFTE] was selected by NASA and it flew on STS [space transport system] 51-B, STS 51-C (1984) and Spacelab-1 (1992).

Woman of the Year, and in 1992 she received the *Ebony* Black Achievement Award. She also received an honorary doctorate from Lincoln University in 1991. Then, in 1992, an alternative public school in Detroit was named The Mae C. Jemison Academy in her honor. During those years she conducted science experiments for NASA and kept up her interests in medicine and science with various board memberships, including a one-year appointment (1990–92) to the Board of Directors of the World Sickle Cell Foundation. (Sickle cell anemia is an inherited disease affecting African Americans in which unusually shaped red blood cells do not carry oxygen properly.) Jemison also held memberships in the American Medical Association, the American Chemical Society, and the American Association for the Advancement of Science. She has gone on to serve on the advisory committee of the American Express Geography Competition and as an honorary board member of the Center for the Prevention of Childhood Malnutrition. Jemison was the subject of a Public Broadcasting System television documentary, *The New Explorers: Endeavour,* and she appeared in an episode of the television show *Star Trek: The Next Generation.*

For More Information

Books

Alagna, Magdalena. *Mae Jemison: The First African American Woman in Space.* New York: Rosen Central, 2004.

Gelletly, LeeAnne. *Mae Jemison.* Philadelphia: Chelsea House Publishers, 2002.

Jemison, Mae. *Find Where the Wind Blows: Moments from My Life.* New York: Scholastic, 2001.

Naden, Corinne J., and Rose Blue. *Mae Jemison: Out of This World.* Brookfield, CT: Millbrook Press, 2003.

Periodicals

"Dr. Mae Jemison: First in Space." *SuperScience* (February 2001): p. 10.

Eze, Paschal. "Mae Jemison Honoured." *New African* (February 2002): p. 25.

Giovanni, Nikki. "Shooting for the Moon." *Essence* (April 1993): pp. 58+.

Leach, Susan Llewelyn. "How One Woman Is Bringing Space Technology Down to Earth." *Christian Science Monitor* (April 5, 2001): p. 14.

Marshall, M. "Child of 60s Set to Become First Black Woman in Space." *Ebony* (August 1989): pp. 50+.

Sykes, Tanisha A., and Sonya A. Donaldson. "A Space-Age Idea." *Black Enterprise* (July 2003): p. 43.

Web Sites

Cowings, Patricia S. "Women of NASA." *NASA.* http://quest.arc.nasa.gov/people/bios/women/pc.html (accessed on June 30, 2004).

"Dr. Mae Jemison." *NASA Quest: Women of NASA.* http://quest.arc.nasa.gov/women/TODTWD/jemison.bio.html (accessed on June 29, 2004).

"Mae C. Jemison." *The Faces of Science: African Americans in Science.* http://www.princeton.edu/~mcbrown/display/faces.html (accessed on July 2, 2004).

Sergei Korolev

Born December 30, 1906 (Zhitomir, Ukraine)
Died January 14, 1966 (Moscow, Russia)

Russian engineer

During the 1950s and 1960s the former Soviet Union and the United States were engaged in a space race. This competition for superiority in space exploration was part of the Cold War (1945–91), which resulted from political differences that arose between the two superpowers after World War II (1939–45). The Cold War also pitted the Soviet Union and United States against one another in an arms race to gain military domination through advanced weapons technology. In 1957 the Soviets scored a stunning victory by launching *Sputnik 1,* the first artificial space satellite (an object that orbits in space). Realizing that the Soviet Union was now ahead in the space race, the United States immediately responded by integrating U.S. space research agencies into the National Aeronautics and Space Administration (NASA) and establishing an astronaut training program. Then, in 1961, Soviet cosmonaut (astronaut) **Yuri Gagarin** (1934–1968; see entry) made a nearly complete orbit of Earth aboard the spacecraft *Vostok 1.* Gagarin's flight represented yet another a technical triumph for the Soviet Union.

"Not long after [Joseph] Stalin's death, Korolev came to a . . . meeting to report on his work. I don't want to exaggerate, but I'd say we gawked at what he showed us as if we were a bunch of sheep seeing a new gate for the first time."

Nikita Khrushchev, Soviet Premier

Sergei Korolev. *(© Bettmann/Corbis)*

In the 1970s and 1980s Sergei Korolev was a legendary figure in the Russian space program. Soviet officials portrayed
him as being the person who single-handedly invented the
first long-range ballistic missiles, rocket launchers for spacecraft, and the artificial satellite. Russians were also told that
Korolev alone was responsible for Gagarin's successful space
flight. The collapse of the Soviet Union in late 1980s and early
1990s made possible more realistic information about Korolev's career. Although he is still considered an important
force in the Russian space program, it is now known that he
was influenced by the ideas of interplanetary flight put forth

by the Russian inventor **Konstantin Tsiolkovsky** (1857–1935; see entry). Korolev also worked closely with other scientists to train the scientists and engineers who later formed the core of Russia's space program.

Sergei Pavlovich Korolev was born on December 30, 1906 (January 12, 1907, in the Gregorian calendar used in Russia), in the Ukranian town of Zhitomir. As a young child he wanted to be a pilot, and by age seventeen he had designed a glider (an aircraft that relies on air currents to stay aloft). He attended the Kiev Polytechnic Institute before enrolling at the Moscow Higher Technical University. While studying at the university Korolev designed and constructed a series of gliders, the most advanced being a glider called the SK-4, which he made for flying in the stratosphere (outside Earth's atmosphere). Having become interested in rocket-propelled aircraft, he helped to organize the Group for Investigation of Reactive Motion (GIRD) in 1931. GIRD launched the Soviet Union's first liquid-propelled rockets, the GIRD-9 and GIRD-10.

Sent to prison

In 1933 the Soviet military replaced GIRD with the Reaction Propulsion Scientific Research Institute (RNII), which developed rocket-propelled missiles and gliders. Korolev was in charge of aircraft body frames and engineer Valentin Petrovich Glushko (1908–1989) headed rocket-engine design. RNII produced Russia's first rocket-propelled manned aircraft. In 1938, even before the rocket plane could be flown, Soviet authorities sent Korolev and Glushko to the gulag (prison system). At that time Joseph Stalin (1879–1953), the Soviet premier, was waging one of many purges to imprison or execute people he considered enemies of the communist state. (Communism is a political philosophy that advocates state operation of all aspects of society. The Soviet Union had been under communist rule since the Communist Revolution in 1917.) Particular targets were members of the intelligentsia (educated people). After being arrested in March, Glushko denounced Korolev to the Soviet authorities, who arrested Korolev in September. In July 1940 Korolev was sentenced to ten years of hard labor in gold mines in Kolyma, the worst part of the gulag. Two months later another prisoner, aircraft

Rocket Technology Developed

In 1931 Sergei Korolev helped to organize the Group for Investigation of Reactive Motion, which launched the Soviet Union's first liquid-propelled rockets, the GIRD-9 and GIRD-10.

Efforts to develop rocket-propelled aircraft were also underway in the United States and Germany. American physicist **Robert Goddard** (1882–1945; see entry) had already flown liquid-propellant rockets, and German scientists with the Society for Spaceship Travel were testing liquid-fueled rockets. The Society for Spaceship Travel disbanded in 1933, and a few of those scientists—the foremost being **Wernher von Braun** (1912–1977; see entry)—eventually developed the V-2 missile, the forerunner of all liquid-fuel rockets. In the meantime Goddard's work remained generally unknown because Goddard insisted upon keeping his research and experiments secret. After World War II, Soviet researchers headed by Korolev used V-2 technology to develop the R-7, which became the most widely used rocket in the world.

designer Sergei Tupolev (1906–1966), saved Korolev from almost certain death from overwork and starvation.

Develops R-7 rocket

Tupolev had been recruited by Stalin to head a sharashka (bureau) in Moscow, where prisoners were used to build missiles and rockets. World War II (then a conflict waged by Germany and its allies against countries in Europe) had been underway for about a year, and Stalin was preparing for a German invasion. Tupolev recommended Korolev to work in Moscow. In 1942 Korolev was transferred to a sharashka in Kazan and served as deputy director of flight training. Then, two years later, he was given the assignment that began his career as the top Soviet rocket scientist—supervision of sixty engineers who were required to design a Soviet version of the German V-2 missile. The V-2 had a range of 300 kilometers (186 miles; see box on this page) and was ten years ahead of Soviet technology. Korolev's team was given only three days to produce a design. The results were the D-1 and D-2, two-stage, liquid-fuel rockets guided by an automatic pilot. (A two-stage rocket is fired first on takeoff and a second time after it is in the air.)

Progress on a Soviet rocket was slow until 1945, when the war ended with the Allied defeat of Germany. (The major Allies were the United States, Great Britain, and the Soviet Union.) Russian engineers then had a chance to inspect leftover V-2 rockets in German factories. Though Korolev was still a prisoner, he was sent to Germany, where he interviewed German rocket scientists. The following year the Scientific Research Institute NII-88 was established to produce the Soviet version of the V-2. German workers were used as laborers in the rocket factory in Gordodomlya, located between Moscow and Leningrad.

Over the next decade Korolev succeeded in developing the R-7 rocket, which was launched on August 21, 1957. The rocket was a modified Soviet Intercontinental Ballistic Missile (ICBM) about 100 feet (30.48 meters) in length with a weight of 300 tons (272,400 kilograms). It became the most widely used rocket in the world. On October 4, 1957, the R-7 was used to launch *Sputnik 1*, the first artificial satellite to orbit Earth. Another success associated with Korolev was *Luna 3*, a probe satellite that provided the first views of the far side of the Moon. In 1959 it looped around the Moon, took pictures, developed them, and radioed them back to Earth. The *Luna 3* flight improved the prestige of the Soviet Union throughout the world. During this time Korolev was apparently released from prison and declared fully rehabilitated (no longer an enemy of the state).

Korolev then persuaded the Soviets to concentrate exclusively on manned spaceflight. He was authorized to oversee development of *Vostok 1*, the first manned spacecraft, which sent Gagarin into space on April 12, 1961. The Vostok was modified for other space exploits: the first multicrew space flight in 1964 and the first space walk in 1965. Korolev was also in charge of the *Venera 3* mission, the first spacecraft to come in contact with another planet. It landed on Venus in 1966. Even though *Venera 3* failed to return any information due to loss of contact with Earth, it was able to relay extensive information about interplanetary space before it crashed.

Hailed as space hero

The Soviet space program was dealt a stunning blow when Korolev died on January 24, 1966. He had been diagnosed with cancer the previous year but had concealed the news from his colleagues. Korolev was buried in Kremlin Wall, an honor reserved for Russians of exceptional distinction. Two weeks after his death the *Luna 9* made the first soft landing on the Moon, taking the first close-up views of the lunar surface. *Luna 9* sent back television images showing that the feared deep layers of lunar dust did not exist.

Once Korolev's role in the space program was revealed to the public, he became a hero praised for his inexhaustible

The Baikonur Cosmodrome, where all space craft from Russia are launched. Sergei Korolev was influential in the design of, as well as obtaining financial support for, the facility. *(© Reuters NewMedia Inc./Corbis)*

energy and talent as a researcher, his engineering intuition, and his creative boldness in solving difficult tasks. He left behind a group of dedicated and highly trained scientists and engineers, many of whom are still working at space and rocket engineering research institutes and design bureaus. Another Korolev legacy was the Baikonur Cosmodrome, the large complex where all Russian spacecraft have been launched since *Sputnik 1* was sent into orbit in 1957. Yet the Soviet space program essentially died with Korolev, for several complex reasons. No other scientist was able match his skills and dedication, but a more important factor was intense political rivalry within the Soviet system.

Throughout his career Korolev had competed with other rocket researchers, principally Valentin Glushko and Vladimir Nikolayev Chelomei (1914–1984). Along with Korolev, these men are now regarded as the founders of the Soviet space program. Korolev's former colleague Glushko designed innovative rockets that frequently competed with those developed by Korolev. In fact, Korolev's refusal to compromise with Glushko reportedly resulted in the loss of many years of vital new technology. Chelomei had close political ties with Nikita Khrushchev (1894–1971; the Soviet premier who followed Stalin), which he often used against Korolev and other scientists. Equally problematic was the Soviet military, who wanted to use rockets and spacecraft to win the arms race. Finally, the Soviet Union was running out of funds at a crucial time in the space race, which was now being won by the United States. In 1965 the United States initiated Project Gemini (see **Christopher Kraft** [1924–] entry), the manned space program that ultimately led to putting the first humans on the Moon (see **Buzz Aldrin** [1930–] and **Neil Armstrong** [1930–] entries). After *Luna 9* the Soviets did not send any other flights to the Moon. Since the fall of the Soviet Union, Russia has trained cosmonauts for the **International Space Station** program (see entry).

For More Information

Books

Harford, James. *Korolev: How One Man Masterminded the Soviet Drive to Beat America to the Moon.* New York: Wiley, 1997.

Periodicals

Gautier, Daniel James. "Sergei Pavlovich Korolev." *As Astra.* (July/August 1991): p. 27.

Heppenheimer, T.A., and Peter Gorin. "Match Race." *Air and Space Smithsonian.* (February/March 1996): pp. 78+.

Web Sites

"Sergei Korolev." *Encyclopedia Astronautica.* http://www.astronautix.com/astros/korolev.htm (accessed on June 29, 2004).

"Sergei Korolev." *Russian SpaceWeb.* www.russianspaceweb.com/korolev.html (accessed on June 29, 2004).

"Sergei Korolev—*Sputnik* Biographies." *NASA.* www.hq.nasa.gov/office/pao/History/sputnik/korolev.html (accessed on June 29, 2004).

Christopher Kraft

Born February 28, 1924 (Phoebus, Virginia)

**American flight director for National Aeronautics and Space
Administration (NASA)**

"With a man on the end
of a rocket, if you're not
shaking, you don't
understand the
problem."

Christopher Kraft played a significant role in the development of the National Aeronautics and Space Administration (NASA). He was recruited by NASA in 1958, at a crucial
time in U.S. history. In 1957 the former Soviet Union surprised the Americans and the rest of the world by launching
the *Sputnik 1* satellite (an object that orbits in space) to study
the atmosphere of Earth. Since the end of World War II (1939–
45), the United States and the Soviet Union had been engaged
in a period of hostile relations known as the Cold War (1945–
91). Not only were the two powers involved in an arms race
for military superiority, but they were also competing for dominance in space. *Sputnik 1* was therefore a sign that the Soviet
Union was moving ahead in the Cold War. The United States
immediately responded by creating NASA, which integrated
all U.S. space research agencies and established an astronaut
training program. Kraft's career as NASA flight director
spanned twenty-four years, encompassing the major achievements of American manned space exploration.

Christopher Kraft. *(© Bettmann/Corbis)*

Joins NASA

Christopher Columbus Kraft Jr. was born in Phoebus, Virginia, on February 28, 1924, the son of Christopher Columbus and Vanda Suddreth Kraft. In 1944 he received a degree in aeronautical engineering from Virginia Polytechnic Institute. The following year he took a job conducting flight tests for new military airplanes at the Langley Aeronautical Laboratory of the National Advisory Committee for Aeronautics at Langley Field, Virginia. In 1950 he married Betty Ann Turnbull, with whom he later had a son and a daughter. Kraft joined NASA in 1958 as a member of the Space Task Group, which was developing Project Mercury. The first stage of the U.S. manned space program, Project Mercury developed the basic technology for manned space flight and investigated a human's ability to survive and perform in space. Kraft remained in Langley until 1962, when he moved with the Space Task Group to Houston, Texas.

Kraft was named flight director for the Mercury missions. He was also put in charge of designing mission control facilities at the Manned Spacecraft Center (now Johnson Space Center) in Houston. The position of flight director was a new concept at the time. Although preparing for a space flight seemed fairly basic, the job turned out to be extremely challenging. Kraft had to develop a system to coordinate hundreds of pieces of equipment for the spacecraft; for the launch pad in Cape Canaveral, Florida; and for the facilities at the ground control center in Houston and at numerous other NASA control sites around the world. The nature of his job was also controversial, because he was in charge of all aspects of a mission.

Directs Mercury flights

The first Mercury flight was made by astronaut Alan Shepard (1923–1998; see box in **John Glenn** entry) on May 5, 1961, from Cape Canaveral. Forty years later Kraft recalled his own experience on that day. In an interview with Barbara Bogave on *Fresh Air,* a National Public Radio program, he revealed that he was nervous. As he prepared to announce the countdown for the launch of Shepard's space capsule, Kraft told Bogave, he was shaking so hard that he could not even see his microphone. "With a man on the end of a rocket," he explained, "if you're not shaking, you don't understand the problem." Kraft managed to announce the countdown, and he continued to do so for the next twenty-one years. His voice was identified with U.S. space flights in the minds of many Americans who grew up during the early days of manned space flight.

The Mercury flight was a success, and Shepard became the first American in space. He piloted the Mercury space capsule 115 miles (185 kilometers) above Earth's surface and 302 miles (486 kilometers) across the Atlantic Ocean. Although the trip lasted for only about fifteen minutes, his journey was almost technically perfect. Shepard was not the first human in space,

". . . It Will Be an Entire Nation."

On May 25, 1961, President John F. Kennedy gave a speech to a joint session of the U.S. Congress in which he announced that the United States would put a man on the Moon. In the following excerpt from the speech, available on the John F. Kennedy Library and Museum Web site, Kennedy asks for the nation's commitment to this goal:

First, I believe that this nation should commit itself to achieving the goal, before this decade is out, of landing a man on the moon and returning him safely to the earth. No single space project in this period will be more impressive to mankind, or more important for the long-range exploration of space; and none will be so difficult or expensive to accomplish. We propose to accelerate the development of the appropriate lunar space craft. We propose to develop alternate liquid and solid fuel boosters [rockets], much larger than any now being developed, until certain which is superior. We propose additional funds for other engine development and for unmanned explorations—explorations which are particularly important for one purpose which this nation will never overlook: the survival of the man who first makes this daring

President John F. Kennedy addresses a joint session of Congress, announcing that the United States faced an "extraordinary challenge" of putting a man on the moon before the next decade. *(© Bettmann/Corbis)*

flight. But in a very real sense, it will not be one man going to the moon—if we make this judgment affirmatively, it will be an entire nation. For all of us must work to put him there.

however: Less than a month earlier, on April 12, Soviet cosmonaut (astronaut) **Yuri Gagarin** (1934–1968; see entry) had made a nearly complete orbit of Earth aboard the spacecraft *Vostok.* Gagarin's flight, which had been surrounded by intense secrecy, represented yet another technical triumph for the Soviet Union. Americans saw this event as a potentially fatal blow to the prestige of the United States.

Immediately confronting the Soviet challenge, on May 25 President John F. Kennedy (1917–1963; served 1961–63) made a momentous speech before a joint session of the U.S.

Congress. He announced that the United States would put a man on the Moon within the next ten years (see box on page 131). Kennedy's vision captured the imagination of the American people, and it greatly expanded the mission of NASA. Kraft had been so focused on the Mercury goal of getting a man into orbit that he was completely surprised by the president's commitment to go to the Moon. "Frankly, it was beyond my comprehension," he admitted in the interview with Bogave.

Recalls Glenn flight

Under pressure to match the Russian feat as soon as possible, NASA chose **John Glenn** (1921–; see entry) to be the first American to orbit Earth. On February 20, 1962, Glenn successfully made three orbits aboard the *Friendship 7*. As Glenn was preparing to land, Kraft and his ground control crew received a signal that the heat shield (a panel that protects the capsule from intense heat) might not be secured to the *Friendship 7*. Many engineers at ground control felt that Glenn should change the original plan of releasing the retrorocket apparatus, a rocket attached to the capsule that is used to slow its descent to Earth. Instead, they argued, the rocket would be kept in place, strapped over the heat shield, to keep the shield from coming loose. Glenn was instructed to leave the rocket on the capsule, then he guided the *Friendship 7* manually back to Earth. The signal was later determined to be a false alarm.

Kraft recalled the heat-shield incident during an interview with MSNBC television correspondent Alan Boyle in 1998. Kraft contended that the event had been made to seem "a lot more dramatic than it was." He knew the heat shield was not loose, and he was more concerned about leaving the retrorocket in place. As a result of this experience Kraft decided that "from then on I was going to make my own . . . decisions about those kinds of things and not worry too much about what other people thought."

In 1964 NASA initiated Project Gemini, and Kraft served as flight director for many of the missions. The Gemini program provided astronauts with experience in returning to Earth from space as well as successfully linking space vehicles and "walking" in space. Gemini also involved the launching of a series of unmanned satellites, which would gain information about the Moon and its surface to determine whether humans could survive there. Gemini was the transition between Mercury's short flights and the Apollo Project, which would safely land a man on the Moon.

Helps land men on Moon

Kraft was appointed chief of flight operations for the Apollo Project. The program's first mission, *Apollo 1* (see entry) ended tragically on January 27, 1967, when three astronauts died in a launch-pad fire in their module. (Two other tragedies later struck NASA programs. In 1986 the space shuttle *Challenger* [see entry] exploded shortly after takeoff. [A space shuttle is a craft that transports people and cargo between Earth and space.] In 2003 the space shuttle *Columbia* disintegrated after it reentered Earth's atmosphere [see box in *Challenger* Crew entry].) Kraft was wearing a headset that transmitted the horrifying sounds of the last moments of the astronauts— Gus Grissom (1926–1967), Edward White (1930–1967), and Roger Chaffee (1935–1967). The cause of the fire was determined to be an electrical short circuit near Grissom's seat. As a result of the accident the program was temporarily delayed while safety precautions were reviewed. The next five Apollo missions were unmanned flights that tested the safety of the equipment. The first manned flight was *Apollo 7* (October 1968) and the last was *Apollo 17* (December 1972). The most famous was *Apollo 11,* which successfully landed **Neil Armstrong** (1930–; see entry) and **Buzz Aldrin** (1930–; see entry) on the Moon.

Kraft told Boyle that his favorite mission was *Apollo 8* because "the firsts associated with that were unbelievable." The first Moon flight in history, *Apollo 8* received considerable public attention, especially because it took place during the Christmas season. The spacecraft was launched on December 21, 1968, from Cape Kennedy (now Cape Canaveral), with Frank Borman (1928–), James Lovell (1928–), and William Anders (1933–) onboard. As the astronauts entered lunar orbit on December 24, they moved to the far side of the Moon, where they were beyond voice contact with Earth. Starting at 7:00 P.M., after they regained contact, they broadcast live pictures from the Moon's surface. That night the crew members read verses one through ten from *Genesis,* the first book in the Old

Testament of the Bible (the holy book of the Jewish and Christian religions). After making ten orbits around the Moon, *Apollo 8* headed back to Earth on Christmas morning, December 25. During the mission Borman, Lovell, and Anders became the first humans to leave Earth's orbit, the first to orbit another world, and the first to reenter Earth's orbit from outer space.

During a conversation with *American History* writer Mark Wolverton in 2001, Kraft revealed that NASA officials had opposed putting television cameras on the Apollo flights. "They thought we could do without it," Kraft recalled, "that the motion picture and still cameras we took along would be sufficient and that it wasn't worth the weight [on the space craft]." He eventually succeeded in persuading NASA to install cameras, thus making it possible for the world to witness such historic moments as Armstrong's first step onto the surface of the Moon. Small color television cameras were not yet available, so the images were in black and white. "It was a lousy picture," Kraft said, "but better than nothing."

Advocates future exploration

After *Apollo 17* the United States did not undertake any other Moon flights. Instead, NASA concentrated its efforts on space shuttle missions in conjunction with Spacelab and the **International Space Station** (ISS; see entry). A space shuttle is a craft that transports people and cargo between Earth and outer space. Spacelab is an orbiting research laboratory operated by the United States. The International Space Station is an orbiting research laboratory operated by the United States and other nations.

Following the Apollo missions, Kraft was promoted to director of the Johnson Space Center, the position he held until his retirement in 1982. Kraft wrote about his NASA experiences in *Flight: My Life in Mission Control*. Discussing the book with Bogave, Kraft said he had been content not to travel into space himself: "I never wanted to go. I was on every flight." In the interview with Wolverton, Kraft expressed his disappointment at the lack of government and public interest in continuing lunar exploration after Project Apollo. "I think we ought to set the goal of going back to the moon and to Mars," he said. NASA should "lay out the steps which would get us a permanent base on the back side of the moon," he continued. "That would lead to the tools to live on Mars." Kraft's hopes seemed closer to becoming a reality in January 2004. Speaking at NASA headquarters in Washington, D.C., President George W. Bush (1946–; served 2001–) announced that he would authorize a new program for exploration of the Moon and Mars.

For More Information

Books

Kraft, Christopher. *Flight: My Life in Mission Control.* New York: Dutton, 2001.

Periodicals

Wolverton, Mark. "Talking with: Chris Kraft." *American History* (August 2000): p. 66.

Web Sites

Bogave, Barbara. Interview with Chris Kraft. *Fresh Air* (March 5, 2001). http://freshair.npr.org/day_fa.jhtml?display=day&todayDate=03/05/2001 (accessed on June 29, 2004).

Boyle, Alan. "Christopher Kraft: The Maestro of Mission Control." http://www.geocities.com/drmwm/wizzbo.html (accessed on June 29, 2004).

"Christopher Kraft." *Encyclopedia Astronautica.* http://www.astronautix.com/astros/kraft.htm (accessed on June 29, 2004).

Kennedy, John F. Special Message to the Congress on Urgent National Needs. *John F. Kennedy Library and Museum.* http://www.cs.umb.edu/jfklibrary/j052561.htm (accessed on July 2, 2004).

Kraft, Christopher. "The Kraft Report on Space Shuttle Operations" (March 15, 1995). *NASA Watch.* http://www.nasawatch.com/shuttle/03.15.95.kraft.sts.html (accessed on June 29, 2004).

Shannon Lucid

Born January 14, 1943 (Shanghai, China)

American astronaut, biochemist, administrator

"What could be more exciting than working in a laboratory that hurtles around the earth at 17,000 miles per hour?"

Women's contributions to space exploration began in 1963, when Russian cosmonaut **Valentina Tereshkova** (1937–; see entry) became the first woman to fly in space. Tereshkova's legacy was continued by such women as American astronauts **Sally Ride** (1951–; see entry) and **Mae Jemison** (1956–; see entry) and French cosmonaut **Claudie Haigneré** (1957–; see entry). More than thirty years after Tereshkova's flight, American astronaut Shannon Lucid achieved another milestone. During a six-month mission on the Russian space station *Mir,* she logged the most flight hours in space by a woman. (A space station is a research laboratory that orbits in space.) She also set the international record for the most flight hours in orbit by a non-Russian.

Combines studies with family life

Shannon Lucid was born on January 14, 1943, in Shanghai, China, the daughter of Joseph and Myrtle Wells. Her parents were American citizens, but they were serving as Baptist missionaries in China during the Second Sino-Japanese War (1937–45; a conflict between China and Japan over territory

Shannon Lucid. *(© Bettmann/Corbis)*

in China). At the time of Shannon's birth, China was occupied by Japan and the family was being held in a Japanese prison camp. She would not have survived had her parents not saved their rations (supply of food) to feed her. When she was nearly a year old, the family moved back to the United States as part of a prisoner exchange program. They returned to China after the war, remaining there until Shannon was six. Once again the Wellses were forced to leave China, this time by the Chinese Communists, who had seized control of the government. They went to Bethany, Oklahoma, where Joseph Wells became an evangelical preacher. He traveled around the country giving sermons, while the family remained in Bethany.

While attending public school in Bethany, Lucid excelled in mathematics and science. She was also interested in space exploration, but she received little encouragement. In *Biography Today* Lucid is quoted as saying, "People thought I was crazy because that was long before America had a space program." When she was in junior high school she discovered a book on **Robert Goddard** (1882–1945; see entry), the father of modern rocketry. She decided to follow in his footsteps, and in eighth grade she even worked on a science experiment to make her own rocket fuel. One junior-high teacher told her girls were not allowed to be rocket scientists, but a high-school science teacher encouraged her to pursue a science career. Lucid also became interested in flying when she was in high school, finally earning her private pilot's license at age twenty. Later she earned commercial, instrument, and multiengine aircraft licenses.

Lucid graduated from Bethany High School in 1960, placing second in her class. She attended the University of Oklahoma, where in 1963 she became the first woman to receive a bachelor of science degree in chemistry. She was a teaching assistant at the university for a year before taking a job as a senior lab technician at the Oklahoma Medical Research Foundation. Lucid left the foundation in 1966 to work as a chemist for Kerr-McGee, where she met her husband, Michael Lucid. They married in 1968, and their first daughter was born about a year later.

Lucid returned to the University of Oklahoma in 1969 as a graduate assistant in the biochemistry and molecular biology department. She earned her master of science and doctor of philosophy degrees in biochemistry in 1970 and 1973, respectively. Lucid was such a dedicated student that she even took an exam the day after the birth of her second daughter. In 1974 Lucid returned as a research associate to the Oklahoma Medical Research Foundation, where she investigated the effect of cancer-causing agents on rats. She remained at the foundation until she joined the astronaut candidate training program in 1978. Her third child, a son, was born in 1976.

Begins astronaut career

Lucid was a member of the first group of women chosen from eight thousand applicants for the National Aeronautics and Space Administration (NASA) astronaut training program. She joined surgeon Margaret Rhea Seddon (1947–), geophysicist Kathryn D. Sullivan (1951–), electrical engineer Judith A. Resnik (1949–1986; see *Challenger* **Crew** entry), physicist Sally Ride, and physician Anna Lee Fisher (1949–). In 1979 Lucid and her five colleagues became the first women to achieve the full rank of astronaut. Yet they were not the first women to be selected as candidates for astronaut training. In the 1960s thirteen women were chosen for Project Mercury, the first stage of the U.S. manned spaceflight mission. Known as the **Mercury 13** (see entry), they were ultimately not allowed to go on to astronaut training because they were not military pilots.

Lucid was trained as a mission specialist (one who conducts research and other specialized tasks) on space shuttles and served in this capacity on all of her space flights. (A space shuttle is a craft that transports people and cargo between Earth and space.) She took her first trip into space on June 17, 1985, aboard the space shuttle *Discovery*. During this seven-day mission the crew deployed (released into orbit) three international communications satellites (objects that orbit in space)—the Morelos for Mexico, the Arabsat for the Arab League, and the AT&T Telstar for the United States. Using the Remote Manipulator System (RMS), they deployed and retrieved the SPARTAN satellite. The SPARTAN performed seventeen hours of x-ray astronomy experiments while separated from the space shuttle. In addition, the crew activated the Advanced Automated Directional Solidification Furnace (AADSF), which determines how gravity-driven convection (transfer of heat) affects alloys (mixtures of two or more materials, usually metal). They also activated six Small, Self-Contained Payloads (also known as Getaway Specials, or GAS payloads), which offer individuals or groups the opportunity to fly small experiments aboard a space shuttle. Finally, they participated in biomedical experiments.

Lucid's next flight was a five-day mission on the space shuttle *Atlantis* in October 1989. She and fellow crew members deployed the *Galileo* spacecraft on its journey to explore

Shannon Lucid in a space shuttle corridor during one of her many trips where she served as a mission specialist conducting scientific experiments. *(© NASA/Roger Ressmeyer/Corbis)*

the planet Jupiter. In addition, they operated the shuttle solar backscatter ultraviolet instrument (SSBUV), which maps ozone (air pollution) in Earth's atmosphere, and performed numerous secondary experiments. In August 1991 Lucid returned to space on a nine-day *Atlantis* mission to deploy the fifth tracking-and-data-relay satellite. This particular satellite provides telecommunication services to orbiting spacecraft. The crew also conducted thirty-two experiments, most of them relating to a U.S. space station called *Freedom*, which was never constructed.

In November 1991, Lucid went into space a fourth time, spending fourteen days aboard the space shuttle *Columbia*. She and the crew tested the effects of space flight on humans and rats and conducted various engineering tests. On this flight

Lucid set a record as the American woman with the most hours in space—a total of 838. The *Columbia* orbited Earth 225 times, traveling 5.8 million miles (9.33 kilometers) in 336 hours.

Prepares for *Mir* mission

Lucid's involvement with the *Mir* program began in 1994. Robert "Hoot" Gibson (1946–), then head of the NASA astronaut office, asked if she would be interested in starting full-time Russian-language instruction with the possibility of going to Russia to train for a *Mir* mission. Lucid accepted the assignment, though this did not necessarily mean she would be going to Russia, much less flying on *Mir*. As she explained in an article for *Scientific American* magazine, "From a personal standpoint, I viewed the Mir mission as a perfect opportunity to combine two of my passions: flying airplanes and working in laboratories. . . . For a scientist who loves flying, what could be more exciting than working in a laboratory that hurtles around the earth at 17,000 miles per hour?"

Lucid was eventually selected to participate in the mission. After three months of intensive language study, she began training at Star City, the cosmonaut instruction center outside Moscow, in January 1995. Every morning she woke at 5:00 to begin studying. She spent most of the day in classrooms listening to lectures on the *Mir* and Soyuz systems—all in Russian. (Soyuz is the longest-serving spacecraft in the world.) In the evenings Lucid continued to study the language and struggled with workbooks written in technical Russian. "I worked harder during that year than at any other time in my life. Going to graduate school while raising toddlers was child's play in comparison," Lucid wrote in *Scientific American*.

In February 1996, after passing the required medical and technical exams, Lucid was certified as a *Mir* crew member by the Russian spaceflight commission. She then traveled to Baikonur, Kazakhstan, to watch the launch of the *Soyuz,* which carried her crewmates, both named Yuri—Commander Yuri Onufrienko (1961–), a Russian air force officer, and Yuri Usachev (1957–), a Russian civilian—to the *Mir* space station. Lucid then went back to the United States for three weeks of training with the crew of the U.S. space shuttle *Atlantis,* which would take her to *Mir*. On March 22, 1996, *Atlantis* lifted off

Shannon Lucid (center) aboard the Russian space station *Mir* with cosmonauts Yuri Usachev and Yuri Onufrienko. Lucid conducted science experiments aboard *Mir* for six months. *(AP/Wide World Photos)*

from the Kennedy Space Center in Cape Canaveral, Florida. Three days later the shuttle docked with *Mir*.

Spends six months in space

Lucid stayed busy while living aboard *Mir*. The day began when the alarm rang at 8:00 A.M. The first activity for the crew members was to put on their headphones and talk with mission control. Next they had breakfast, first adding water to their food and then eating it while floating around a table. In the afternoon they had a long lunch—again floating around the table—which usually consisted of Russian potatoes and meat casseroles. Although the crew had many responsibilities, they still had time for conversations about their own lives and experiences. They also had fun. One time Lucid lost a shoe

Letter from a "Cosmic Outpost"

Shannon Lucid wrote a letter from *Mir* on May 19, 1996. In the excerpt below she described the arrival of the resupply vehicle *Progress.*

> Usually about every six weeks one [a resupply vehicle] is sent to Mir with food, equipment, clothes—everything that, on Earth, you would have to go to the store and buy in order to live. . . .
>
> I saw it [the Progress] first. There were big thunderstorms out in the Atlantic, with a brilliant display of lightening [sic] like visual tom toms. The cities were strung out like Christmas tree lights along the coast—and there was the Progress like a bright morning star skimming along the top!!! Suddenly, its brightness increased dramatically and Yuri

> said, "The engine just fired." Soon, it was close enough that we could see the deployed solar arrays. To me, it looked like some alien insect headed straight toward us. All of a sudden I really did feel like I was in a "cosmic outpost" anxiously awaiting supplies—and really hoping that my family did remember to send me some books and candy!!! . . .
>
> The first things we took out were our personal packages and, yes, I quickly peeked in to see if my family had remembered the books and candy I'd requested. Of course they had. Then we started to unpack. We found the fresh food and stopped right there for lunch. We had fresh tomatoes and onions; I never have had such a good lunch. For the next week we had fresh tomatoes three times a day. It was a sad meal when we ate the last ones!!!

and a cosmonaut found it, so she gave him a gelatin dessert as a reward.

The crew performed thirty-five life science and physical science experiments, such as determining how protein crystals grow in space and how quail embryos develop in zero gravity. Many of the experiments also provided useful data for the engineers designing the **International Space Station** (ISS; see entry). The results from investigations in fluid physics, for example, helped the space station's planners build better ventilation and life-support systems. Research on combustion in microgravity may also lead to improved procedures for fighting fires on the station.

Exercise was essential to counteract the effects of weightlessness. Lucid spent two hours every day running on a treadmill, attaching herself to the machine with a bungee cord. This prevented significant weight and muscle loss normally encountered by astronauts. When Lucid returned to Earth aboard the *Atlantis* on September 26, she was in such good physical shape that she was able to walk off the space shuttle without assistance. She had flown 75.2 million miles (121 kilometers) in 188 days, 4 hours, and 14 seconds, setting a new record for a woman—a total of 5,354 hours (223 days) in space. The previous female record, 170 days, had been held by Russian cosmonaut Yelena Vladimirovna Kondakova (1957–).

Honored for achievements

In 2002, NASA named Lucid the new chief scientist of the Solar System Exploration division of the Jet Propulsion Laboratory, a NASA agency based in California. In this position she oversaw the agency's science agenda, leading a three-person science council that would shape the future of U.S. space exploration. Lucid is the only woman to be awarded the U.S. Congressional Space Medal of Honor. She also received the Order of Friendship Medal, one of the most prestigious Russian civilian honors and the highest award that can be presented to a non-citizen. In 1997 the Freedom Forum presented Lucid the Free Spirit Award in recognition of her work and accomplishments in the space program.

For More Information

Books

Atkins, Jeannine. *The Story of Women in Space*. New York: Farrar, Straus and Giroux, 2003.

Crouch, Tom D. *Aiming for the Stars: The Dreamers and Doers of the Space Age*. Washington, DC: Smithsonian Institution Press, 1999.

Harris, Laurie, and Cherie Abbey, eds. *Biography Today, Scientists and Inventors Series*. Detroit: Omnigraphics, Inc., 1998.

Woodmansee, Laura S. *Women Astronauts*. Burlington, Ontario: Collector's Guide Publishing, 2002.

Periodicals

Danes, Mary K. "Space Woman on *Mir*." *Hopscotch* (October/November 2002): p. 2.

"Just Let Her Fly." *Discover* (April 1999): p. 18.

Lucid, Shannon. "Six Months on Mir." *Scientific American* (May 1998): pp. 46–55.

Web Sites

"Astronaut Bio: Shannon Lucid." *Johnson Space Center, NASA.* http://www.jsc.nasa.gov/Bios/htmlbios/lucid.html (accessed on June 29, 2004).

"Pink Socks and Jello: Shannon Lucid Writes a Letter Home." http://www.geocities.com/CapeCanaveral/4411/lucid.htm (accessed on June 30, 2004).

Mercury 13
1960–61

"**M**ercury 13" is the popular name given to a group of thirteen women who were tested for Project Mercury astronaut training in 1960 and 1961. They passed the same seventy-five tests that were taken by their famous male counterparts, the Mercury 7 astronauts. The women never had a chance to fly in space, however, because the National Aeronautics and Space Administration (NASA) and the U.S. military were unwilling to accept women into their ranks. By the early twenty-first century, women had been regularly serving as astronauts for over twenty years. Historians have credited the Mercury 13, as well as the doctor and the brigadier general who initiated the women's testing program, as a pioneering event in the U.S. space program.

Mercury 7 are heroes

In 1958 the United States established NASA, which integrated U.S. space research agencies and started an astronaut training program. The formation of NASA was a direct response to *Sputnik 1,* an artificial satellite (an object that orbits in space) that the former Soviet Union had launched

Seven crew members of Mercury 13 in 1995 (from left): Gene Nora Jessen, Mary Wallace "Wally" Funk, Geraldyn "Jerrie" Cobb, Jerri Truhill, Sarah Ratley, Myrtle "K" Cagle, and Bernice "B" Steadman. *(NASA)*

the previous year. This event sent shock waves through American society because at the time the United States and the Soviet Union were engaged in a political standoff known as the Cold War (1945–91). Not only were the two superpowers involved in an arms race for military superiority, but they were also competing for dominance in space. *Sputnik 1* was a sign that the Soviet Union was winning the space race.

Determined to move ahead of the Soviets, NASA developed a manned space flight program with the goal of sending the first person into Earth orbit. According to the plan, the program would progress in three stages: Project Mercury, Project Gemini, and Project Apollo. Project Mercury developed the basic technology for manned space flight and investigated

The original seven members of the Mercury Project (from left): (front row) Walter M. Schirra Jr., Donald "Deke" K. Slayton, John Glenn, M. Scott Carpenter; (back row) Alan Shepard, Virgil I. "Gus" Grissom, and Leroy G. Cooper. *(© NASA/Roger Ressmeyer/Corbis)*

a human's ability to survive and perform in space. Project Gemini provided astronauts with experience in returning to Earth from space as well as successfully linking space vehicles and "walking" in space. Integrating the information and experience gained from Mercury and Gemini, Project Apollo would land a person safely on the Moon.

NASA aggressively promoted Project Mercury, seeking a pool of applicants from whom a few would be selected to train as the first U.S. astronauts. NASA administrator T. Keith Glennan (1905–1995) convinced President Dwight D. Eisenhower (1890–1969; served 1953–61) that military jet test pilots would be the most qualified astronauts, so experience as a military pilot became the primary requirement. In April 1959, after applicants had been screened and tested, Glennan presented seven astronaut candidates—all males and all military test pilots—to the American public. Called the "Mercury 7" and immediately acclaimed as heroes, they were Malcolm Scott Carpenter (1925–), Leroy G. Cooper Jr. (1927–), **John Glenn** (1921–; see entry), Virgil I. "Gus" Grissom (1926–1967), Walter M. Schirra Jr. (1923–), Alan Shepard (1923–1998; see box in **John Glenn** entry), and Donald "Deke" K. Slayton (1924–1993).

Cobb leads the way

The Mercury 7 had undergone extensive medical testing at the Lovelace Foundation in Albuquerque, New Mexico, and at Wright-Patterson Air Force Base in Dayton, Ohio. The medical testing program, which involved three phases, was designed by Dr. W. Randolph Lovelace II (1929–), chair of the NASA Life Sciences Committee, and Brigadier General Donald Flickinger (1907–1997) of the U.S. Air Force. When the Mercury 7 were selected, Lovelace and Flickinger had for some time been interested in testing women as astronauts. The main reason was that women generally weigh less than men. Women's lighter body weight could offer several advantages in space, such as reducing the load in the capsule, increasing the booster power of the rocket that propels the capsule, and decreasing the amount of food and oxygen required during a flight. Lovelace and Flickinger were also intrigued by the possibility that women could match men in physical stamina and endurance. In addition, the Soviet Union was rumored to be training women cosmonauts (astronauts), so the doctor and the general were keenly aware that the United States must not lag behind the Soviets again in the space race.

Lovelace and Flickinger initiated a secret search for women they could test for the astronaut program. In late 1959 they met their ideal applicant: Oklahoma native Geraldyn "Jerrie" Cobb (1931–). An experienced pilot, Cobb had already set three world records for distance and speed in a twin-engine Aero Commander plane. She was the first woman test pilot hired by the manufacturer of the Commander, and she had flown a variety of aircraft, including crop dusters, gliders, blimps, and B-17s. Lovelace and Flickinger were impressed with Cobb's credentials, so they asked her to report to the Lovelace Clinic for the first phase of NASA astronaut qualification tests. By the time Cobb arrived at the clinic in early 1960, she had logged ten thousand flight hours, more than twice the number accumulated by some of the Mercury 7 astronauts. Cobb underwent the same seventy-five tests that had been administered to male candidates. The tests evaluated heart rate; lung capacity; loneliness level; pain level; noise tolerance; sensory deprivation; and spinning, tilting, and dropping into water tanks to measure resistance to vertigo (a state of extreme dizziness). Placing in the top 2 percent of all applicants, Cobb proceeded to phase two testing at the Naval School of Aviation at Pensacola, Florida.

In the meantime, the Lovelace Clinic had recruited twenty-five other women for testing. The criteria included being in good health, having a college education, and logging a significant number of flying hours. In 1961, after undergoing the first phase of testing, twelve of the women met NASA qualifications. Like Cobb, they were all licensed pilots. They had varying degrees of flying experience, and many had logged more flying hours than had the Mercury 7 astronauts. Ranging in age from twenty-one to forty, a few were married but most were single at the time. Many of the women never met one another. The testing program had not been revealed to the public, so the women signed a pledge that they would keep it secret.

The Mercury 13

In addition to Cobb, the women who became known as the Mercury 13 were Myrtle "K" Cagle (1922–), Jan Dietrich (1924–), Marion Dietrich (1924–1974), Mary Wallace "Wally" Funk (1938–), Jane (Janey) Briggs Hart (1920–), Jean Hixson (1921–1962), Gene Nora Stumbough Jessen (1934–), Irene Leverton (1924–), Sarah Lee Gorelick Ratley (1931–), Bernice "B" Steadman (1923–), Jerri Sloan Truhill (1928–), and Rhea Allison Woltman (1928–).

Myrtle Cagle, age thirty-six, was a flight instructor in Macon, Georgia. Having flown a variety of airplanes since she was twelve, she had logged 4,300 hours of flying time. Jan and Marion Dietrich were thirty-four-year-old identical twins who had degrees from the University of California at Berkeley. After graduation Jan became a flight instructor and commercial pilot, logging eight thousand flight hours by 1961.

Marion was a reporter and writer for a newspaper in Oakland, California, and she pursued flying in her spare time. When she came to the Loveland Clinic she had logged 1,500 flight hours.

The youngest member of the training group was Wally Funk. Age twenty-one, she was a civilian flight instructor at Fort Sill, a military base in Oklahoma. She placed second, after Cobb, in the phase-one tests. Janey Hart, at age forty, was the oldest—and the mother of eight children. The first licensed female pilot in the state of Michigan, she was married to Phil Hart (1912–1976), a U.S. senator from Michigan. The most experienced member of the group was Jean Hixson, age thirty-seven. She had served in the WASP (the women's branch of the Army Air Force) during World War II. After the war she worked as a flight instructor, earned a college degree, and became a school teacher in Ohio.

Gene Nora (pronounced Janora) Stumbough Jessen was serving on the faculty at the University of Oklahoma when she entered the Lovelace program. Although she passed the phase-one tests at age twenty-four, she was not aware at the time that she had qualified for astronaut training. She quit her job to take the phase-two tests in 1962, but the program was discontinued a few days later. Irene Leverton, a thirty-four-year-old flight instructor from the University of Oklahoma, held a commercial pilot's license. She had logged more than nine thousand flight hours when she arrived at Lovelace. Kansas City native Sarah Ratley, who was twenty-eight, had a bachelor's degree in mathematics. Working as an electrical engineer at AT&T, she held a commercial pilot's license and had won women's air races such as the Powder Puff Derby and the International Air Race.

Jerri Sloan Truhill, who began taking flying lessons as a teenager, was an experienced pilot when she entered the Lovelace program at age thirty-two. In partnership with Joe Truhill (whom she later married), she tested Terrain Following Radar (TFR) and "smart bombs" for Texas Instruments, a company based in Dallas, Texas. Rhea Allison Woltman was a professional pilot with licenses to fly a variety of aircraft. She had also towed gliders for cadets at the U.S. Air Force Academy in Colorado, where she was a flight instructor.

Two Would-be "Astronettes"

Mercury 13 members Jerrie Cobb and Janey Hart actively protested against NASA's cancellation of the women's astronaut testing program. In 1962, when they realized that NASA was not going to change its position, they met with Vice President Lyndon B. Johnson (1908–1973; served as vice president 1961–63) and asked him to intervene on their behalf. Johnson had been a major force in establishing the space agency, so his word would carry considerable weight. In the following excerpt from her book *The Mercury 13: The Untold Story of Thirteen American Women and the Dream of Space Flight,* writer Martha Ackmann describes the end of the meeting, when the vice president dismisses Cobb and Hart.

Many minority groups were asking for attention from NASA, the Vice President [told Cobb and Hart]. They want to be astronauts, too. If the United States allowed women in space, then blacks, Mexicans, Chinese, and other minorities would want to fly too. . . . Leaning toward the women with a pained expression on his face, Lyndon Johnson looked directly at Cobb and Hart and gave them his final thought. As much as he would like to help the cause of women astronauts, it was really an issue for [NASA administrator] James Webb (1906–1992) and those at NASA. It hurt him to have to say it because he was eager to help, but the question was not his to address. Johnson called an end to the meeting and started talking on his private phone.

Hart and Cobb left Johnson's chambers and met with a crowd of reporters outside in the Capitol hallway. Hart stood with her arms tightly folded across her chest, her pocketbook stuffed into the crook of her arm. Her goal at this point seemed to be to mind her manners and hold her temper in

Women's program canceled

Cobb, Funk, and Woltman passed phase-two testing. Cobb and Funk completed phase three, which means that they achieved equal status with their male counterparts, the Mercury 7. Yet they were never accepted into the astronaut corps, and they never flew in space. In July 1961, while Cobb and Funk were waiting for the next stage of training, NASA canceled the women's testing program. No explanation was given. Many people protested NASA's decision and pressured the U.S. Congress to hold hearings on discrimination against women in the space program. A Congressional subcommittee reviewed the matter and asked NASA for clarification of its policies. NASA officials responded by saying that the women trainees were ineligible to become astronauts because they had not gone through the military jet-pilot training program at Ed-

check. Cobb leaned near the wall, her face set rigidly in a practiced smile. "I'm hoping that something will come of these meetings," she politely said as reporters scribbled into their notebooks. Later, newspaper reporters declared that two would-be "astronettes" had pleaded their case in Washington. The vice president—using the current jargon from Cape Canaveral [the NASA launch site in Florida]—had said the women were "A-OK" but the decision was not his to make.

Ironically, people from all of the groups mentioned by Johnson—women, blacks, Mexicans, and Chinese—eventually became U.S. astronauts (see separate entries): **Sally Ride** (1951–) was the first American woman; **Guy Bluford** (1946–) was the first African American male, and **Mae Jemison** (1956–) was the first African American woman; **Ellen Ochoa** (1958–) was the first Hispanic woman, and **Franklin Chang-Díaz** (1950–) is of Chinese-Hispanic descent.

Jerrie Cobb (left) and Janey Hart (right) lobby for women's participation in the U.S. space program. *(© Bettmann/Corbis)*

wards Air Force Base in California. Since women were not allowed to train as military pilots at the time, historians note that NASA was simply making an excuse. The truth was that male military officers, both in the armed forces and at NASA, did not want women to fly in space.

In April 1961 Soviet cosmonaut **Yuri Gagarin** (1934–1968; see entry) became the first man in space, setting this record one month before Mercury astronaut Alan Shepard made a successful flight into space. Then in 1963, the year after NASA canceled the women's astronaut testing program, the Soviet Union scored yet another victory in the space race: Cosmonaut **Valentina Tereshkova** (1937–; see entry) became the first woman to travel in orbit. No American woman was given a chance to accomplish this feat until 1983, when **Sally Ride** (1951–; see entry) flew aboard the space shuttle *Challenger.* (A space shuttle is a craft that transports people and cargo between Earth and space.)

The Mercury 13 returned to active private lives, remaining in the aviation field as commercial pilots, flight instructors, owners of aviation-related businesses, air race competitors, and flying hobbyists. In 1995 ten of the Mercury thirteen members, some meeting for the first time, gathered at Cape Canaveral, Florida. They were there to witness the launch of Eileen Collins (1956–), the first American woman pilot astronaut to travel in space. Before entering the space shuttle *Discovery,* Collins paid tribute to the Mercury 13 pioneers, saying, "They gave us [women astronauts] a history."

Although most of the Mercury 13 were disappointed about NASA's decision to cancel the testing program, they did not make any further efforts to pursue a career in spaceflight. Jerrie Cobb and Wally Funk were the exceptions: Hoping to fly in space one day, both stayed physically fit and were still flying airplanes as they approached the age of seventy. In 1998, when Mercury 7 hero John Glenn took his second flight at age seventy-six, Cobb and her supporters started a movement to pressure NASA to give her a mission in space. Once again, NASA ignored her. In 2001 Funk signed a contract with a civilian space launch company, Interorbital Systems, to take a suborbital flight. Her trip had been delayed several times by 2004, but she remained optimistic about finally traveling in space.

For More Information

Books

Ackmann, Martha. *The Mercury 13: The Untold Story of Thirteen American Women and the Dream of Space Flight.* New York: Random House, 2003.

Cobb, Jerrie. *Jerrie Cobb, Solo Pilot.* Sun City, FL: Jerrie Cobb Foundation, 1997.

Nolen, Stephanie. *Promised the Moon: The Untold Story of the First Women in the Space Race.* New York: Four Walls Eight Windows, 2003.

Periodicals

"'Mercury 13' Project Helped Pave Way for Female Astronauts." *Government CustomWire* (April 8, 2004).

"Star Struck." *Weekly Reader—Senior* (April 2, 2004): pp. 2–3.

"Stars in Their Eyes." *People* (July 7, 2003): pp. 111–14.

Web Sites

Burbank, Sam. "Mercury 13's Wally Funk Fights for Her Place in Space." *National Geographic.com.* http://news.nationalgeographic.com/news/2003/07/0709_030709_tvspacewoman.html (accessed on June 29, 2004).

DeFrange, Ann. "State-Born Aviatrix Yearns for Space. 2nd Astronaut Bid Supported." *The Sunday Oklahoman* (May 17, 1998): pp. 1–2. http://freepages.genealogy.rootsweb.com/ñswokla/family/jerricobb.html (accessed on June 29, 2004).

Funk, Wally. "The Mercury 13 Story." *The Ninety-Nines, Inc.* www.ninety-nines.org/mercury.html (accessed on June 29, 2004).

"Mercury 13—The Women of the Mercury Era." http://www.mercury13.com/ (accessed May 22, 2004).

Hermann Oberth

Born June 25, 1894 (Hermannstadt, Transylvania)
Died December 29, 1989 (Nuremberg, West Germany)

Austro-Hungarian-born German scientist

"Because that is the goal: To secure any place on which life can exist and prosper, give life to any dead world, and to give purpose to any living world."

German scientist Hermann Oberth ranks with Russian aerospace engineer **Konstantin Tsiolkovsky** (1857–1935; see entry) and American physicist **Robert Goddard** (1882–1945; see entry) as one of the founders of space flight. Tsiolkovsky and Goddard made many discoveries before Oberth, but Oberth's writings on a variety of subjects reached a wider audience. His most important contributions were two books that led first to the development of the German V-2 long-range guided missile (a rocket that carries a weapon) and then to human spaceflight. Oberth also published and expressed intriguing but often controversial views. These included claims that unidentified flying objects could be space vehicles carrying intelligent people from beyond our world.

Becomes fascinated by spaceflight

Hermann Julius Oberth was born on June 25, 1894, in the German town of Hermannstadt, Transylvania; formerly a part of Austria-Hungary, the town is now known as Sibiu, Romania. His father, Julius Gotthold Oberth, was a medical doctor who was the director and chief surgeon of the county hospi-

Hermann Oberth. *(AP/Wide World Photos)*

tal in Schässburg, Transylvania, where Oberth grew up. His mother, Valerie Emma (Krassner) Oberth, was the daughter of a doctor who had prophesied accurately in July 1869 that humans would land on the Moon in a hundred years. In an autobiographical piece published in *Astronautics* journal, Oberth recalled that "at the age of eleven, I received from my mother as a gift the famous books, *From the Earth to the Moon* and *Travel to the Moon* by Jules Verne [1828–1905], which I . . . read at least five or six times and, finally, knew by heart." Fascinated by space flight as a child, he began to perform various calculations about how humans could travel to the Moon.

Although Oberth learned infinitesimal calculus (calculus is a variety of methods of mathematical calculation using symbols) at the Schässburg secondary school, he taught himself differential calculus, and he successfully verified the magnitude of escape velocity (the minimum force needed to propel a rocket out of Earth orbit into space).

Oberth began studying medicine at the University of Munich in Germany in 1913, but he also attended lectures in physics (the study of energy and matter and their interactions) and related subjects at the nearby technical institute. His education was interrupted by World War I (1914–18), in which he served with an infantry regiment (soldiers trained and armed to fight on foot). After being wounded in 1916, he was assigned to a reserve hospital, where he continued experiments with weightlessness that he had begun as a teenager. He also experimented on himself with drugs, including scopolamine, which is still used to treat motion sickness.

When Oberth left the army he worked on solutions to the problems posed by space flight. In 1918 he submitted a proposal to the German Ministry of Armament for a long-range rocket that could be used as a weapon. Powered by ethyl alcohol, water, and liquid air, the rocket was larger and less complicated than the V-2 missile, which Oberth later developed with engineer **Wernher von Braun** (1912–1977; see entry). The ministry turned down Oberth's proposal. On June 6, 1918, Oberth married Mathilde Hummel, with whom he later had four children. Two of the children died during World War II (1939–45).

Publishes rocket theories

In 1919 Oberth resumed his schooling, this time studying physics at the University of Klausenburg in Transylvania. He soon returned to the University of Munich and the nearby technical institute, then he attended the University of Göttingen, and finally he completed his studies for a Ph.D. at the University of Heidelberg. He submitted his doctoral dissertation (a long research paper on a specialized topic) on rockets and spaceflight theory at Heidelberg, but it was not accepted. From 1922 until 1938 Oberth taught physics and mathematics at secondary schools in Transylvania. In 1923 the University of Klausenburg granted him the title of professor. Five

From the Earth to the Moon

Hermann Oberth enjoyed reading science fiction. One of his favorite works was *From the Earth to the Moon: Passage Direct in Ninety-seven Hours and Twenty Minutes,* (1865) by the French novelist Jules Verne (1828–1905). It is a tale about the adventures of members of the Baltimore Gun Club, who travel to the Moon onboard a gigantic cannon that they had made into a rocket. In the final chapter the cannon becomes a satellite (an object that orbits in space), an event that is witnessed by their friends J. Belfast and J. T. Maston "thanks to the gigantic reflector of Long's Peak!" Belfast sends a note of confirmation to the Observatory of Cambridge. At the close of the chapter Maston contemplates the significance of the Gun Club's achievement:

> When the dispatch from Long's Peak had once become known, there was but one universal feeling of surprise and alarm. Was it possible to go to the aid of these bold travelers? No! for they had placed themselves beyond the pale of humanity, by crossing the limits imposed by the Creator on his earthly creatures. They had air enough for two *months;* they had victuals enough for twelve;—but after that? There was only one man who would not admit that the situation was desperate—he alone had confidence; and that was their devoted friend J. T. Maston.
>
> Besides, he never let them get out of sight. His home was henceforth the post at Long's Peak; his horizon, the mirror of that immense reflector. As soon as the moon rose above the horizon, he immediately caught her in the field of the telescope; he never let her go for an instant out of his sight, and followed her assiduously [steadily worked at tracking the Moon] in her course through the stellar spaces. He watched with untiring patience the passage of the projectile across her silvery disc, and really the worthy man remained in perpetual communication with his three friends, whom he did not despair of seeing again some day.
>
> "Those three men [members of the Gun Club]," said he, "have carried into space all the resources of art, science, and industry. With that, one can do anything; and you will see that, some day, they will come out all right."

years later Oberth published his doctoral dissertation as a book titled *Die Rakete zu den Planeträumen* (*The Rocket into Planetary Space*).

Although filled with complicated equations, Oberth's book sold well. He set forth the basic principles of space flight and discussed possible solutions to a number of specific problems. For instance, he examined such matters as liquid-propellant rocket construction and the use of propellants for different stages of rockets. (A liquid-propellant rocket is fired with liquid fuel. Prior to the twentieth century rockets were fired with gun powder, known as solid fuel.) He discussed the use of pumps to inject propellants into a rocket's combustion chamber and speculated on the effects of space flight upon humans. He also proposed the idea of a space station. In 1929 Oberth published a considerably expanded version of this book, now titled *Wege zur Raumschiffahrt* (*Ways to Spaceflight*). Both the German version and the English translation of the book provided inspiration to other spaceflight pioneers. One of the most important consequences was the German Rocket Society (Verein für Raumschiffahrt), which was founded in 1927 to raise money for Oberth's rocket experiments. Oberth served as president from 1929 until 1930.

The German Rocket Society provided practical training in rocketry to several of its members. Among them was von Braun, who later joined the German army's rocket center at Peenemünde, where he participated in developing the V-2 guided missile. As public interest in space flight increased, the German film director Fritz Lang (1890–1976) made the movie *Frau im Mond* (*Woman on the Moon*), with Oberth as the technical advisor. Lang and his film company also provided funds for Oberth to construct a liquid-propellant rocket that would be launched at the movie's premier. Oberth was unable to meet the deadline. During production of the film Oberth lost the sight in his left eye while conducting an experiment. He went on to build a rocket that never flew, but it did undergo a static test on July 23, 1930. Although his rocket design was certified by the Government Institute for Chemistry and Technology, Oberth returned to teaching in Romania when he could not obtain funding to develop it. The German Rocket Society continued its work, benefiting from the certification of Oberth's design.

Describes space ships

After 1930 Oberth resumed liquid-propellant rocket experiments. He succeeded in launching one rocket in 1935, but he remained outside the mainstream of rocket development. In 1938 he received an appointment to the Technical Institute in Vienna, Austria, to work on liquid-propellant rockets under a contract with the German Air Force. He was unable to accomplish anything of significance because he did not have adequate facilities or sufficient staff. In 1940 he was transferred to the Technical Institute of Dresden in Germany to develop a fuel pump for what turned out to be the V-2 rocket. The rocket system, including a fuel pump, had already been designed, so Oberth went to Peenemünde to work with von Braun. By this time, however, the V-2 rocket was essentially developed. Since Oberth had become a German citizen in 1941, he was put in charge examining patents and other technical information for possible use on rockets. After doing some analytical work with a supersonic wind tunnel at Peenemünde in 1943, he began work on an anti-aircraft rocket, using a solid propellant. He was then transferred to a firm that dealt in solid fuels, Westfälisch-Anhaltische Sprengstoff A.G., where he remained until the end of the war.

After World War II, Oberth moved to Feucht in what became West Germany. In 1948 he took a position in Switzerland as an advisor and technical writer on matters related to rocketry. Two years later he was hired by the Italian navy to develop a solid-propellant rocket, but the project was discontinued in 1953. Returning to Feucht, he published *Menschen im Weltraum* (*Man into Space*) the following year. In the book he discussed electric spaceships and a vehicle for moving about on the Moon, as well as many of the topics covered in his previous books. In 1955 Oberth published *Das Mondauto* (*The Moon Car*), in which he elaborated on his conception for a vehicle to operate on the Moon. That year Oberth also went to the United States to work with von Braun at the U.S. Army Ballistic Missile Agency (ABMA) at Redstone Arsenal in Huntsville, Alabama. Shortly before the war ended in 1945,

Hermann Oberth meets with engineer Werner von Braun. During his time with von Braun, Oberth helped to develop propulsion for rockets, guidance devices for spacecrafts, and vehicles for use in zero gravity.

(© Bettmann/Corbis)

von Braun and 112 of his Peenemünde colleagues had surrendered to American military forces. They had been taken to the United States to work on rockets for the U.S. weapons and space programs, and von Braun was now head of the ABMA.

Contributes to Moon exploration

At ABMA, Oberth was involved in advanced planning for projects in space, including electrical and thermonuclear (energy produced from the nucleus of an atom with high temperatures) propulsion for rockets, guidance devices, and vehicles for the Moon. Von Braun believed that Oberth had inspired the roving vehicle used on the *Apollo 15* flight to the Moon. Inspiration is what best characterizes Oberth's other designs at Huntsville as well, for they seem to have contributed little directly to the space effort. In 1958 he returned to Feucht, where he resided for the rest of his life. He returned briefly to the United States in July 1969 to witness the launch of *Apollo 11,* which carried the first humans to the Moon (see **Buzz Aldrin** [1930–] and **Neil Armstrong** [1930–] entries).

In recognition of his contributions to space flight, Oberth was the first recipient of the international R. E. P. Hirsch Astronautics Prize in 1929. He also received the Diesel medal of the Association of German Inventors in 1954, the American Astronautical Society Award in 1955, and the Federal Service Cross First Class from the German Federal Republic in 1961. Of the three preeminent founders of spaceflight, Oberth alone lived to witness the results of his early ideas. He died at age ninety-five in Nuremberg, West Germany, on December 29, 1989. Throughout his life he remained committed to the dream of human exploration of space. In 1954, thirty-five years before his death, he wrote in *Men into Space,* "Because that is the goal: To secure any place on which life can exist and prosper, give life to any dead world, and to give purpose to any living world."

For More Information

Books

Freeman, Marsha, Christina Huth, and Konrad Dannenberg, eds. *How We Got to the Moon: The Story of German Space Pioneers.* Washington, DC: Twenty-First Century Science Associates, 1994.

Heppenheimer, T.A. *Countdown: A History of Space Flight.* New York: John Wiley & Sons, 1987.

Oberth, Hermann. *Men into Space.* Translated by G.P.H. De Freville. New York: Harper, 1957.

Oberth, Hermann. *The Moon Car.* Translated by Willy Ley. New York: Harper, 1959.

Walters, Helen B. *Hermann Oberth: Father of Space Travel.* New York: Macmillan, 1962; 2003.

Periodicals

Frazier, Allison. "They Gave Us Space: Space Pioneers of the 20th Century." *Ad Astra* (January/February 2000): pp. 25–26.

Oberth, Hermann. "From My Life." *Astronautics* (June 1959): pp. 38–39, 100–105.

Winter, Frank H. "Was Hermann Oberth the True Father of Spaceflight?" *Ad Astra* (November/December 1996): pp. 40+.

Yeomans, Donald. "'Space Travel Is Utter Bilge.'" *Astronomy* (January 2004): pp. 48+.

Web Sites

The Hermann Oberth Raumfahrt Museum. http://www.oberth-museum.org/index_e.html (accessed on June 29, 2004).

Lethbridge, Cliff. "History of Rocketry Chapter 3: Early 20th Century—Hermann Oberth." *Spaceline.* http://spaceline.org/history/25.html (accessed on June 29, 2004).

Strange, Christiaan. "Hermann Oberth: Father of Space Travel." http://www.kiosek.com/oberth (accessed on June 29, 2004).

Verne, Jules. "Chapter 28. The Star." *From the Earth to the Moon.* http://vesuvius.jsc.nasa.gov/er/seh/chapter28.htm (accessed June 29, 2004).

Ellen Ochoa

Born May 10, 1958 (Los Angeles, California)

American astronaut, electrical engineer

"I never got tired of watching the Earth, day or night, as we passed over it."

Ellen Ochoa began training as an astronaut in 1990, twelve years after the program was opened to women. In 1993 she became the first Latina (woman of Hispanic descent) to travel in space, and by 2002 she had participated in three more missions. An inventor and optics expert (one who studies the origin and uses of light), Ochoa continues her active career in the National Aeronautics and Space Administration (NASA). Her achievements have made her a popular role model for other Hispanics, yet she prefers to see herself simply as an astronaut. After her first trip into space, Ochoa was given a medal by the Congressional Hispanic Caucus. In her acceptance speech she said, "What everyone in the astronaut corps shares in common is not gender or ethnic background, but motivation, perseverance, and desire—the desire to participate in a voyage of discovery."

Begins career as engineer

Ellen Ochoa was born on May 10, 1958, in Los Angeles, California, the third of five children of Rosanne Deardorff Ochoa and Joseph Ochoa. She grew up in La Mesa, a suburb

Ellen Ochoa. *(AP/Wide World Photos)*

of San Diego. Her father, a native of Mexico, was the manager of a retail store and her mother was a homemaker. When Ellen was in junior high school, Joseph left the family and Rosanne struggled to raise five children alone. Described by Ellen as a "super-mentor," Rosanne took college courses in her spare time and, over a period of twenty years, earned three degrees. Ellen, her sister, and her three brothers were outstanding students in the public schools. During high school Ellen gained recognition as an outstanding classical flutist, and she was the valedictorian of her graduation class in 1975. (The valedictorian is generally the highest ranking student in

Rodolfo Neri Vela

Mexican astronaut Rodolfo Neri Vela became the first Latino to go into space in 1985. Flying aboard the space shuttle *Atlantis,* he participated in a seven-day, joint NASA–European Space Agency (ESA) mission. A specialist in communications technology, he carried out multiple experiments and placed in orbit the Mexican satellite Morelos 2. From 1989 until 1990 Neri Vela worked on the **International Space Station** (ISS; see entry) for the ESA in Holland. He later held academic positions at universities in Mexico and other countries, teaching courses on satellites and astronautics. He has written numerous articles and published ten books on subjects such as communications satellites, the solar system, and space travel.

the class who has earned the right to give the farewell speech during the graduation ceremony.) Although she was offered a four-year scholarship to Stanford University in Palo Alto, she chose instead to attend San Diego State University. She wanted to stay near her two younger brothers, who were still in high school at the time.

Ochoa was planning to study journalism when she entered college, but she eventually changed her major to physics. After graduating from San Diego State in 1980—once again as valedictorian—she enrolled in graduate school at Stanford University. She earned a master's degree in electrical engineering in 1981 and a doctorate in the same field in 1985. During this time she also performed as a flute soloist with the Stanford Symphony Orchestra. Ochoa became interested in the NASA astronaut training program when several other graduate students submitted applications. NASA had been accepting women and minorities into the candidates' program only since the late 1970s (see **Guy Bluford** [1942–] and **Sally Ride** [1951–] entries). The first Latino astronaut, Rodolfo Neri Vela (1952–; see box on this page), flew his first space shuttle mission in 1985, the same year Ochoa applied to the program. (A space shuttle is a craft that transports people and cargo between Earth and space.)

Takes first trip in space

While awaiting acceptance as an astronaut candidate, Ochoa took a research position at Sandia National Laboratories in Albuquerque, New Mexico. In 1987 she learned she was among one hundred finalists for the NASA training program. The following year she was hired as chief of the Intelligent Systems Technology Branch at Ames Research Center at Moffett Field Naval Air Station in Mountain View, California. During this period she was the coinventor of three patented

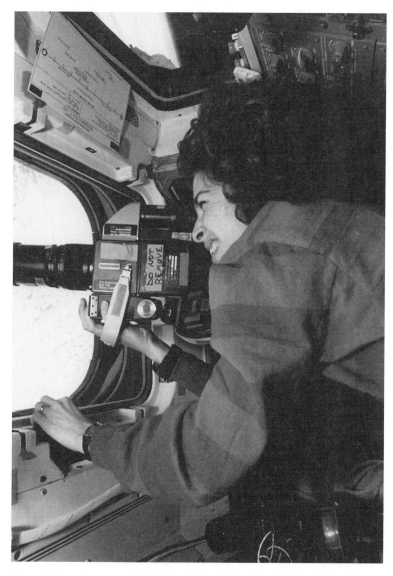

Ellen Ochoa photographing one of Earth's oceans from aboard the *Discovery* **space shuttle during her first mission in 1993.** *(NASA)*

devices: one for an optical inspection system, a second for an optical object recognition method, and a third for a method to reduce noise in images. In her spare time, Ochoa took flying lessons and became a certified private pilot.

Ochoa continued to persevere throughout the lengthy and difficult NASA selection process. She finally achieved her goal in 1990, becoming the first female Hispanic astronaut in NASA history. Training began in late 1990 at the Johnson Space Center in Houston, Texas. The program was physically and mentally demanding, involving academic subjects such as geology, oceanography, meteorology, astronomy, orbital mechanics, and medicine as well as land and water survival techniques and even parachuting. Each astronaut also devoted considerable time to learning about the space shuttle itself. Ochoa passed the rigorous course and officially became an astronaut in July 1991. She began as a flight software specialist in the development of robots (remote-controlled devices that perform human activities). She was also involved in flight testing and training.

Ochoa participated in her first mission, a nine-day flight aboard the space shuttle *Discovery,* in April 1993. The only woman on the five-member crew, she was a specialist for the second mission of ATLAS (Atmospheric Laboratory for Applications and Science). Ochoa and her crewmates conducted research on solar activity to gain a better understanding of Earth's climate and environment. She operated the Remote Manipulator System (RMS), a fifty-foot (15.42 meters) robotic arm, to deploy (release into orbit) and capture the *Spartan* satellite, which retrieved data about the solar corona (colored circle around the Sun) and solar winds (plasma continuously ejected from the Sun's surface into and through planetary space). Ochoa later recalled that observing the universe from the shuttle's windows was an awe-inspiring experience. "I never got tired of watching the Earth, day or night, as we passed over it," she told Nora López, a reporter for *Latina* magazine. "Even though we brought back some pretty incredible pictures, they don't quite compare with being there."

Helps assemble space station

Ochoa's next space flight, an eight-day trip, took place in November 1994 on the space shuttle *Atlantis.* As payload commander, she again collected data on solar energy. Her third mission, aboard the *Discovery* in 1999, was a ten-day journey (May 27–June 6) for which she served as a mission specialist and flight engineer. The seven-person crew included representatives from the Canadian Space Agency, the Russian Space Agency, and a French representative of the ESA. May 29 was a particularly momentous day, in that it marked the first time the shuttle docked with the **International Space Station** (ISS; see entry), an orbiting research laboratory being constructed for use by many nations.

The *Discovery* crew was preparing for the arrival of the first crew to live onboard the space station the following year. Ochoa's responsibilities included coordinating the transfer of nearly two tons of supplies such as clothing, sleeping bags, medical equipment, spare parts, and water from *Discovery* to the ISS craft. She also operated the RMS during a lengthy space walk by two of her fellow astronauts. Ochoa's most recent space journey, in April 2002, was on the *Atlantis,* which visited the ISS and marked the thirteenth shuttle flight to the space station. During the eleven-day mission the three-person crew installed the S-Zero (SO) truss on the ISS. The truss was the first segment of the main backbone of the station, which would be expanded to carry solar panel wings and radiators. The crew also moved around the station for the first time. Between space shuttle flights, Ochoa has held a variety of other positions with NASA at the Johnson Space Center. She has tested flight software, served as crew representative for robotics, and worked at mission control (communications base for all spaceflight) as spacecraft communicator. She also directed the crew involved in the ISS project, a high priority for NASA in the twenty-first century. In 2003 she held the position of deputy director of flight crew operations.

Shares experiences with students

In addition to receiving the Congressional Hispanic Caucus Medallion of Excellence Role Model Award in 1993, Ochoa holds numerous other honors for her achievements. These include Space Act Tech Brief Awards in 1992; Space Flight Medals in 1993, 1994, and 1999; an Outstanding Leadership Medal in 1995; and an Exceptional Service Medal in 1997. Others are the Women in Aerospace Outstanding Achievement Award, the Hispanic Engineer Albert Baez Award for Outstanding Technical Contribution to Humanity, and the Hispanic Heritage Leadership Award. In addition, Ochoa has served as a member of the Presidential Commission on the Celebration of Women in American History. Ochoa is frequently asked to speak to students and teachers about her career and the success she has achieved as NASA's first Hispanic female astronaut. She regards this part of her job as an unexpected bonus and enjoys having the chance to inspire young people to study mathematics and science. Ochoa and her husband, Coe Fulmer Miles, have two children. She flies her own single-engine plane for recreation, and still plays the flute, as she did in high school.

As a veteran of four shuttle flights and countless hours of training, Ochoa compares her experiences with the life of a student. "Being an astronaut allows you to learn continuously, like you do in school," she remarked in an article published in the *Stanford University School of Engineering Annual Report, 1997–98*. "One flight you're working on atmospheric research. The next, it's bone density studies or space station design." But she readily admitted that other components of space flight such as the launch, weightlessness, and seeing Earth from afar have a strong appeal as well: "What engineer wouldn't want those experiences?"

For More Information

Books

Camp, Carole Ann. *American Women Inventors*. Berkeley Heights, NJ: Enslow, 2004.

Machamer, Gene. *Hispanic American Profiles*. New York: Ballantine Books, 1996.

Stille, Darlene R. *Extraordinary Women Scientists*. New York: Scholastic Library, 1995.

Periodicals

López, Nora. "La Primera Astronaut [The First Astronaut]." *Latina*. (May 1998): pp. 60–63.

Web Sites

"Astronaut Bio: Ellen Ochoa." *Johnson Space Center, NASA.* http://www.jsc.nasa.gov/Bios/htmlbios/ochoa.html (accessed on June 29, 2004).

"Ellen Ochoa." *Inventors.About.com.* http://inventors.about.com/library/inventors/blochoa.htm (accessed on June 29, 2004).

"Ellen Ochoa." *Stanford University School of Engineering Annual Report, 1997–98.* http://soe.stanford.edu/AR02-03/index.html (accessed on June 29, 2004).

"Rodolfo Neri Vela." *Encyclopedia Astronautica.* http://www.astronautix. com/astros/nerivela.htm (accessed on June 29, 2004).

Other Sources

Ochoa, Ellen. Speech to Congressional Hispanic Caucus, 1993. Cited in *Contemporary Heroes and Heroines, Book IV.* Detroit: Gale Group, 2000.

Sally Ride

Born May 26, 1951 (Encino, California)

American astronaut

Sally Ride was the first American woman to travel into outer space. With this feat she became, at age thirty-one, the youngest American sent into orbit. For women, Ride's historic flight was a significant step forward. It also represented the end to a story that began more than twenty years earlier with the **Mercury 13** (see entry). Thirteen women fliers had met the same qualifications as the first male astronauts, but they were not permitted to enter the training program. After her ventures into space, Ride rose to prominence within the National Aeronautics and Space Administration (NASA). She currently holds an academic position, and she is a vital force in promoting math and science education for young students.

Trains as astronaut

Sally Kristen Ride was born on May 26, 1951, in Encino, California, near Los Angeles. She is the older daughter of Dale Burdell, a political science professor, and Carol Joyce (Anderson) Ride. During her childhood, Sally's parents encouraged her curiosity and sense of adventure. When she was nine years old, her father took a sabbatical (temporary leave) from his

Sally Ride. *(NASA)*

teaching position at Santa Monica Community College and the family traveled throughout Europe for a year. An outstanding athlete who started playing tennis at age ten, Ride won a scholarship to Westlake School for Girls in Los Angeles. Ride eventually ranked eighteenth nationally on the junior circuit. After graduating from Westlake in 1968, Ride enrolled at Swarthmore College in Pennsylvania, but she soon dropped out to pursue a tennis career. Within three months, however, she decided she did not have the skills to become a professional player. Ride then entered Stanford University in California, where she received two bachelor's degrees—in science and in literature—in 1973. She remained at Stanford, earning a master's degree in physics two years later and a doctorate degree in physics, astronomy, and astrophysics in 1978.

After completing her Ph.D. dissertation (a long research paper on a topic in one's field of specialization) in 1978, Ride applied for astronaut training. She simply responded to a NASA advertisement seeking applicants for the program, which had recently begun accepting women. Ride told interviewers for *Scholastic Scope* magazine that "In the 1970s, many professions were being opened to women. And NASA recognized that this was a time of change. There was no reason a woman couldn't become an astronaut." Ride was working as a research assistant when she was chosen as one of thirty-five candidates (six of them women) from an original field of eight thousand applicants. Even after three years of studying X-ray astrophysics, she had to go back to the classroom to gain skills to be part of a team of astronauts. The program included basic science and math, meteorology, guidance, navigation, and computers as well as flight training on a T-38 jet trainer and other operational simulations. Ride was selected as part of the ground-support crew for the second (November 1981) and third (March 1982) space shuttle flights. (A space shuttle is a craft that transports people and cargo between Earth and space.) Among her duties was being the capsule communicator, or "capcom," which involves relaying commands from the ground to the shuttle crew. This experience prepared her to be an astronaut.

Makes historic flight

Ride took her first trip into space in 1983 aboard the space shuttle *Challenger*. The mission was launched on June 18 from Cape Canaveral in Florida, orbited Earth for six days, and landed on June 24 at Edwards Air Force Base in California. Among the shuttle team's tasks were the deployment (the release while in orbit) of international satellites (objects that orbit in space) and numerous research experiments supplied by a range of groups, such as a naval research lab and various high school students. Ride and fellow crew member John M. Fabian (1939–) operated the shuttle's robot arm, accomplishing the first satellite deployment and retrieval using such a device. Ride's second flight, again on the *Challenger*, took place between October 5 and October 13, 1984. This time, the robot arm was put to some unusual applications, including "ice-busting" (removing ice) on the shuttle's exterior and readjusting a radar antenna. Objectives during this longer period in orbit covered scientific observations of Earth, demonstrations of potential satellite refueling techniques, and deployment of (releasing into orbit) a satellite.

Sixteen years after her first venture into space, Ride reflected on the experience in the *Scholastic Scope* interview. "The thing I'll remember most about the flight," she said, "is that it was fun. I'm sure it was the most fun I'll ever have in my life." When asked what she thought about being the only woman in a five-member crew, she answered, "It was like flying with four brothers, except there were no fights."

Ride was preparing for a third flight, but training was cut short in January 1986, when the ***Challenger*** (see entry) exploded in midair shortly after takeoff. The entire crew was killed. President Ronald Reagan (1911–2004; served 1981–89) immediately formed the Rogers Commission to investigate the disaster, and he appointed Ride as the only astronaut member of the panel. According to the commission's final report the 12-foot rubber washers called O-rings, which are placed between the steel segments of booster rockets, had failed under stress. The O-rings had long been considered a problem by NASA technicians. According to a *Chicago Tribune* article at the time, many people at NASA began to feel that their safety had been endangered without their knowledge. Ride was quoted as saying, "I think that we may have been misleading people into thinking that this [a space shuttle flight] is a routine operation."

Following her work on the Rogers Commission, Ride was named special assistant for long-range and strategic planning to NASA administrator James C. Fletcher (1919–1991) in Washington, D.C. Ride created the Office of Exploration, a task force on the future of the space program, and wrote a status report titled *Leadership and America's Future in Space*. In the report Ride proposed changing NASA goals in order to prevent a "space race" mentality that might pressure management and personnel into taking risks. She suggested that NASA take environmental and international research goals into consideration, and that the agency pledge to inform the public about space missions. In addition, Ride cited the lack of math and science proficiency among American high school graduates as a potential problem. For instance, only 6 percent of Americans tested that they had competent knowledge in these fields, compared with up to 90 percent in other nations.

Serves on disaster commissions

Ride left NASA in 1987 to join the Center for International Security and Arms Control at Stanford. Two years later she became the director of the California Space Institute and a physics professor at the University of California at San Diego. In 2003 Ride was once again called upon to provide her expertise in the investigation of a NASA disaster. On February 1 the space shuttle *Columbia* (see box in **Challenger Crew** entry) broke apart over the western United States while returning to Earth from a sixteen-day mission. The day after the accident NASA administrator Sean O'Keefe (1956–) organized the Columbia Accident Investigation Board (CAIB). By the end of the month, however, the board had not made significant progress. After special hearings the U.S. Congress determined that, among other shortcomings, board members lacked sufficient technical knowledge. Pressured to bring in outside experts, in early March O'Keefe appointed Ride; Douglas Osheroff (1945–), a Nobel prizewinner in physics; and John Logsdon (1937–), director of the Space Policy Institute. On August 26 the CAIB issued a final report stating that the *Columbia* accident was caused in large part by deficiencies within NASA and by a lack of government oversight.

Promotes math and science education

In addition to her professional duties, Ride is active in promoting math and science education for children and young adults. Interviewed by *T. H. E. Journal* in 1999, Ride was asked how boys and girls could be encouraged to become interested in scientific exploration. "It's pretty clear," Ride responded, "that the key is to start very early, in elementary school and middle school. Kids are naturally curious when they're in second and third and fourth grade. . . . You can start them on a path toward scientific literacy [knowledge] and appreciating that these are interesting topics. Then, as they get older, they'll appreciate that they're important topics."

Sally Ride's Club and Science Festivals

In collaboration with Imaginary Lines Inc., in 2001 Sally Ride launched the Sally Ride Club and the Sally Ride Science Festival. These organizations were created for girls who want to learn more about science. Sally Ride Clubs have been started in cities throughout the country by teachers, YM-CAs, Girl Scouts, Girls Clubs, and even Boys Clubs. Activities and materials are provided by Imaginary Lines. Using the club's interactive Web site, participants can chat with one another and send suggestions for space projects to astronauts.

The Sally Ride Science Festival is held each year in several U.S. cities. At these events girls have a chance to interact with Ride, participate in workshops, and build projects. Typical projects include recreating a volcano, using kitchen chemicals, and making a rocket out of Legos. According to an article in the *Christian Science Monitor,* six hundred girls, teachers, and parents attended the San Diego festival in 2002.

Sally Ride showing her website for the Sally Ride Club. *(AP/Wide World Photos)*

The Sally Ride Club Web site is http://www.sallyrideclub.com; the Sally Ride Science Festival Web site is http://www.sallyridefestivals.com.

After serving for a year as president of space.com, an information Web site for the space industry, Ride founded EarthKAM in 1999. This Internet-based NASA project provides middle-school students with an opportunity to take pictures of Earth from space and then download them. Ride's most recent endeavor is Imaginary Lines, an organization that encourages girls to become interested in science, math, and technology through the Sally Ride Club and the Sally Ride Science Festivals (see box on this page). Ride is also the author or coauthor of five books for children: *To Space and Back, Voyager: An Adventure to the Edge of the Solar System, The Third*

Planet: Exploring the Earth from Space, The Mystery of Mars, and *Exploring Our Solar System.*

For her work in education Ride was presented the Jefferson Award for Public Service by the American Institute for Public Service in 1984. Among her other honors are two National Spaceflight Medals in recognition of her two groundbreaking shuttle missions in 1983 and 1984. She also served on the transition team of newly elected president Bill Clinton (1946–; served 1993–2001) in 1992. Her most recent honor came in 2003, when she was inducted into the Astronaut Hall of Fame at Kennedy Space Center in Florida. Besides being the first American woman astronaut and the youngest American astronaut, Ride was the first to marry another astronaut during active duty. In 1982 she married Steven Alan Hawley (1951–), a Ph.D. from the University of California, who had joined NASA with a background in astronomy and astrophysics. They were divorced five years later.

For More Information

Books

Holden, Henry M. *Pioneering Astronaut Sally Ride.* Berkeley Heights, NJ: Enslow, 2004.

Hurwitz, Sue. *Sally Ride: Shooting for the Stars.* New York: Fawcett, 1989.

Woodmansee, Laura S. *Women Astronauts.* Burlington, Ontario: Collector's Guide, 2002.

Periodicals

Cohen, Russell, and Laine Falk. "On Top of the World." *Scholastic Scope* (March 11, 2002): p. 12.

"From the Cosmos to the Classroom: Q and A with Sally Ride." *T. H. E. Journal* (March 1999): pp. 20+.

Rowley, Storer, and Michael Tackett. "Internal Memo Charges NASA Compromised Safety." *Chicago Tribune* (March 6, 1986): section 1, p. 8.

Steindorf, Sara. "Sally Ride Enters New Frontier: Convincing Girls That Science Is Cool." *Christian Science Monitor* (March 19, 2002): p. 12.

Web Sites

"Sally Kristen Ride: First American Woman in Space." *Lucidcafé.* http://www2.lucidcafe.com/lucidcafe/library/96may/ride.html (accessed on June 29, 2004).

Sally Ride Science Club. http://www.sallyrideclub.com (accessed on June 29, 2004).

Sally Ride Science Festival. http://www.sallyridefestivals.com (accessed on June 29, 2004).

Other Sources

Intimate Portrait: Sally Ride. Unapix Video, 2000.

Women in Space. Vision Quest Video, 2000.

Valentina Tereshkova

Born March 6, 1937 (Maslennikovo, Russia)

Russian cosmonaut

"I'm trying to memorize, fix all the feelings, the peculiarities of this descending, to tell those, who will be conquering space after me."

Valentina Tereshkova made history by becoming the first woman to fly in space. She accomplished this feat in 1963, at the height of the former Soviet Union's space program. In 1957 the Soviets had launched *Sputnik 1*, the first man-made satellite (an object that orbits in space), and in 1961 cosmonaut **Yuri Gagarin** (1934–1968; see entry) had made the first successful orbit of Earth onboard the spacecraft *Vostok 1.* These triumphs took place during the Cold War (1945–91), a period of hostile relations between the Soviet Union and the United States. Since World War II (1939–45) the two super-powers had been engaged in an arms race for military superiority. Now the competition included a space race, and the Soviets were winning. The United States had sent its first astronaut, Alan Shepard (1923–1998; see box in **John Glenn** [1921–] entry), into orbit, but this was the only real U.S. space accomplishment so far. Tereshkova's flight therefore had added significance because it represented yet another Soviet victory.

Tereshkova did not participate in any other space missions, but she became an instant celebrity throughout the world. After the fall of the Soviet Union in 1989, however,

Valentina Tereshkova. *(© Bettmann/Corbis)*

there was minimal publicity about her outside of Russia. At the turn of the twenty-first century, attention was once again focused on the first woman in space, who celebrated the fortieth anniversary of her flight in 2003. That year the American journal *Quest: The History of Spaceflight* published the English translation of Tereshkova's memoir, originally titled "Stars Are Calling," which she wrote in 1963.

Applies to cosmonaut program

Valentina Vladimirovna Tereshkova was born on March 6, 1937, in the small village of Maslennikovo near the Russian city of Yaroslavl. Her father, Vladimir Tereshkova, was a tractor driver on a collective farm and her mother, Elena Fyodorovna Tereshkova, worked at the Krasny Perekop cotton mill. Vladimir was killed while serving with the Soviet army in World War II, leaving Elena to raise two-year-old Valentina and two other children—a daughter, Ludmilla, and a son, Vladimir. Valentina was not able to attend school until she was ten because she stayed at home to help her mother. Eventually Elena moved the family to Yaroslavl, where she found work in a textile factory.

At age sixteen Valentina was an apprentice (a person being trained for a skill) in the Yaroslavl tire factory, and in 1955 she took a job as a loom operator at the Red Canal Cotton Mill. In the meantime she graduated from the Light Industry Technical School after taking correspondence courses. She was also politically active, first joining the Komsomol (Young Communist League) and then advancing to membership in the Communist Party (the political organization that controlled the Soviet Union). In 1959 she joined the Yaroslavl Air Sports Club and became a skilled amateur parachutist, making 126 successful jumps. Recalling her first parachute jump in the article published in *Quest,* she wrote, "I came home later than usual. Perhaps there was something unusual in my appearance, because mom asked, 'Has anything happened? You are so strange today.' To tell her that I joined the parachute club was too hard for me. I didn't want to trouble her; besides, I was not completely sure about the success of my new adventure."

Following the Soviet Union's first successful unmanned space launch in May 1960, Tereshkova became interested in the idea of space flight. After Gagarin made the first manned space flight, she was so enthusiastic that she wrote a letter to the Soviet Space Commission asking to be considered for cosmonaut training. The Space Commission filed her letter along with several thousand others it had received. In early 1962, however, **Sergei Korolev** (1907–1966; see entry), head of the Soviet Space commission, came up with the idea that the Soviet Union could score an important public relations coup against the United States by sending a woman into space. (The United States did not accept women for astronaut training for another twenty years; see **Sally Ride** [1951–] entry.)

Trains as cosmonaut

Although Korolev had originated the idea of sending a woman into space, Soviet premier Nikita Khrushchev (1894–1971) made the final decision. He wanted the choice to be an ordinary Russian worker, so he was not interested in applicants who were highly skilled scientists or airplane pilots. On February 16, 1962, Tereshkova and four other women were chosen for cosmonaut training. Tereshkova was instructed not to tell her friends or family what she would be doing. Instead she told them that she was training for a women's precision skydiving team. All five candidates participated in an intensive, eighteen-month training program at the Baikonur space center. They worked in a centrifuge and an isolation chamber, underwent tests in weightless conditions, and made 120 parachute jumps in spacesuits. They were also given jet pilot training. Since Tereshkova had no scientific background, she had difficulty with rocket theory and spacecraft engineering. Nevertheless, she reportedly applied herself to the course and mastered it.

Makes historic flight

At 12:30 P.M. on June 16, 1963, Junior Lieutenant Tereshkova became the first woman to be launched into space. Her radio call sign, Chaika (Seagull), would become the nickname by which Russians know her even today. Tereshkova reported the view from space, remarking on the beauty of Earth and the universe. She was later seen smiling on Soviet and European television, pencil and logbook floating weightlessly before her face. *Vostok 6* made forty–eight orbits (1.2 million miles; 1.93 million kilometers) in 70 hours, 50 minutes, coming within 3.1 miles (4.98 kilometers) of *Vostok 5*. The *Vostok 5* had been launched on June 14 in a separate orbit and was piloted by Valery Bykovsky (1934–). A dual female flight had been planned, but Bykovsky, a male cosmonaut, had been substituted at the last minute (see box on page 184).

While in space the two cosmonauts conversed through radio contact and sent television pictures back to Earth. Tereshkova carried out a series of physiological tests to learn about the effects of weightlessness and space travel on humans. To return to Earth she fired the retro-engine to brake the rocket. As the space capsule reentered Earth's atmosphere, flames surrounded the capsule. In her memoir Tereshkova described this

Plan for Dual Female Flight Canceled

While the first women cosmonauts underwent training, Soviet officials were having intense discussions behind the scenes. When Sergei Korolev suggested sending a woman into space, officials had conceived an even more dramatic idea—a dual female flight, with women pilots for both the *Vostok 5* and the *Vostok 6*. The two spacecraft would be launched a day apart and fly for three days in March and April 1963. There was a problem with the plan, however. Tereshkova was an acceptable choice for *Vostok 5,* but some officials were concerned about the candidate for *Vostok 6.*

The candidate was Valentina Leonidovna Ponomaryova (1933–), a Ukranian who had scored the best test results. But officials considered her to be too aggressive and not sufficiently loyal to the Soviet cause. In response to the question "What do you want from life?" she said in *Encyclopedia As-*
tronautica, "I want to take everything it can offer." This answer proved that she was promoting herself and not committed to glorifying the Communist Party. Ponomaryova also traveled without a male escort, which was regarded as unseemly behavior for a woman. The idea for a dual female flight was finally discarded at the last minute. It was decided that Tereshkova would pilot *Vostok 6* and a male cosmonaut, Valery Bykovsky (1934–), would pilot *Vostok 5.* The flights were delayed two months, until June.

Ponomaryova and the three other women cosmonauts never flew in space. A civilian pilot and a member of the Academy of Sciences, Ponomaryova left space service in 1969. She works in orbital mechanics at the spaceflight training center. Ponomaryova is married to cosmonaut Yuri Ponomaryov (1932–), with whom she has two children.

moment: "Again the pressure pushes me in the chair, shuts my eyes. I notice the dark red tongues of flame outside the windows. I'm trying to memorize, fix all the feelings, the peculiarities of this descending, to tell those who will be conquering space after me." The spacecraft stabilized under a small parachute, and Tereshkova was ejected through the side hatch. She landed with the aid of a regular parachute. Her flight confirmed Soviet test results that women had the same resistance as men to the physical and psychological stresses of space.

Becomes world celebrity

After their return, Tereshkova and Bykovsky were hailed in Moscow's Red Square. On June 22, at the Kremlin,

Valentina Tereshkova and fellow cosmonaut Valery Bykovsky are honored by the Soviet Premier Nikita Khrushchev for their historic space flight that made Tereshkova the first woman in space.

(© Bettmann/Corbis)

Tereshkova was named a Hero of the Soviet Union and was decorated by Presidium Chairman Leonid Brezhnev (1906–1982) with the Order of Lenin and the Gold Star Medal. A symbol of emancipated Soviet women, she toured the world as a goodwill ambassador promoting the equality of the sexes in the Soviet Union. She received a standing ovation at the United Nations. With Gagarin, she traveled to Cuba in October as a guest of the Cuban Women's Federation, and then went to the International Aeronautical Federation Conference in Mexico.

On November 3, 1963, Tereshkova married Soviet cosmonaut Colonel Andrian Nikolayev (1929–), who had orbited Earth sixty-four times in 1962 onboard the *Vostok 3*. Their daughter Yelena Adrianovna Nikolayeva was born on June 8,

1964, and was carefully studied by doctors, who were fearful that her parents' space exposure may have damaged her. No ill effects were found. After the flight, Tereshkova continued as an aerospace engineer in the space program, while at the same time becoming active in Soviet politics, feminism, and culture. She was a deputy to the Supreme Soviet (1966–89), a People's Deputy (1989–91), and a member of the Supreme Soviet Presidium (1974–89). She also served on the Soviet Women's Committee (1968–87), becoming its head in 1977. Tereshkova led the USSR's International Cultural and Friendship Union (1987–91) and chaired the Russian Association of International Cooperation. In 2003 she held the rank of general and headed the Russian Centre for International Science and Cultural Cooperation.

Tereshkova summarized her views on women and science in "Women in Space," an article published in the American journal *Impact of Science on Society*: "I believe a woman should always remain a woman and nothing feminine should be alien to her," Tereshkova wrote. "At the same time I strongly feel that no work done by a woman in the field of science or culture or whatever, however vigorous or demanding, can enter into conflict with her ancient 'wonderful mission'—to love, to be loved—and with her craving for the bliss of motherhood. On the contrary, these two aspects of her life can complement each other perfectly."

For More Information

Books

Edmonson, Catherine M. *Extraordinary Women: Women Who Have Changed History*. Avon, MA: Adams Media Corp., 1999.

Oberg, James E. *Red Star in Orbit*. New York: Macmillan, 1977.

Woodmansee, Laura S. *Women Astronauts*. Burlington, Ontario: Collector's Guide Publishing, 2002.

Periodicals

Block, Jen, and Marissa Ferrari. "Who Knew?" *Ms.* (December 1999/January 2000): pp. 52+.

"The Extraordinary Destiny of an 'Ordinary' Woman." *Russian Life* (May/June 2003): pp. 19–20.

O'Neil, Bill. "Whatever Became of Valentina Tereshkova?" *New Scientist* (August 14, 1993): pp. 21+.

Tereshkova, Valentina. "The First Lady of Space Remembers." *Quest: The History of Spaceflight Quarterly* 10, No 2 (2003): pp. 6–21.

"Women in Space." *Impact of Science on Society.* (January–March, 1970): pp. 5–12.

Web Sites

"Valentina Leonidovna Ponomaryova."*Encyclopedia Astronautica.* http://www.astronautix.com/astros/ponryova.htm (accessed on June 30, 2004).

"Valentina Tereshkova." *Encyclopedia Astronautica.* http://www.astronautix.com/astros/terhkova.htm (accessed on June 29, 2004).

"Valentina Tereshkova." *Fun Social Studies.* http://www.funsocialstudies.learninghaven.com/articles/valentina_tereshkova.htm (accessed on June 29, 2004).

"Valentina Tereshkova." *StarChild.* http://starchild.gsfc.nasa.gov/docs/StarChild/whos_who_level1/tereshkova.html (accessed on June 29, 2004).

Konstantin Tsiolkovsky

Born September 17, 1857 (Izhevskoye, Russia)
Died September 19, 1935 (Kaluga, Russia)

Russian aerospace engineer

"I had to figure out
everything by myself."

Konstantin Tsiolkovsky (pronounced KAHN-stan-tyeen tsee-ohl-KAHV-skee) was one of the greatest Russian scientists of the early twentieth century. Along with American physicist **Robert Goddard** (1882–1945; see entry) and German physicist **Hermann Oberth** (1894–1989; see entry), he is considered a founding father of spaceflight. Almost entirely self-educated, Tsiolkovsky studied and wrote about a wide range of scientific topics, but he is best known for his pioneering work in astronautics. In the 1890s he began calculations on the mathematics and physics of spaceflight, which he saw as the first step in the colonization of space by humans.

Throughout his life Tsiolkovsky saw himself as a scientist who not only worked on abstract problems but also strived for the betterment of human existence. On October 4, 1957, twenty-two years after his death, the Soviet Union launched *Sputnik 1,* the world's first artificial satellite (an object that orbits in space; see **Sergei Korolev** [1907–1966] entry). Soviet officials attempted to send the satellite into space on September 17, the one hundredth anniversary of Tsiolkovsky's birth. Although that deadline was not met, the flight was dedicated to Tsiolkovsky.

Konstantin Tsiolkovsky. *(Library of Congress)*

Loses his hearing

Konstantin Eduardovich Tsiolkovsky was born on September 17, 1857, in the Russian village of Izhevskoye in the province of Ryazan. His mother was the former Maria Yumasheva and his father, Eduard Tsiolkovsky, was a forester, teacher, and minor government official. The Tsiolkovsky family moved frequently while Konstantin was young, and their financial situation was often difficult. Until age ten he led a typical childhood, playing games, ice skating, flying kites, and climbing fences. Then disaster struck in 1867, when Tsiolkovsky became seriously ill and lost his hearing. For a long time he was deeply depressed about his misfortune, but he gradually worked his way through this difficult period. He then pursued an intense interest in science, teaching himself at every step along the way. In his autobiography Tsiolkovsky explained that "there were very few books, and I had no teachers at all. . . . There were no hints, no aid from anywhere; there was a great deal that I couldn't understand in those books and I had to figure out everything by myself."

In 1873 Tsiolkovsky's father acquired enough money to send him to Moscow. Tsiolkovsky continued his self-education in the rich intellectual environment of the city. He devised an ear trumpet that enabled him to hear lectures, but he could not afford to enroll in a formal college or university program. At the end of three years in Moscow, Tsiolkovsky returned to his hometown. He continued to teach himself science, building models of various kinds of machines and carrying out original experiments.

Writes about his ideas

In 1879 Tsiolkovsky passed the examination for a teacher's license and took a job as instructor of arithmetic and geometry at the Borovsk Uyzed School in Kaluga. Continuing his research, in 1880 he wrote his first scientific paper, "The Graphical Depiction of Sensations," an effort to express human sensations in strict mathematical formulas. A year later Tsiolkovsky wrote "The Theory of Gasses," which he submitted to the Russian Physico-Chemical Society. The group admired his work and offered support for his future research but decided that the paper did not qualify for publication. In 1883 he completed "On the Theoretical Mechanics of Living," an analysis of the ways natural forces, such as gravity, affect the structure and movement of human beings. Although this paper was not published, the Physico-Chemical Society was impressed and accepted Tsiolkovsky as a member.

Tsiolkovsky started the next phase of his work, developing theories of flight and aircraft, in the mid-1880s. His interest in flight can be traced at least to age fifteen, when he posed for himself the problem of determining the size a balloon must be in order to carry people into the air. More than a decade later he wrote on this subject in "The Theory and Experiment of a Horizontally Elongated Balloon." He designed a metal lighter-than-air machine, now called a dirigible, but he could not obtain funding to build a working model. Those who granted money for scientific research saw no practical use for such an invention.

Tsiolkovsky was also thinking about heavier-than-air craft. One of his first papers on the subject was "On the Problem of Flying by Means of Wings," which he wrote in 1890. In this work he completed one of the earliest mathematical studies of forces operating on the wings and body of an aircraft. He then produced studies on the shape of aircraft fuselages (FYOO-seh-lahg-ez; the main bodies of airplanes), the use of internal engines, the shape of wings, and other important features of heavier-than-air machines. During this time he married Barbara E. Sokolova, the daughter of a local preacher. They later had three daughters and four sons.

Tsiolkovsky was aware that most of his ideas needed to be tested in actual experiments. Taking a step toward this goal, he designed the first wind tunnel built in Russia. Put in operation in Kaluga in 1897, the wind tunnel produced a stream of air that could be forced over aircraft bodies and wings of various sizes, shapes, and designs. Tsiolkovsky described the preliminary results of his experiments in "Air Pressure on Surfaces Introduced into an Artificial Air Flow." Encouraged by his success, he appealed to the Russian Academy of Sciences for a grant that would allow him to expand his wind tunnel experiments. He was successful in getting an award of 470 rubles (about $235 at the time) to build a larger wind tunnel. In May 1900 he began construction of a larger wind tunnel, and he undertook experiments before the end of that year.

Develops theories of space travel

Tsiolkovsky will be remembered probably best for his accomplishments in the field of astronautics, or space travel. He had started thinking about space travel during his stay in Moscow. By the late 1870s he was producing ideas about spacecraft and space travel at an astonishing rate, touching on virtually every aspect of the subject. In about 1879, for example, he designed an instrument for measuring the effects of gravitational acceleration (an increase in the force of gravity) on the human body. Four years later, he outlined the mechanism by which a jet rocket could carry an object into space.

Launch of *Gemini 3* **in 1965.** *(NASA)*

In the early 1890s Tsiolkovsky wrote about travel to the Moon, other planets, and beyond. Published in 1895, his paper "Dreams of the Earth and Sky and the Effects of Universal Gravitation" introduced the concept of an artificial Earth. He described it as being somewhat similar to the Moon. By the following year Tsiolkovsky had identified the mathematical formulas needed to describe the movement of a spacecraft. A year later he worked out the fundamental relationship between the velocity (speed) and mass of a rocket and the exhaust velocity of the propellant used to send it into space. That formula is now known as the basic rocket equation.

As a result of his research Tsiolkovsky realized that the most efficient way of placing rockets into space is to arrange them in packets, or "cosmic rocket trains." Writing about rocket trains in an article in 1929, he originated the concept that is today called "rocket staging." This process involves a series of rocket engines being fired at specific intervals to put an object into space. By the end of his life Tsiolkovsky had investigated virtually every technical question pertaining to space travel. He determined the kinds of fuels that would work best as rocket propellants, eventually settling on a mixture of liquid hydrogen and liquid oxygen as the best choice.

Envisions colonization of space

In 1903 Tsiolkovsky completed a historic paper, "Investigations of Outer Space by Reaction Devices," which summarized his work. The paper did not actually appear in print until it was published in the journal *Vestnik vozdukhoplavaniya* (*Herald of Aeronautics*; 1911–12). This paper also outlined Tsiolkovsky's views on the colonization of space. He argued that space travel should not be viewed as some abstract scientific experiment but as a way of creating new human communities outside Earth. In 1920 Tsiolkovsky published *Beyond the Earth,* a popular book that described space travel and living in space to nonscientists.

Tsiolkovsky's first sixty years were extremely difficult, not only because he lived in poverty but also because his colleagues were indifferent to his work. The October Revolution (an overthrow of the Russian monarchy by the Communist Party) of 1917 brought a dramatic change in Tsiolkovsky's situation. He was elected a member of the Socialist Academy and given a pension by the Council of the Peoples' Commissariats of the Russian Federation. For the first time in his life he could concentrate on scientific research with some degree of comfort. An indication of the impact of this pension on Tsiolkovsky's productivity is the fact that about 25 percent of his more than five hundred papers were written in the six decades between 1857 and 1917. He wrote the remaining 75 percent in the last two decades of his life.

In the late 1920s Tsiolkovsky spent more time on problems of aeronautics (the science of flight). Typical of his papers from this period were "A New Airplane" and "Reactive Airplane" as well as studies of topics unrelated to air and space travel. Among them were a common alphabet, the future of Earth and humanity, and solar energy. During his lifetime he also wrote science-fiction books, including *On the Moon*

(1895), *Dreams of the Earth and Sky* (1895), and *Beyond the Earth* (1920). In an effort to secure a pension for his family, on September 13, 1935, Tsiolkovsky willed his books and papers to the Communist Party and the Soviet government. He died at his home in Kaluga six days later, and the government honored him with a state funeral. He was buried in the Kaluga cemetery near his home, which was later made into a museum. During World War II (1939–45) the museum was badly damaged. After the launching of *Sputnik 1,* the Tsiolkovsky home-museum became a popular sightseeing stop for visitors.

For More Information

Books

Dickson, Paul. *Sputnik: The Launch of the Space Race.* Toronto, Ontario: MacFarlane, Walter & Ross, 2002.

Heppenheimer, T. A. *Countdown: A History of Space Flight.* New York: John Wiley & Sons, 1987.

Tsiolkovsky, Konstantin. *K. E. Tsiolkovsky: Selected Works.* Translated by G. Yankovsky. Moscow: Mir, 1968.

Periodicals

Frazier, Allison. "They Gave Us Space: Space Pioneers of the 20th Century." *Ad Astra* (January/February 2000): pp. 25–26.

Yeomans, Donald. "'Space Travel Is Utter Bilge.'" *Astronomy* (January 2004): pp. 48+.

Zak, Anatoly. "Konstantin Tsiolkovsky Slept Here." *Air & Space Smithsonian* (August/September 2002): pp. 62+.

Web Sites

"Konstantin Tsiolkovsky." *Inventors.About.com* http://www.inventors.about.com/library/inventors/blrocketTsiolkovsky.htm (accessed on June 29, 2004).

Lethbridge, Cliff. "Konstantin Eduardovitch Tsiolkovsky." *Spaceline.* http://www.spaceline.org/history/21.html (accessed on July 2, 2004).

The Life of Konstantin Eduardovitch Tsiolkovsky, 1857–1935. www.informatics.org/museum/tsiol.html (accessed on June 29, 2004).

Wernher von Braun

Born March 23, 1912 (Wirsitz, Germany)
Died June 16, 1977 (Alexandria, Virginia)

German-born American rocket engineer

Wernher von Braun was the most famous rocket engineer of the twentieth century. He began his career in Germany, where he developed the revolutionary V-2 rocket during World War II (1939–45). Fleeing to the United States at the end of the war, he became an important figure in the American rocket and space programs. Teams of engineers under his direction designed the Redstone, Jupiter, and Pershing missiles (rockets that carry weapons). Von Braun then led development of the Jupiter C, Juno, and Saturn launch vehicles, which carried early U.S. satellites (objects that orbit in space) and spacecraft beyond Earth's atmosphere and ultimately to the Moon. Von Braun was both a celebrity and a national hero in the United States.

"To millions of Americans, [Wernher von Braun's] name was inextricably linked to our exploration of space and to the creative application of technology."

President Jimmy Carter

Begins developing rockets

Wernher Magnus Maximilian von Braun was born on March 23, 1912, in the town of Wirsitz (later Wyrzysk, Poland) in eastern Germany. He was the second of three sons of Baron Magnus Alexander Maximilian von Braun, a banker and government official, and Emmy (von Quistorp) von Braun, an

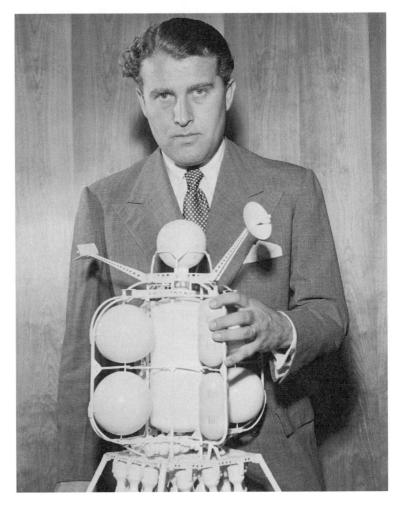

Wernher von Braun. *(© Bettmann/Corbis)*

accomplished musician and talented amateur astronomer (one who studies stars and planets). She encouraged her son's fascination with spaceflight by giving him a telescope and books by science-fiction writers Jules Verne (1828–1905) and **H. G. Wells** (1866–1946; see entry). Wernher attended the French Gymnasium (high school), where he excelled in languages but failed physics (the science that deals with matter and energy and their interactions) and mathematics. He then attended the Hermann Lietz School at Ettersburg Castle, a school famous for its advanced teaching methods and emphasis on practical trades. At age thirteen he attempted to read *Rockets* to *Planetary Space* by the space pioneer **Hermann Oberth** (1894–1989; see entry), but he could not understand Oberth's complicated mathematical formulas. He then vowed to master math and physics. Before he graduated, he was teaching mathematics and tutoring struggling students.

In 1930 von Braun enrolled at the Charlottenburg Institute of Technology in Berlin. He also joined the German Rocket Society, which was founded in part by Oberth. Von Braun soon became Oberth's student assistant, and together they successfully developed a small rocket engine. Funding for the project ended, however, and Oberth returned to his native Romania. Von Braun and his associates continued their work at an abandoned field outside Berlin, using the old buildings for laboratories and living quarters. For a time von Braun attended the Institute of Technology in Zurich, Switzerland. There he began the study of the physiological effects of space flight, conducting crude experiments with mice in a centrifuge (a machine used for simulating gravitational force). The experiments convinced him that humans could withstand the rapid acceleration and deceleration of space flight. He then returned to Charlottenburg Institute and to his work at the field where he launched his rockets.

Develops V-2 rocket

While von Braun and his associates were developing their rocket, Adolf Hitler (1889–1945) had manipulated his way to power as head of the Nazi Party. Elected chancellor of Germany on January 30, 1933, Hitler took over the parliament (legislative body) and suspended the constitution. He began ruling by decree (an order that has the force of law) and rebuilding the German army, which had been virtually dismantled by the Treaty of Versailles at the end of World War I (1914–18). The treaty had forbidden Germany to have any gun, cannon, or weapon with a bore (barrel) exceeding three inches. But the Nazis saw a loophole. The treaty did not envision rockets and made no mention of them, so German military planners hoped to develop rockets as weapons. German army ordnance (weapons) experts began frequent visits to von Braun's rocket field and monitored his team's rocket development work. Impressed with von Braun's knowledge and the scope of his imagination, ordnance officials invited him to continue his research at the army's facilities at Kummersdorf.

On October 1, 1932, von Braun officially joined the German Army Ordnance Office rocket program. Two years later he received a doctorate in physics from the University of Berlin. By that time he was technical director at Kummersdorf with a staff of eighty scientists and technicians. They had completed the preliminary design for the A-4 rocket, which became known as the V-2. This was an ambitious undertaking, since the missile was to be 45 feet (13.7 meters) long, deliver a one-ton (.97 metric ton) warhead (the section of a missile containing the explosive or chemical) to a target nearly 160 miles (257.4 kilometers) away. The rocket motor was also far more powerful than the largest liquid-fueled rocket motors then available. It could deliver a 25-ton (22.6 metric ton) thrust (upward force) for 60 seconds, compared to the 1.5 tons (1.36 metric tons) of thrust supplied by other rockets. The following year the group moved to new military facilities at Peenemünde, a town on the Baltic coast.

When Hitler started World War II by invading Poland in 1939, Germany gave rocket development the highest priority. Hitler envisioned using this new weapon in his quest to take over Europe. Von Braun's team encountered difficulties in perfecting their rocket, however, so the first launch did not occur at Peenemünde until October 3, 1942. Failures continued to plague the project, and fully operational V-2s were not fired until September 1944. By the end of the war in June 1945, approximately six thousand rockets were manufactured at an underground production site named *Mittelwerk*. The factory used the slave labor of concentration camp inmates and prisoners of war. (Concentration camps were compounds where the Nazis imprisoned and executed millions of people, including Jews and other "enemies of the state.") Although several thousand V-2s struck London, England; Antwerp, Belgium; and other Allied targets, they were not strategically significant in the German war effort. (The Allies were military forces led by Great Britain, the United States, and the Soviet Union.)

Heads U.S. rocket program

The Nazis wanted the rocket as a weapon of war, but von Braun had a different vision: space travel. His interest in space

Von Braun's Nazi Connections

Wernher Von Braun's prominence in American spaceflight efforts often overshadows his responsibility in the suffering and loss of life associated with the German V-2 rocket. Although he always gave credit to his team for the technical success of this and other programs, he clearly played a key role in the development of the missile. He and his army superior, General Walter Dornberger (1895–1980), were also successful in obtaining funding and other support for the V-2. Although he had no direct responsibility for production at *Mittelwerk,* von Braun was aware of conditions in the concentration camp that provided the factory's labor. Moreover, he had joined the Nazi Party on May 1, 1937, and became an officer in the elite SS (an abbreviation of *Schutzstaffel,* German for "Protective Corps") in 1940. (The SS started as Hitler's bodyguards, but under Heinrich Himmler [1900–1945] it came to control military police activities, Nazi intelligence, and the administration and maintenance of the death camps.)

While historians note that more research is needed on this subject, available American records support von Braun's claim that he was forced to join both organizations to avoid abandoning his rocketry work. He further stated that his motivation in building army missiles was their ultimate use in space travel and scientific endeavors. He said he was arrested by the Nazis in 1944 because he was not interested in using the V-2 as a weapon.

exploration rather than military application led to his arrest and imprisonment by the German secret police in 1944. The Nazis released him only after they realized that jailing their leading rocket scientist was an unwise political move. The program lurched backward without von Braun's leadership, disrupting Hitler's timetable for the war. When Germany was near collapse, von Braun led his associates and their families from Peenemünde to the Bavarian coast so they could surrender to the Americans. He reasoned that the United States was the nation most likely to use its resources for space exploration. The rocket team surrendered to U.S. forces on May 2, 1945, just before the Russians advanced into the abandoned rocket development center.

During interrogation by Allied intelligence officers, von Braun prepared a report in which he forecast trips to the Moon, orbiting satellites, and space stations. Recognizing the scope of von Braun's work, the U.S. Army authorized the

Various images of the V-2 rocket as it is launched during altitude tests at White Sands Proving Ground, near Las Cruces, New Mexico. Wernher von Braun, the creator of the V-2, helped the United States to improve their own missile capabilities as well as adapt the technology for use in space travel. *(AP/Wide World Photos)*

transfer of von Braun, 112 of his engineers and scientists, 100 V-2 rockets, and rocket technical data to the United States. They went to Fort Bliss near El Paso, Texas, as part of a military operation called Project Paperclip. (Project Paperclip was a program in which the United States military employed and protected numerous Nazi scientists and intelligence agents.) In 1946 they worked on rocket development and used captured V-2s for high-altitude research at the nearby White Sands Proving Ground in New Mexico.

Promotes spaceflight

In his free time von Braun wrote about space travel and corresponded with his family and his cousin, Maria von Quistorp. In early 1947 he obtained permission to return to Germany to marry Maria. The couple returned to Texas after the wedding; they later had three children. Von Braun continued work on V-2 launchings, conducting some of the earliest experiments in recording atmospheric conditions, photographing Earth from high altitudes, perfecting guidance systems, and conducting medical experiments with animals in space. He also completed his book, *The Mars Project,* an account of planetary exploration, but he was unable to interest a publisher until much later. In 1950 the von Braun team transferred to the Redstone Arsenal near Huntsville, Alabama, where between April 1950 and February 1956 it developed the Redstone rocket. On April 15, 1955, von Braun and forty of his associates became naturalized U.S. citizens.

The Redstone eventually played a significant role in America's early space program. During the 1950s, however, the Russian space program moved ahead of U.S. efforts. This development caused considerable alarm in the United States. Immediately after World War II, the United States and the former Soviet Union became engaged in the Cold War (1945–91), a period of political hostility that resulted in an arms race to achieve military superiority and a space race to be the first to send humans into space. Von Braun repeatedly warned American officials of Soviet advances in the space race, but his requests for permission to orbit a satellite (a man-made object that orbits in space) were denied.

Satellite delayed by politics

When the Soviet Union successfully orbited the *Sputnik 1* satellite in 1957, the U.S. government finally authorized von Braun's group to work on a satellite. Within ninety days the team developed the *Explorer 1* satellite from a modified Redstone rocket (the Jupiter C), with the cooperation of the Jet Propulsion Laboratory of the California Institute of Technology. The *Explorer 1* was launched into orbit on January 31, 1958.

Nearly four decades later, newly released government documents revealed information that had been kept secret: The administration of Dwight D. Eisenhower (1890–1969; served 1953-61), the U.S. president at the time of the *Sputnik 1* launch, had deliberately delayed production of an American satellite. This political strategy, unknown to von Braun, was a gamble to gain an edge over the Soviets in the use of spy satellites. In 1995 *Christian Science Monitor* reporter Robert C. Cowen published an article about the documents after they were declassified, or made public. According to Cowen, "when Sputnik 1 caught most Americans napping on Oct. 4, 1957, it also helped fulfill one of the Eisenhower administration's secret strategic goals. It helped legalize the future use of spy satellites." Soviet leader Nikita Khrushchev (1894–1971), Cowen wrote, "basked in a propaganda coup . . . [but he] also implicitly acknowledged a new limit to nation sovereignty. It ends short of the lowest orbit in which an earth satellite can travel. And that meant that the Soviet Union had nothing to complain about when the United States later orbited unarmed reconnaissance [spy] satellites."

Heads space center

In 1958 the United States created the National Aeronautics and Space Administration (NASA). Two years later von Braun was appointed director of the George C. Marshall Space Flight Center, a NASA agency at Huntsville. On October 27, 1961, NASA launched the first *Saturn 1* vehicle. It was 162 feet (49.37 meters) long, weighed 460 tons (417 metric tons) at liftoff, and rose to a height of 85 miles (136.76 kilometers). On November 9, 1967, the newer *Saturn 5* made its debut, and it was more than twice as long as the *Saturn 1.* Just before Christmas in 1968, a *Saturn 5* launch vehicle, developed under von Braun's direction, launched *Apollo 8,* the world's first spacecraft to travel to the Moon (see **Buzz Aldrin** [1930–] and **Neil Armstrong** [1930–] entries). In 1970 NASA transferred von Braun to its headquarters in Washington, D.C., where he became deputy associate administrator.

Von Braun resigned from NASA in 1972 to become vice president for engineering and development with Fairchild Industries of Germantown, Maryland. Besides his work for that aerospace firm, he promoted human space flight, helping to found the National Space Institute in 1975 and serving as its first president. An enthusiastic advocate for spaceflight, von Braun published numerous books and magazine articles, served as a consultant for television programs and films, and testified before the U.S. Congress about the possibilities of space flight. Perhaps most important in this regard were his contributions, with others, to a series of *Collier's* magazine articles (1952–53) and to a Walt Disney television series (1955–57). The articles and the series were enormously influential and, along with the fears aroused by the Soviet space program, energized American efforts to conquer space.

Von Braun received numerous awards, including the first Robert H. Goddard Memorial Trophy in 1958. The award was named for American physicist **Robert Goddard** (1882–1945; see entry), who was conducting rocket experiments around the time von Braun began working on the A-4. Goddard was highly secretive and rarely shared his research, but some historians suggest that the Germans may have managed to learn about his work. Von Braun also received the Distinguished Federal Civilian Service Award (presented by President Dwight D. Eisenhower) in 1959 and the National Medal of Science in 1977. In addition to his role as a space pioneer, von Braun pursued a wide range of interests. An accomplished musician, he played the piano and cello. He was also an ardent outdoorsman who enjoyed scuba diving, fishing, hunting, sailing, and flying. Von Braun died of cancer at a hospital in Alexandria, Virginia, on June 16, 1977.

For More Information

Books

Hunt, Linda. *Secret Agenda: The United States Government, Nazi Scientists, and Project Paperclip, 1945 to 1990.* New York: St. Martin's Press, 1991.

Ward, Bob. *Mr. Space: The Life of Wernher von Braun.* Washington, DC: Smithsonian Press, 2004.

Periodicals

Cowan, Robert C. "Declassified Papers Show U.S. Won Space Race After All." *Christian Science Monitor* (October 23, 1999): p. 15.

"Previously Unpublished von Braun Drawings." *Ad Astra* (July/August 2000): pp. 46–47.

Von Braun, Wernher. "Man on the Moon—The Journey." *Collier's* (October 18, 1952): pp. 52–60.

Von Braun, Wernher, with Cornelius Ryan. "Baby Space Station." *Collier's* (June 27, 1953): pp. 33–40.

Von Braun, Wernher, with Cornelius Ryan. "Can We Get to Mars?" *Collier's* (April 30, 1954): pp. 22–28.

Web Sites

Graham, John F. "A Biography of Wernher von Braun." *Marshall Space Flight Center, NASA.* http://liftoff.msfc.nasa.gov/academy/history/VonBraun/VonBraun.html (accessed on June 29, 2004).

"Wernher von Braun." http://www.spartacus.schoolnet.co.uk/USAbraun.htm (accessed on June 29, 2004).

H. G. Wells

Born September 21, 1866 (Bromley, Kent, England)
Died August 13, 1946 (London, England)

British writer

"Those who have never seen a living Martian can scarcely imagine the strange horror of its appearance."

The War of the Worlds

British writer H. G. Wells made significant contributions to the literary genre of science fiction. Although science fiction was not new to the modern age—scholars have traced its roots back to ancient mythology—writers of scientific fantasy had a profound influence in the late nineteenth and twentieth centuries. For instance, spaceflight pioneers **Hermann Oberth** (1894–1989; see entry) and **Konstantin Tsiolkovsky** (1857–1935; see entry) read science-fiction novels and stories by such writers as Wells and French novelist Jules Verne (1828–1905). Most writers at that time, however, concentrated mainly on bizarre tales of alien beings, spaceships, and trips to the Moon and other worlds.

A committed socialist (advocate of state control of production and services), Wells provided an added dimension in his novels, which he called scientific romances: He depicted the dark side of human nature and warned about the misuse of technology. In these and other works he predicted devastating global conflicts, the development of atomic weaponry, and the advent of chemical warfare. Wells is best remembered today for four of his early science-fiction novels—*The Time*

H. G. Wells. *(AP/Wide World Photos)*

Machine: An Invention, The War of the Worlds, The Invisible Man: A Grotesque Romance, and *The Island of Doctor Moreau: A Possibility.* During an extremely prolific career that spanned fifty years, Wells wrote other types of novels as well as social criticism, journalism, literary criticism, film scripts, and political manifestos (statements of belief).

Education shapes his ideas

Herbert George Wells was born in Bromley, Kent, England, on September 21, 1866. He was the youngest of three sons of

Joseph Wells and Sarah Neal Wells. Joseph was a well-known cricket player who worked as a gardener for an upper-class employer, and he had once been an unsuccessful shopkeeper. Sarah Wells was a housekeeper and lady's maid who wanted a better life for her sons. Wells entered Morley's School in Bromley at age seven. In 1880, at his mother's insistence, he left when he was fourteen to become an apprentice to a draper (a clothing and dry goods merchant). Wells hated the job, and three years later his mother let him take a pupil-teacher position at a private school. In 1884 he won a scholarship to the Normal School of Science at South Kensington. Although he studied all branches of science, he was interested only in the classes taught by biologist Thomas Huxley (1825–1895), one of the founders of the school. (A biologist is a scientist who studies living organisms.)

Wells's thinking was shaped by Huxley, who supported the theory of evolution, which states that species (forms of life) evolve through natural selection (survival of dominant traits) over long periods of time. This idea was controversial because it contradicted the teachings of the Christian religion, which stated that all of nature was created at the beginning of time by a divine being. Huxley's students, including Wells, came to think of science in general and biology in particular as revolutionary, and they began to question previously held views. Huxley's definition of biology also took in social and cultural studies, now classified as sociology (the science of social institutions and other aspects of society) and anthropology (the study of human cultures), providing the basis for Wells's later political views.

The Normal School was important for Wells because it gave him a way to escape his lower-middle-class origins by obtaining a higher education. Schools like Oxford and Cambridge, where scholarships were usually limited to the sons of gentlemen, were far beyond the means of families like the Wellses. In addition, these elite schools tended to concentrate on classics and humanities (Latin, Greek, theology, and literature) rather than on the sciences, which were regarded as lower-class studies. Even after Wells became famous, with a worldwide reputation, some of his contemporaries regarded him as a "counter-jumper," a former draper's assistant unworthy of being ranked among the great men of the British nation.

Begins writing career

Wells left Kensington without a degree in 1887 and returned to teaching in private schools in London and Wales for three years. While living in Wales, a serious sports injury prevented him from returning to teaching full time. One of his kidneys was severely damaged and his lungs hemorrhaged (bled excessively), the latter leading to tuberculosis (a severe lung infection) from which he suffered for the rest of his life. Wells received his degree from the University of London in 1890, and the next year he married his cousin, Isabel Mary Wells. Settling with his wife in a suburb of London, he began teaching at a correspondence college and writing articles on education. In 1893 he suffered another severe lung hemorrhage that eventually forced him to leave teaching altogether. As he slowly recovered, he struck up a close friendship with one of his biology students, Amy Catherine Robbins. Wells obtained a divorce from Isabel in 1895 and married Robbins the same year.

Wells had not planned to make his living by writing, but his bouts of tuberculosis left him few other options. His work for newspapers and magazines led to a position as fiction reviewer for the English *Saturday Review* magazine. He worked at this job for three years but gave it up to concentrate on his own writing. His first project was to revise and expand a story he had published in his college paper in 1888, under the title "The Chronic Argonauts." In 1895 he published the story as *The Time Machine,* the first of his scientific novels. *The Time Machine* tells the tale of an inventor, known only as the Time Traveller, who creates a machine that can navigate into the past or into the future. When the machine is completed, the Time Traveller takes a journey into the distant future, to the year 802,701 C.E. He discovers a world inhabited by pretty, childlike beings called the Eloi, who enjoy lives of pure leisure. He also discovers an underworld inhabited by the Morlocks. The Morlocks manage the technology that keeps the Eloi in comfort and in turn use the Eloi as a food source. The Time Traveller makes friends with an Eloi named Weena and loses the time machine to the Morlocks. After returning to share his story with his friends on Earth, he starts on another voyage in time. He is never seen again.

In Wells's second scientific novel, *The Island of Doctor Moreau* (1896), a young diplomat is found floating adrift af-

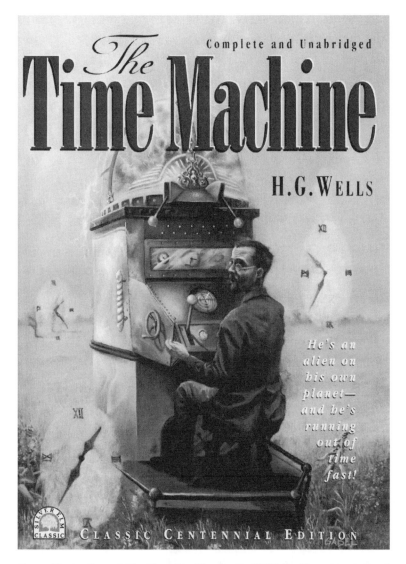

Cover illustration of *The Time Machine* by H. G. Wells. The story tells of a man who is able to conquer time travel but also provides a political commentary on the dangers of technology and their misuse. *(Illustration by Matt Gabel. © Worthington Press)*

ter a tragic shipwreck. His rescuer is an assistant of the infamous Doctor Moreau, a scientist who fled his homeland because of charges of unethical treatment of animals. Moreau has created half-human and half-animal Beast People by means of a surgical process that involves assembling body parts with plastic surgery. The Beast People are frightened of him and worship him only so they can hold onto their human characteristics. After Moreau's death, the Beast People return to being animals. Wells's next novel, *The Invisible Man* (1897) is about a character named Griffin who, like Moreau, is a "mad scientist." Griffin invents a way to make skin, bones, and blood invisible. He then uses the formula on himself so he can go anywhere and threaten anyone without being seen. He can never become visible again, however, and he goes insane.

Today, Wells is best known for *The War of the Worlds* (1898), which describes a Martian invasion of Earth. The story takes place over a ten-day period in England during the late nineteenth century. As the novel opens, astronomers observe a series of large explosions on the surface of the planet Mars. Within a few days, huge cylinder-shaped objects begin landing outside London. From the cylinders emerge the Martians: giant octopuslike creatures possessed of greatly superior technology. The Martians attack and drive the inhabitants of London out of the city. Only two or three Martians are killed by resisting people, but suddenly they begin to die from the Earth's microorganisms (bacteria), which cause them to rot and decay. Forty years later *The War of the Worlds* was the basis of one of the most memorable events of the twentieth century: On an October evening in 1938, the actor Orson Welles (1825–1895) and his Mercury Theater players broadcast a live radio dramatization of the novel. The performance was so realistic that listeners in New Jersey fled their homes in panic, believing they were actually being invaded by Martians.

Promotes worldwide socialism

Wells considered his scientific romances to be unimportant, and most critics agreed with him at the time. Wells was more respected for his comic novels, including *Kipps* (1905) and *The History of Mr. Polly* (1909), and his social criticism, such as *Tono-Bungay* (1908). These works gained Wells a reputation as the foremost British novelist of the early twentieth century. He wrote his best science fiction before 1901, when he was firmly established as a professional writer. By that time he had earned enough from sales of his writing to build a home, Spade House, near the English coast in the county of

The War of the Worlds

In this excerpt from Chapter 4 of *The War of the Worlds,* the narrator expresses his horror upon seeing Martians for the first time.

I think everyone expected to see a man emerge—possibly something a little unlike us terrestrial men, but in all essentials a man. I know I did. But, looking, I presently saw something stirring within the shadow: greyish billowy movements, one above another, and then two luminous disklike eyes. Then something resembling a little grey snake, about the thickness of a walking stick, coiled up out of the writhing middle, and wriggled in the air towards me—and then another. . . .

A big greyish rounded bulk, the size, perhaps, of a bear, was rising slowly and painfully out of the cylinder. As it bulged up and caught the light, it glistened like wet leather.

Two large dark-coloured eyes were regarding me steadfastly. The mass that framed them, the head of the thing, was rounded, and had, one might say, a face.

There was a mouth under the eyes, the lipless brim of which quivered and panted, and dropped saliva. The whole creature heaved and pulsated convulsively. A lank tentacular appendage gripped the edge of the cylinder, another swayed in the air.

Those who have never seen a living Martian can scarcely imagine the strange horror of its appearance. The peculiar V-shaped mouth with its pointed upper lip, the absence of brow ridges, the absence of a chin beneath the wedgelike lower lip, the incessant quivering of this mouth, the Gorgon groups of tentacles, the tumultuous breathing of the lungs in a strange atmosphere, the evident heaviness and painfulness of movement due to the greater gravitational energy of the earth—above all, the extraordinary intensity of the immense eyes— were at once vital, intense, inhuman, crippled and monstrous. There was something fungoid in the oily brown skin, something in the clumsy deliberation of the tedious movements unspeakably nasty. Even at this first encounter, this first glimpse, I was overcome with disgust and dread.

Kent. As social conditions in England changed, his novels became less relevant. He turned instead to a long, drawn-out campaign to promote worldwide socialism, but the works he wrote in support of socialism were not taken seriously.

Wells had more success with *Outline of History* (1920), which he wrote with the assistance of prominent advisors. It was the first attempt to present the story of human existence using biological, anthropological, and sociological studies. It proposed world socialism as a means of promoting world peace. If *The Outline of History* was taught in schools, Wells believed, people would reject such empty values as nationalism and patriotism in favor of a world society based on socialism. The work was enormously popular. History for Wells was not simply a story about the past, however, and he revealed his ideas and hopes for the future in a film script, *The Shape of Things to Come*. The motion picture was filmed by director Alexander Korda (1893–1956) in 1936. It was the first big-budget science-fiction film, an ancestor of *2001: A Space Odyssey* and *Star Wars*. *Things to Come* failed at box offices, mainly because its message about the "war to end all wars" was regarded as unconvincing and meaningless.

Wells lived mainly in France between the years 1924 and 1933, but he had returned to London by the outbreak of World War II (1939–45). During the German blitz (air bombardment) he refused to be driven out of the city, remaining at his house in Regent's Park. He contributed to the war effort with the book *The Rights of Man* (1940), which later formed the basis for the United Nations' Declaration of Human Rights. Although Wells made lasting contributions to the problem of human rights abuses, his last book, *Mind at the End of its Tether* (1945), expressed his gloomy outlook about the future of the human race. He died in London on August 13, 1946. His body was cremated in accordance with his wishes, and his ashes were scattered over the English Channel. In the 1960s Wells's science-fiction novels finally began receiving serious attention.

For More Information

Books

Wells, H.G. *The Invisible Man: A Grotesque Romance* (first published serially in *Pearson's Weekly,* June–July, 1897). New York: Arnold, 1897; large print edition, Waterville, ME: G. K. Hall (Thorndike), 1996; edited by David Lake, with an introduction by John Sutherland, New York: Oxford University Press, 1996.

Wells, H.G. *The Island of Doctor Moreau: A Possibility*. New York: Stone & Kimball, 1896; expanded, with notes by Leon E. Stover, Jefferson, NC: McFarland, 1996.

Wells, H.G. *The Time Machine: An Invention* (first published in *Science Schools Journal* as "The Chronic Argonauts," 1888). London: Heinemann, 1895, and New York: Holt, 1895; reprinted, New York: Dover, 1995.

Wells, H.G. *The War of the Worlds* (first published serially in *Pearson's Magazine,* April-December, 1897). New York: Harper, 1898; large print edition, Waterville, ME: G. K. Hall (Thorndike), 1995.

Periodicals

Achenbach, Joel. "The World According to Wells." *Smithsonian* (April 2001): p. 110.

Web Sites

The Complete War of the Worlds Web site. http://www.war-of-the-worlds. org (accessed on June 29, 2004).

Wells, H. G. "Chapter Four: The Cylinder Opens." *The War of the Worlds.* http://www.online-literature.com/wellshg/warworlds/4/ (accessed on June 30, 2004).

Other Sources

Welles, Orson. *The War of the Worlds.* 1938 Mercury Theatre Broadcast. Radio Spirits, 2001.

Yang Liwei

Born June 21, 1965 (Suizhong, Liaoning, China)

Chinese astronaut

"To establish myself as a qualified astronaut, I have studied harder than in my college years and have received training much tougher than for a fighter pilot."

On October 15, 2003, Yang Liwei became the first Chinese man to travel in space. His flight on the *Shenzhou-5* marked a historic moment: China was now the third nation in the world capable of developing and launching a manned space vehicle. Since 1961, when Soviet cosmonaut **Yuri Gagarin** (1934–1968; see entry) and American astronaut Alan Shepard (1923–1998; see box in **John Glenn** [1921–] entry) became the first humans to orbit Earth, the former Soviet Union and the United States had been the dominant forces in space exploration. This is not to say astronauts and cosmonauts from other countries had never traveled into space. France and Germany had operated astronaut programs since the 1970s and had recruited astronauts of many nationalities. The European Space Agency established an astronaut corps in 1998 (see **Claudie Haigneré** [1957–] entry), providing an even greater global reach. Yet no other nation maintained its own fleet of spacecraft, so space adventurers flew aboard vehicles originating only in the United States and Russia. Yang's achievement, coming forty-two years after those of Gagarin and Shepard, was therefore hailed throughout the world as a step forward in the exploration of space.

Yang Liwei. *(AP/Wide World Photos)*

Undergoes rigorous training

Yang Liwei (pronounced yahng lee-way) was born on June 21, 1965, in Suizhong, a county in the Liaoning province of northeast China. As a child he dreamed of flying, and at age eighteen he entered a People's Liberation Army (PLA) Air Force college, where he obtained a bachelor's degree in 1987. After graduation he became a fighter pilot. In 1998, Yang, now a lieutenant colonel, was chosen as one of fourteen (some sources state twelve, others thirteen) astronaut candidates from 1,500 applicants. By this time he had accumulated 1,350 flight-hours as a pilot. He was also married and had an eight-

From Rockets to Space

Historians note it is only fitting that China should have a space program, since the first projectile—the rocket—was invented by the ancient Chinese. They fired their rockets by igniting black powder, an explosive mixture similar to gunpowder. Basic rocket technology did not change until the early twentieth century, when Western (non-Asian) scientists perfected the liquid-propellant rocket. This revolutionary technological advance provided the foundation of future space flight. Pioneers in liquid-propellant rocket development and spaceflight theory include **Konstantin Tsiolkovsky** (1857–1935), **Robert Goddard** (1882–1945), **Hermann Oberth** (1894–1989), and **Wernher von Braun** (1912–1977) (see entries). In 1955 Chinese engineer Tsien Hsue-Shen (1911–), who had been working on rocket research in the United States, returned to his native country. He brought with him the advanced technology he had helped to develop in America. The following year China started its own rocket and space programs, paving the way for Yang Liwei's flight in 2003.

year-old son. Yang's wife, Zhang Yumei, is a teacher who served in China's space program.

As preparation for navigating the Project 921 spacecraft (later called *Shenzhou*), Yang and the other candidates went to the Astronaut Training Base in Beijing for five years of training. In addition to undergoing rigorous physical exercises, they studied aviation dynamics, air dynamics, geophysics, meteorology, astronomy, space navigation, and the design principles and structure of rockets and spacecraft. They also practiced on spaceflight simulators and learned skills for surviving under extreme conditions in the event that their capsule crashed on Earth or at sea. Reflecting on this experience, Yang later told an interviewer for *China Through a Lens* that the training was a difficult challenge. "To establish myself as a qualified astronaut," Yang said. "I have studied harder than in my college years and have received training much tougher than for a fighter pilot."

Flight surrounded in secrecy

The candidates began training on the actual *Shenzhou-5* spacecraft in September 2003, at the Jiuquan Launch Center in the Gobi desert in the Gansu Province of northwest China. The following month Yang was chosen as one of three finalists for the position of astronaut on the twenty-one-hour flight aboard *Shenzhou-5*. The selection was finally narrowed to Yang, but he was not informed until October 14, the evening before liftoff. The morning of October 15 dawned with perfect weather and a clear blue sky. The flight had been made public shortly before the scheduled 9:00 A.M. launch. A few selected Chinese journalists had gathered outside the main building of the launch center when Yang walked to the spacecraft. (The Chinese government continued to surround the details of the mission in secrecy until Yang had landed safely. No foreign journalists were permitted to witness the event.) Waving and smiling to the crowd, he entered the *Shenzhou-5* launch capsule at 9:00 A.M. (Beijing time) on the dot. Liftoff also took place on time, and ten minutes after launch the *Shenzhou-5* went into orbit. Naval rescue vessels stood by in ports on the Sea of Japan.

The mission plan required Yang to remain in the reentry capsule of the *Shenzhou-5* throughout the flight. For this reason he did not enter the orbital module. (The spacecraft consisted of two components, or modules—the reentry capsule, which would take Yang back to Earth, and an orbital module, which would be released into space before returning to Earth.) During the mission he took two three-hour rest periods and had two meals. He maintained communication with ground control via links, including color television, with four tracking ships stationed in the oceans throughout the world. He also spoke with his wife and son by telephone. As reported in *China Through a Lens,* he told his son, "I caught the sight of our beautiful home [Earth] and recorded all that I've seen there."

When the *Shenzhou-5* was in its fourteenth orbit, the reentry capsule separated from the orbital module. The orbital module would stay in space for six months to conduct a reconnaissance (military information) mission. Then the retrorocket (the rocket that fired the reentry capsule on its return trip) was sent back to Earth by a triggering device on a tracking ship in the Atlantic Ocean off the coast of Africa. The *Shenzhou-5* landed only 4.8 kilometers (less than 60 miles) from its targeted destination in Inner Mongolia. Yang ejected from the capsule and as he floated to the ground with the aid of a parachute, he was sighted by recovery forces before his landing. He had spent twenty-one hours and twenty-three minutes in space.

Becomes national hero

Yang was an instant national hero in China. His achievement was praised worldwide, and congratulations came in from space agencies and astronauts in the United States and

The *Shenzhou-5* capsule, the first manned space craft launched by China. Yang Liwei flew in the *Shenzhou-5* when he became the first Chinese man to travel in space. *(AP/Wide World Photos)*

Russia. Among them were Russian cosmonaut **Valentina Tereshkova** (1931–; see entry), the first woman to travel in space, and American astronaut **Buzz Aldrin** (1930–; see entry), the second person to walk on the Moon. In 2004 the high school in his hometown was renamed the Liwei Senior High School of Suizong County in his honor. That year the government also made an announcement pertaining to an important discovery Yang made during his flight. At that time Chinese elementary-school textbooks contained an essay claiming that a cosmonaut (Russian astronaut) had seen two structures from space—a Dutch sea wall and the Great Wall of China. Yang reported, however, that he could not see the Great Wall of China from space. (The Great Wall is one of the most famous structures in China. Stretching 1,500 miles [2,414 kilometers] across the northern part of the country, it was built as a fortification against invaders in the third century B.C.E.) The government ordered that the essay be removed in 2004.

The Chinese space agency is planning to build space shuttles and a space station and has set a goal to send astronauts to the Moon. (A space shuttle is a craft that transports people and cargo between Earth and space; a space station is a scientific research laboratory that orbits in space.) In 2004 the government also announced that it was recruiting women astronauts, one of whom will be the nation's first woman in space.

For More Information

Periodicals

"China to Correct Great-Wall-in-Space Myth." Associated Press (March 12, 2004).

Lynch, David J. "China's 'Space Hero' Returns to Earth." *USA Today* (October 16, 2003): A13.

"School Changes Name to Honor China's First Astronaut." Xinhua News Agency (January 10, 2004).

Yardley, Jim. "China in Space: The Return." *New York Times* (October 16, 2003): p. A10.

Web Sites

"China's Astronaut Returns Safely." *CNN.com* (October 16, 2003). http://www.cnn.com/2003/TECH/space/10/15/china.launch/ (accessed June 29, 2004).

"China's First Spaceman Yang Liwei." Translated by Li Xiao. *China Through a Lens* (October 20, 2003). http://service.china.org.cn/link/wcm/Show_Text?info_id=77494&p_qry=Yang%20and%20Liwei (accessed on June 29, 2004).

"Yang Liwei." *Encyclopedia Astronautica.* http://www.astronautix.com/astros/yanliwei.htm (accessed on June 29, 2004).

Where to Learn More

Books

Aaseng, Nathan. *The Space Race*. San Diego, CA: Lucent, 2001.

Andronik, Catherine M. *Copernicus: Founder of Modern Astronomy*. Berkeley Heights, NJ: Enslow, 2002.

Asimov, Isaac. *Astronomy in Ancient Times*. Revised ed. Milwaukee: Gareth Stevens, 1997.

Aveni, Anthony. *Stairways to the Stars: Skywatching in Three Great Ancient Cultures*. New York: John Wiley and Sons, 1997.

Baker, David. *Spaceflight and Rocketry: A Chronology*. New York: Facts on File, 1996.

Benson, Michael. *Beyond: Visions of the Interplanetary Probes*. New York: Abrams, 2003.

Bille, Matt, and Erika Lishock. *The First Space Race: Launching the World's First Satellites*. College Station, TX: Texas A&M University Press, 2004.

Bilstein, Roger E. *Orders of Magnitude: A History of the NACA and NASA, 1915–1990*. Washington, DC: National Aeronautics and Space Administration, 1989.

Boerst, William J. *Galileo Galilei and the Science of Motion*. Greensboro, NC: Morgan Reynolds, 2003.

Bredeson, Carmen. *NASA Planetary Spacecraft: Galileo, Magellan, Pathfinder, and Voyager.* Berkeley Heights, NJ: Enslow, 2000.

Caprara, Giovanni. *Living in Space: From Science Fiction to the International Space Station.* Buffalo, NY: Firefly Books, 2000.

Catchpole, John. *Project Mercury: NASA's First Manned Space Programme.* New York: Springer Verlag, 2001.

Chaikin, Andrew L. *A Man on the Moon: The Voyages of the Apollo Astronauts.* New York: Penguin, 1998.

Christianson, Gale E. *Edwin Hubble: Mariner of the Nebulae.* Chicago, IL: University of Chicago Press, 1996.

Clary, David A. *Rocket Man: Robert H. Goddard and the Birth of the Space Age.* New York: Hyperion Press, 2003.

Cole, Michael D. *The Columbia Space Shuttle Disaster: From First Liftoff to Tragic Final Flight.* Revised ed. Berkeley Heights, NJ: Enslow, 2003.

Collins, Michael. *Carrying the Fire: An Astronaut's Journeys.* New York: Cooper Square Press, 2001.

Davies, John K. *Astronomy from Space: The Design and Operation of Orbiting Observatories.* Second ed. New York: Wiley, 1997.

Dickinson, Terence. *Exploring the Night Sky: The Equinox Astronomy Guide for Beginners.* Buffalo, NY: Firefly Books, 1987.

Dickson, Paul. *Sputnik: The Shock of the Century.* New York: Walker, 2001.

Ezell, Edward Clinton, and Linda Neuman Ezell. *The Partnership: A History of the Apollo-Soyuz Test Project.* Washington, DC: National Aeronautics and Space Administration, 1978.

Florence, Ronald. *The Perfect Machine: Building the Palomar Telescope.* New York: HarperCollins, 1994.

Fox, Mary Virginia. *Rockets.* Tarrytown, NY: Benchmark Books, 1996.

Gleick, James. *Isaac Newton.* New York: Pantheon Books, 2003.

Hall, Rex, and David J. Shayler. *The Rocket Men: Vostok and Voskhod, the First Soviet Manned Spaceflights.* New York: Springer Verlag, 2001.

Hall, Rex D., and David J. Shayler. *Soyuz: A Universal Spacecraft.* New York: Springer Verlag, 2003.

Hamilton, John. *The Viking Missions to Mars.* Edina, MN: Abdo and Daughters Publishing, 1998.

Harland, David M. *The MIR Space Station: A Precursor to Space Colonization.* New York: Wiley, 1997.

Harland, David M., and John E. Catchpole. *Creating the International Space Station.* New York: Springer Verlag, 2002.

Holden, Henry M. *The Tragedy of the Space Shuttle Challenger.* Berkeley Heights, NJ: MyReportLinks.com, 2004.

Jenkins, Dennis R. *Space Shuttle: The History of the National Space Transportation System.* Third ed. Cape Canaveral, FL: D. R. Jenkins, 2001.

Kerrod, Robin. *The Book of Constellations: Discover the Secrets in the Stars.* Hauppauge, NY: Barron's, 2002.

Kerrod, Robin. *Hubble: The Mirror on the Universe.* Buffalo, NY: Firefly Books, 2003.

Kluger, Jeffrey. *Moon Hunters: NASA's Remarkable Expeditions to the Ends of the Solar System.* New York: Simon and Schuster, 2001.

Kraemer, Robert S. *Beyond the Moon: A Golden Age of Planetary Exploration, 1971–1978.* Washington, DC: Smithsonian Institution Press, 2000.

Krupp, E. C. *Beyond the Blue Horizon: Myths and Legends of the Sun, Moon, Stars, and Planets.* New York: Oxford University Press, 1992.

Launius, Roger D. *Space Stations: Base Camps to the Stars.* Washington, DC: Smithsonian Institution Press, 2003.

Maurer, Richard. *Rocket! How a Toy Launched the Space Age.* New York: Knopf, 1995.

Miller, Ron. *The History of Rockets.* New York: Franklin Watts, 1999.

Murray, Charles. *Apollo: The Race to the Moon.* New York: Simon and Schuster, 1989.

Naeye, Robert. *Signals from Space: The Chandra X-ray Observatory.* Austin, TX: Raintree Steck-Vaughn, 2001.

Orr, Tamra B. *The Telescope.* New York: Franklin Watts, 2004.

Panek, Richard. *Seeing and Believing: How the Telescope Opened Our Eyes and Minds to the Heavens.* New York: Penguin, 1999.

Parker, Barry R. *Stairway to the Stars: The Story of the World's Largest Observatory.* New York: Perseus Publishing, 2001.

Reichhardt, Tony, ed. *Space Shuttle: The First 20 Years—The Astronauts' Experiences in Their Own Words.* New York: DK Publishing, 2002.

Reynolds, David. *Apollo: The Epic Journey to the Moon.* New York: Harcourt, 2002.

Ride, Sally. *To Space and Back.* New York: HarperCollins, 1986.

Shayler, David J. *Gemini: Steps to the Moon.* New York: Springer Verlag, 2001.

Shayler, David J. *Skylab: America's Space Station.* New York: Springer Verlag, 2001.

Sherman, Josepha. *Deep Space Observation Satellites.* New York: Rosen Publishing Group, 2003.

Sibley, Katherine A. S. *The Cold War*. Westport, CT: Greenwood Press, 1998.

Slayton, Donald K., with Michael Cassutt. *Deke! An Autobiography*. New York: St. Martin's Press, 1995.

Sullivan, Walter. *Assault on the Unknown: The International Geophysical Year*. New York: McGraw-Hill, 1961.

Tsiolkovsky, Konstantin. *Beyond the Planet Earth*. Translated by Kenneth Syers. New York: Pergamon Press, 1960.

Voelkel, James R. *Johannes Kepler and the New Astronomy*. New York: Oxford University Press, 1999.

Walters, Helen B. *Hermann Oberth: Father of Space Travel*. Introduction by Hermann Oberth. New York: Macmillan, 1962.

Ward, Bob. *Mr. Space: The Life of Wernher von Braun*. Washington, DC: Smithsonian Institution Press, 2004.

Wills, Susan, and Steven R. Wills. *Astronomy: Looking at the Stars*. Minneapolis, MN: Oliver Press, 2001.

Winter, Frank H. *The First Golden Age of Rocketry: Congreve and Hale Rockets of the Nineteenth Century*. Washington, DC: Smithsonian Institution Press, 1990.

Wolfe, Tom. *The Right Stuff*. New York: Farrar, Straus, and Giroux, 1979.

Web Sites

"Ancient Astronomy." *Pomona College Astronomy Department*. http://www.astronomy.pomona.edu/archeo/ (accessed on September 17, 2004).

"Ancients Could Have Used Stonehenge to Predict Lunar Eclipses." *Space.com*. http://www.space.com/scienceastronomy/astronomy/stonehenge_eclipse_000119.html (accessed on September 17, 2004).

"The Apollo Program." *NASA History Office*. http://www.hq.nasa.gov/office/pao/History/apollo.html (accessed on September 17, 2004).

"The Apollo Soyuz Test Project." *NASA/Kennedy Space Center*. http://www-pao.ksc.nasa.gov/kscpao/history/astp/astp.html (accessed on September 17, 2004).

"Apollo-Soyuz Test Project." *National Aeronautics and Space Administration History Office*. http://www.hq.nasa.gov/office/pao/History/astp/index.html (accessed on September 17, 2004).

"The Apollo-Soyuz Test Project." *U.S. Centennial of Flight Commission*. http://www.centennialofflight.gov/essay/SPACEFLIGHT/ASTP/SP24.htm (accessed on September 17, 2004).

"Biographical Sketch of Dr. Wernher Von Braun." *Marshall Space Flight Center*. http://history.msfc.nasa.gov/vonbraun/index.html (accessed on September 17, 2004).

"Cassini-Huygens: Mission to Saturn and Titan." *Jet Propulsion Laboratory, California Institute of Technology.* http://saturn.jpl.nasa.gov/index.cfm (accessed on September 17, 2004).

"CGRO Science Support Center." *NASA Goddard Space Flight Center.* http://cossc.gsfc.nasa.gov/ (accessed on September 17, 2004).

"Chandra X-ray Observatory." *Harvard-Smithsonian Center for Astrophysics.* http://chandra.harvard.edu/ (accessed on September 17, 2004).

"Cold War." *CNN Interactive.* http://www.cnn.com/SPECIALS/cold.war/ (accessed on September 17, 2004).

The Cold War Museum. http://www.coldwar.org/index.html (accessed on September 17, 2004).

"The Copernican Model: A Sun-Centered Solar System." *Department of Physics and Astronomy, University of Tennessee.* http://csep10.phys.utk.edu/astr161/lect/retrograde/copernican.html (accessed on September 17, 2004).

"Curious About Astronomy? Ask an Astronomer." *Astronomy Department, Cornell University.* http://curious.astro.cornell.edu/index.php (accessed on September 17, 2004).

European Space Agency. http://www.esa.int/export/esaCP/index.html (accessed on September 17, 2004).

"Explorer Series of Spacecraft." *National Aeronautics and Space Administration Office of Policy and Plans.* http://www.hq.nasa.gov/office/pao/History/explorer.html (accessed on September 17, 2004).

"Galileo: Journey to Jupiter." *Jet Propulsion Laboratory, California Institute of Technology.* http://www2.jpl.nasa.gov/galileo/ (accessed on September 17, 2004).

"The Hubble Project." *NASA Goddard Space Flight Center.* http://hubble.nasa.gov/ (accessed on September 17, 2004).

HubbleSite. http://www.hubblesite.org/ (accessed on September 17, 2004).

"International Geophysical Year." *The National Academies.* http://www7.nationalacademies.org/archives/igy.html (accessed on September 17, 2004).

"International Space Station." *Boeing.* http://www.boeing.com/defensespace/space/spacestation/flash.html (accessed on September 17, 2004).

"International Space Station." *National Aeronautics and Space Administration.* http://spaceflight.nasa.gov/station/ (accessed on September 17, 2004).

"Kennedy Space Center: Apollo Program." *NASA/Kennedy Space Center.* http://www-pao.ksc.nasa.gov/kscpao/history/apollo/apollo.htm (accessed on September 17, 2004).

"Kennedy Space Center: Gemini Program." *NASA/Kennedy Space Center.* http://www-pao.ksc.nasa.gov/kscpao/history/gemini/gemini.htm (accessed on September 17, 2004).

"Kennedy Space Center: Mercury Program." *NASA/Kennedy Space Center.* http://www-pao.ksc.nasa.gov/history/mercury/mercury.htm (accessed on September 17, 2004).

"The Life of Konstantin Eduardovitch Tsiolkovsky." *Konstantin E. Tsiolkovsky State Museum of the History of Cosmonautics.* http://www.informatics.org/museum/tsiol.html (accessed on September 17, 2004).

"Living and Working in Space." *NASA Spacelink.* http://spacelink.nasa.gov/NASA.Projects/Human.Exploration.and.Development.of.Space/Living.and.Working.In.Space/.index.html (accessed on September 17, 2004).

"Mars Exploration Rover Mission." *Jet Propulsion Laboratory, California Institute of Technology.* http://marsrovers.jpl.nasa.gov/home/index.html (accessed on September 17, 2004).

Mir. http://www.russianspaceweb.com/mir.html (accessed on September 17, 2004).

Mount Wilson Observatory. http://www.mtwilson.edu/ (accessed on September 17, 2004).

"NASA: Robotic Explorers." *National Aeronautics and Space Administration.* http://www.nasa.gov/vision/universe/roboticexplorers/index.html (accessed on September 17, 2004).

NASA's History Office. http://www.hq.nasa.gov/office/pao/History/index.html (accessed on September 17, 2004).

National Aeronautics and Space Administration. http://www.nasa.gov/home/index.html (accessed on September 17, 2004).

National Radio Astronomy Observatory. http://www.nrao.edu/ (accessed on September 17, 2004).

"Newton's Laws of Motion." *NASA Glenn Learning Technologies Project.* http://www.grc.nasa.gov/WWW/K-12/airplane/newton.html (accessed on September 17, 2004).

"Newton's Third Law of Motion." *Physics Classroom Tutorial, Glenbrook South High School.* http://www.glenbrook.k12.il.us/gbssci/phys/Class/newtlaws/u2l4a.html (accessed on September 17, 2004).

"One Giant Leap." *CNN Interactive.* http://www.cnn.com/TECH/specials/apollo/ (accessed on September 17, 2004).

"Paranal Observatory." *European Southern Observatory.* http://www.eso.org/paranal/ (accessed on September 17, 2004).

"Project Apollo-Soyuz Drawings and Technical Diagrams." *National Aeronautics and Space Administration History Office.* http://www.hq.nasa.gov/office/pao/History/diagrams/astp/apol_soyuz.htm (accessed on September 17, 2004).

"The Race for Space: The Soviet Space Program." *University of Minnesota.* http://www1.umn.edu/scitech/assign/space/vostok_intro1.html (accessed on September 17, 2004).

"Remembering *Columbia STS-107.*" *National Aeronautics and Space Administration.* http://history.nasa.gov/columbia/index.html (accessed on September 17, 2004).

"Rocketry Through the Ages: A Timeline of Rocket History." *Marshall Space Flight Center.* http://history.msfc.nasa.gov/rocketry/index.html (accessed on September 17, 2004).

"Rockets: History and Theory." *White Sands Missile Range.* http://www.wsmr.army.mil/pao/FactSheets/rkhist.htm (accessed on September 17, 2004).

Russian Aviation and Space Agency. http://www.rosaviakosmos.ru/english/eindex.htm (accessed on September 17, 2004).

Russian/USSR spacecrafts. http://space.kursknet.ru/cosmos/english/machines/m_rus.sht (accessed on September 17, 2004).

"Skylab." *NASA/Kennedy Space Center.* http://www-pao.ksc.nasa.gov/kscpao/history/skylab/skylab.htm (accessed on September 17, 2004).

Soyuz Spacecraft. http://www.russianspaceweb.com/soyuz.html (accessed on September 17, 2004).

"Space Race." *Smithsonian National Air and Space Museum.* http://www.nasm.si.edu/exhibitions/gal114/gal114.htm (accessed on September 17, 2004).

"Space Shuttle." *NASA/Kennedy Space Center.* http://www.ksc.nasa.gov/shuttle/ (accessed on September 17, 2004).

"Space Shuttle Mission Chronology." *NASA/Kennedy Space Center.* http://www-pao.ksc.nasa.gov/kscpao/chron/chrontoc.htm (accessed on September 17, 2004).

"Spitzer Space Telescope." *California Institute of Technology.* http://www.spitzer.caltech.edu/ (accessed on September 17, 2004).

"Sputnik: The Fortieth Anniversary." *National Aeronautics and Space Administration Office of Policy and Plans.* http://www.hq.nasa.gov/office/pao/History/sputnik/ (accessed on September 17, 2004).

"Tsiolkovsky." *Russian Space Web.* http://www.russianspaceweb.com/tsiolkovsky.html (accessed on September 17, 2004).

United Nations Office for Outer Space Affairs. http://www.oosa.unvienna.org/index.html (accessed on September 17, 2004).

"Vanguard." *Naval Center for Space Technology and U.S. Naval Research Laboratory.* http://ncst-www.nrl.navy.mil/NCSTOrigin/Vanguard.html (accessed on September 17, 2004).

"Voyager: The Interstellar Mission." *Jet Propulsion Laboratory, California Institute of Technology.* http://voyager.jpl.nasa.gov/ (accessed on September 17, 2004).

"Windows to the Universe." *University Corporation for Atmospheric Research.* http://www.windows.ucar.edu/ (accessed on September 17, 2004).

W. M. Keck Observatory. http://www2.keck.hawaii.edu/ (accessed on September 17, 2004).

Index

X

Y

Z